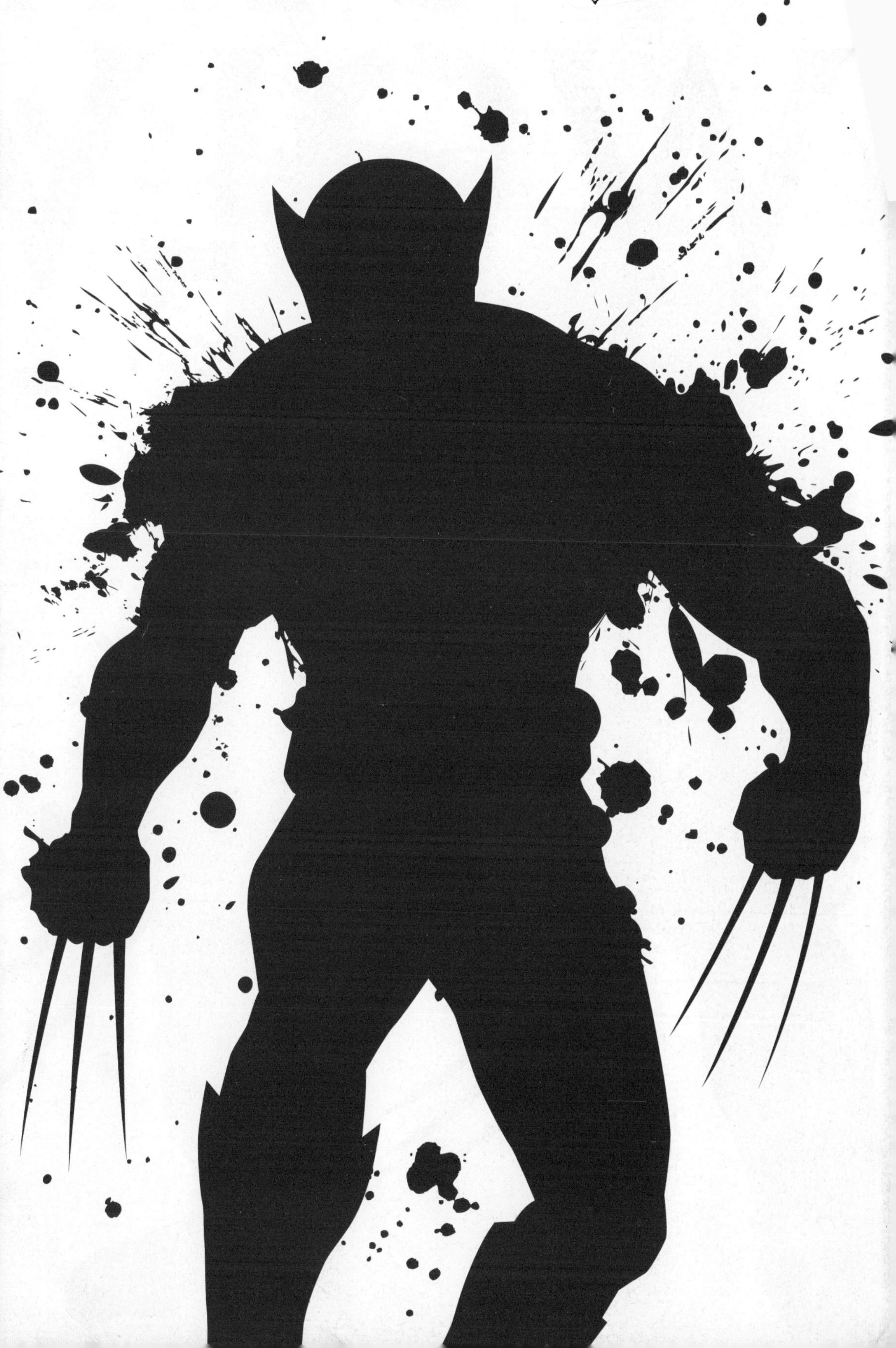

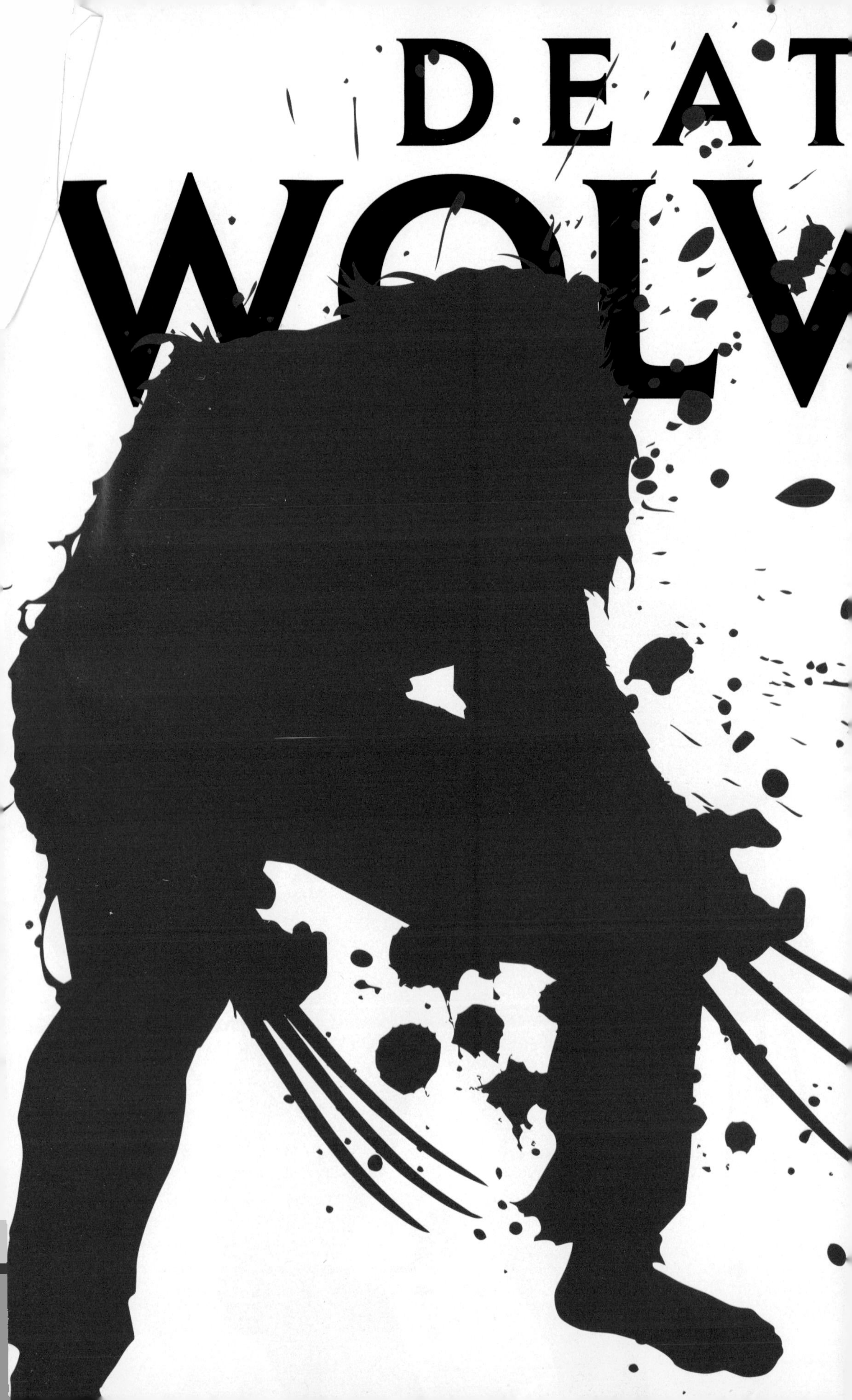
DEAT
WOLV

THE WEAPON X PROGRAM

WEAPON X PROGRAM #1-5

WRITER
CHARLES SOULE

ARTIST, #1-3
SALVADOR LARROCA

PENCILERS, #4-5
ANGEL UNZUETA WITH
IBAN COELLO (#5)

INKERS, #4
MARC DEERING &
JUAN VLASCO

INKERS, #5
DREW GERACI &
IBAN COELLO

COLORIST
FRANK D'ARMATA

LETTERERS
VC'S CORY PETIT WITH
JOE SABINO (#2)

LIFE AFTER LOGAN

"YOU"
WRITER
JEFF LOVENESS

ARTIST
MARIO DEL PENNINO

COLORIST
DAVID CURIEL

LETTERER
**VC'S JOE
CARAMAGNA**

"IN HIS HONOR"
WRITER
**JOSHUA HALE
FIALKOV**

ARTIST
IBAN COELLO

COLORIST
JIM CHARALAMPIDIS

LETTERER
**VC'S JOE
CARAMAGNA**

"A LITTLE PIECE OF YOU"
WRITER
REX OGLE

PENCILER
**PATRICK
SCHERBERGER**

INKER
MARC DEERING

COLORIST
**RACHELLE
ROSENBERG**

LETTERER
**VC'S JOE
CARAMAGNA**

COVER ART
SALVADOR LARROCA
& **JAVIER PULIDO**

EDITORS
**KATIE KUBERT,
MIKE MARTS
& XANDER JAROWEY**

COLLECTION EDITOR: **ALEX STARBUCK** • ASSISTANT EDITOR: **SARAH BRUNSTAD**

EDITORS, SPECIAL PROJECTS: **JENNIFER GRÜNWALD** & **MARK D. BEAZLEY** • SENIOR EDITOR, SPECIAL PROJECTS: **JEFF YOUNGQUIST**

SVP PRINT, SALES & MARKETING: **DAVID GABRIEL** • BOOK DESIGNER: **NELSON RIBEIRO**

EDITOR IN CHIEF: **AXEL ALONSO** • CHIEF CREATIVE OFFICER: **JOE QUESADA**

PUBLISHER: **DAN BUCKLEY** • EXECUTIVE PRODUCER: **ALAN FINE**

DEATH OF WOLVERINE: THE WEAPON X PROGRAM. Contains material originally published in magazine form as DEATH OF WOLVERINE: THE WEAPON X PROGRAM #1-5 and DEATH OF WOLVERINE: LIFE AFTER LOGAN #1. First printing 2015. ISBN# 978-0-7851-9260-2. Published by MARVEL WORLDWIDE, INC., a subsidiary of MARVEL ENTERTAINMENT, LLC. OFFICE OF PUBLICATION: 135 West 50th Street, New York, NY 10020. Copyright © 2014 and 2015 Marvel Characters, Inc. All rights reserved. All characters featured in this issue and the distinctive names and likenesses thereof, and all related indicia are trademarks of Marvel Characters, Inc. No similarity between any of the names, characters, persons, and/or institutions in this magazine with those of any living or dead person or institution is intended, and any such similarity which may exist is purely coincidental. **Printed in the U.S.A.** ALAN FINE, EVP - Office of the President, Marvel Worldwide, Inc. and EVP & CMO Marvel Characters B.V.; DAN BUCKLEY, Publisher & President - Print, Animation & Digital Divisions; JOE QUESADA, Chief Creative Officer; TOM BREVOORT, SVP of Publishing; DAVID BOGART, SVP of Operations & Procurement, Publishing; C.B. CEBULSKI, SVP of Creator & Content Development; DAVID GABRIEL, SVP Print, Sales & Marketing; JIM O'KEEFE, VP of Operations & Logistics; DAN CARR, Executive Director of Publishing Technology; SUSAN CRESPI, Editorial Operations Manager; ALEX MORALES, Publishing Operations Manager; STAN LEE, Chairman Emeritus. For information regarding advertising in Marvel Comics or on Marvel.com, please contact Niza Disla, Director of Marvel Partnerships, at ndisla@marvel.com. For Marvel subscription inquiries, please call 800-217-9158. **Manufactured between 1/9/2015 and 2/16/2015 by R.R. DONNELLEY, INC., SALEM, VA, USA.**

10 9 8 7 6 5 4 3 2 1

1 PHASE ONE: QUESTION

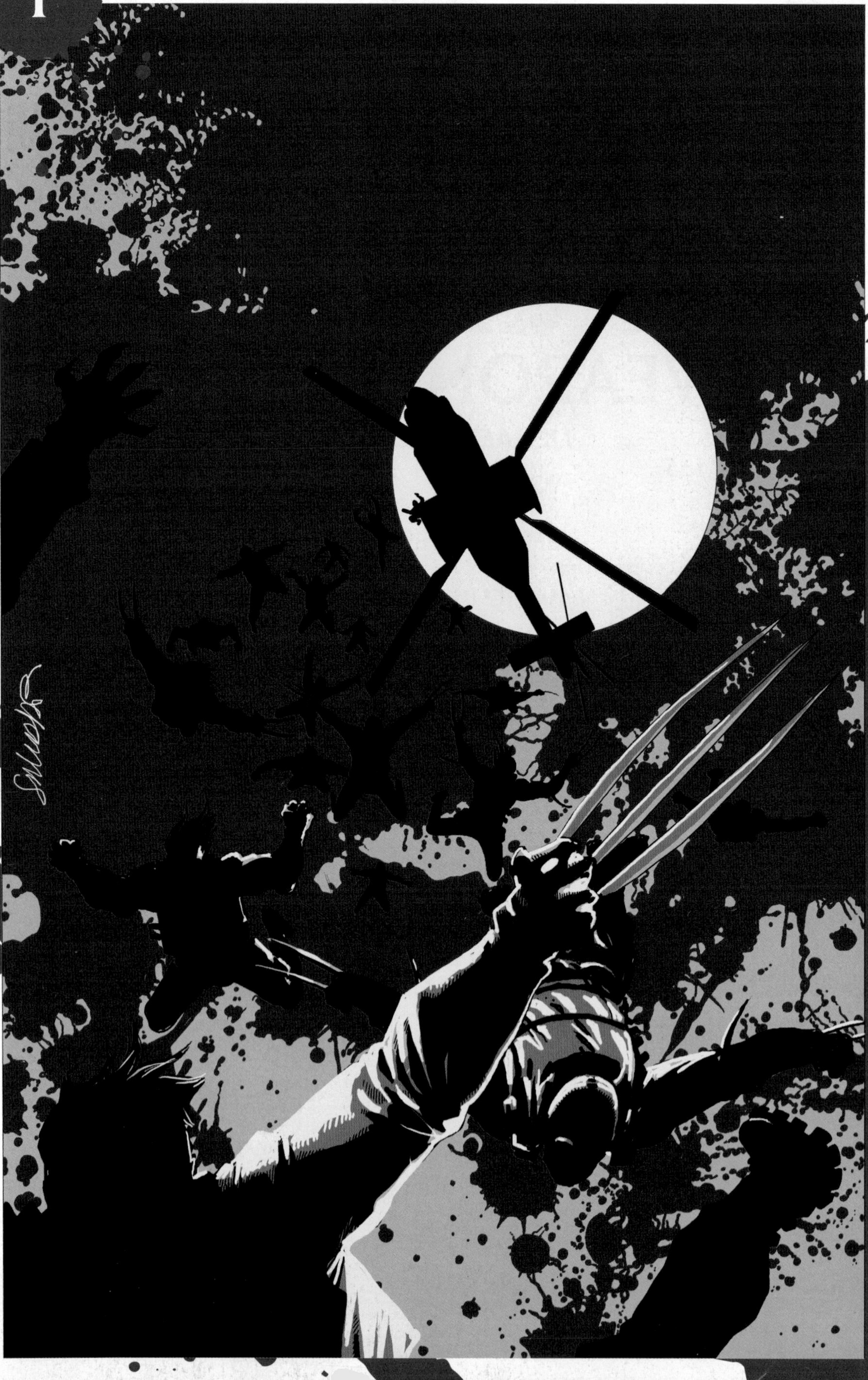

WOLVERINE IS DEAD...

HE DIED HERE, IN THE PARADISE FACILITY, SURROUNDED BY THE FAILED EXPERIMENTS OF THE NOW DECEASED DR. ABRAHAM CORNELIUS.

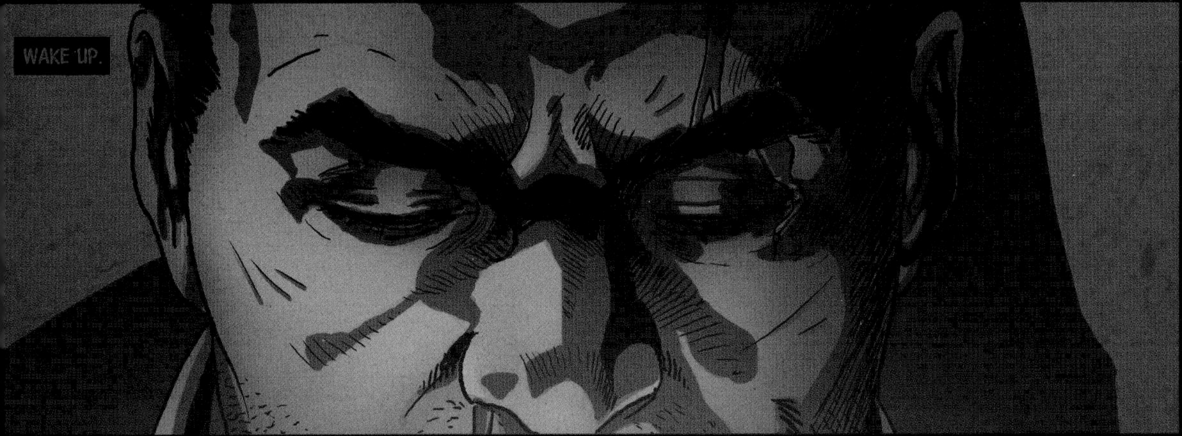
WAKE UP.

THEIR STORY BEGINS HERE...

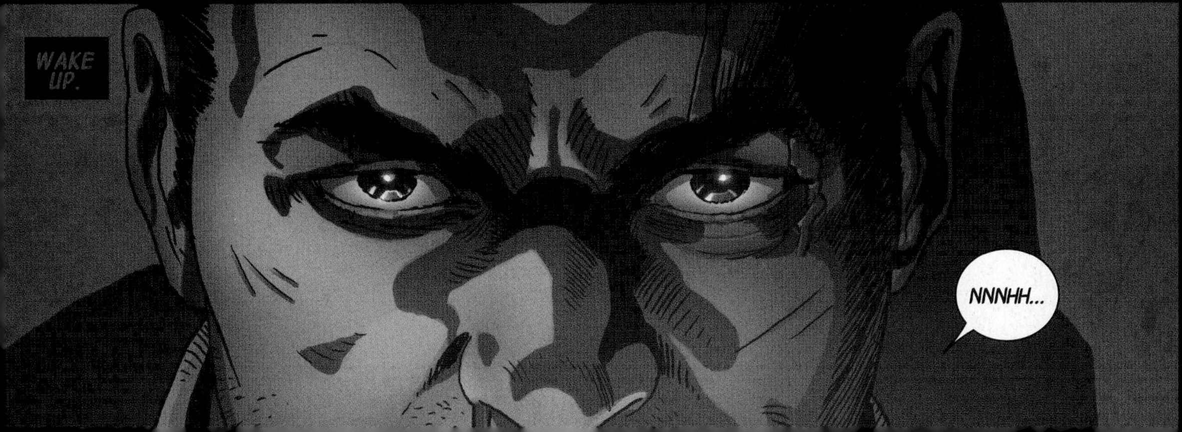
WAKE UP.
NNNHH...

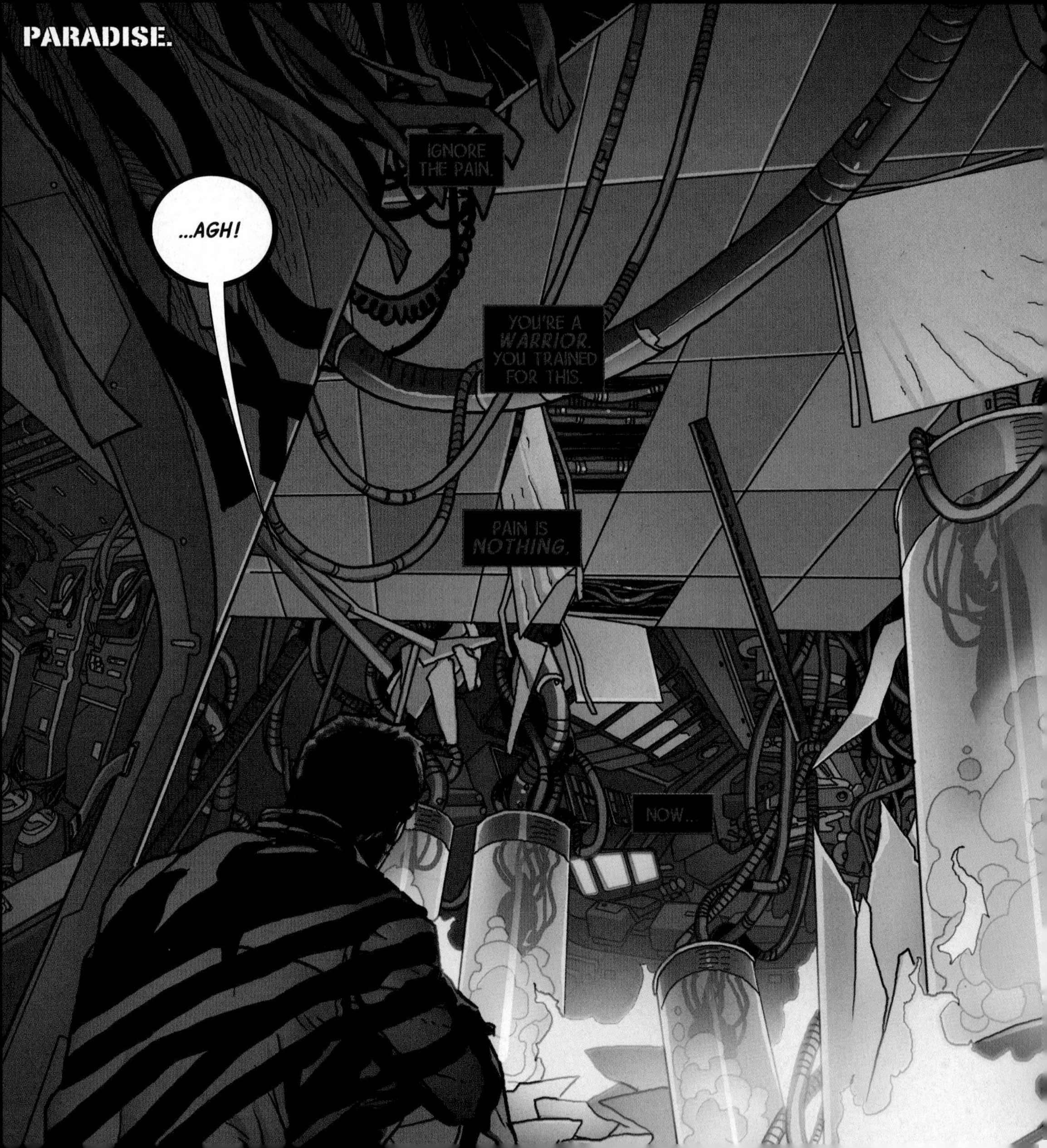
PARADISE.
IGNORE THE PAIN.
...AGH!
YOU'RE A *WARRIOR*. YOU TRAINED FOR THIS.
PAIN IS *NOTHING*.
NOW...

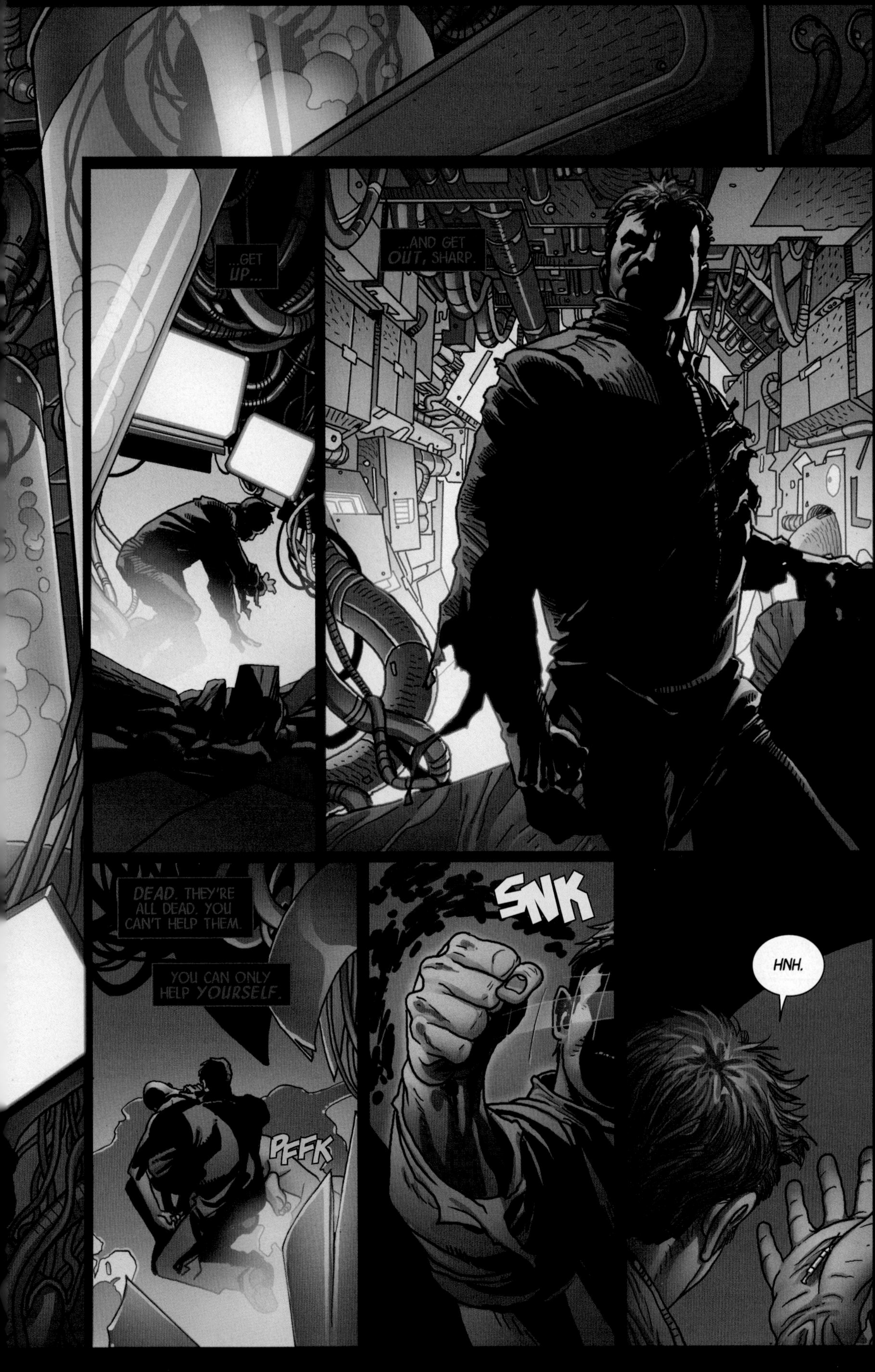
...GET UP...
...AND GET OUT, SHARP.
DEAD. THEY'RE ALL DEAD. YOU CAN'T HELP THEM.
YOU CAN ONLY HELP YOURSELF.
PFFK
SNK
HNH.

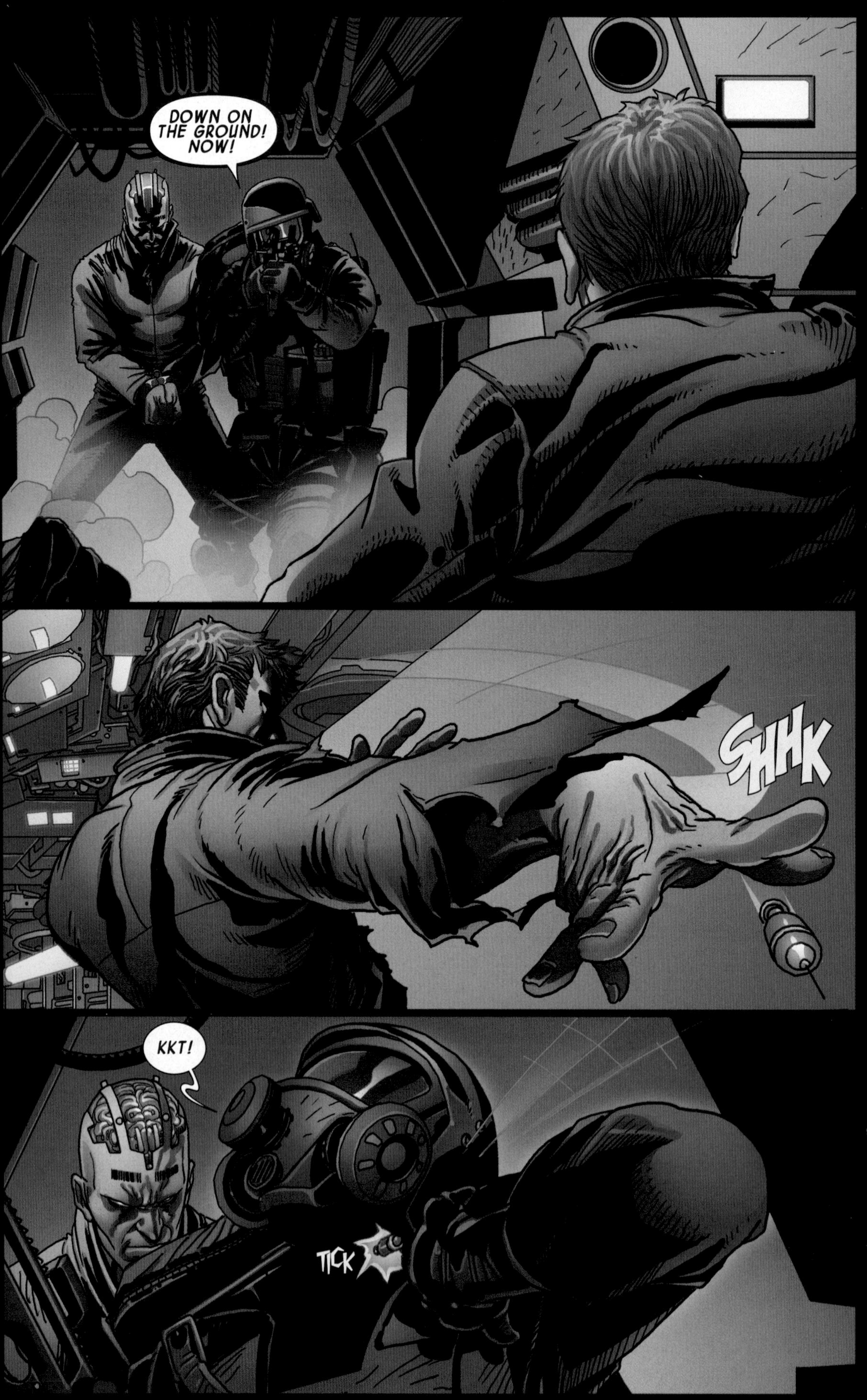
DOWN ON THE GROUND! NOW!
SHHK
KKT!
TICK

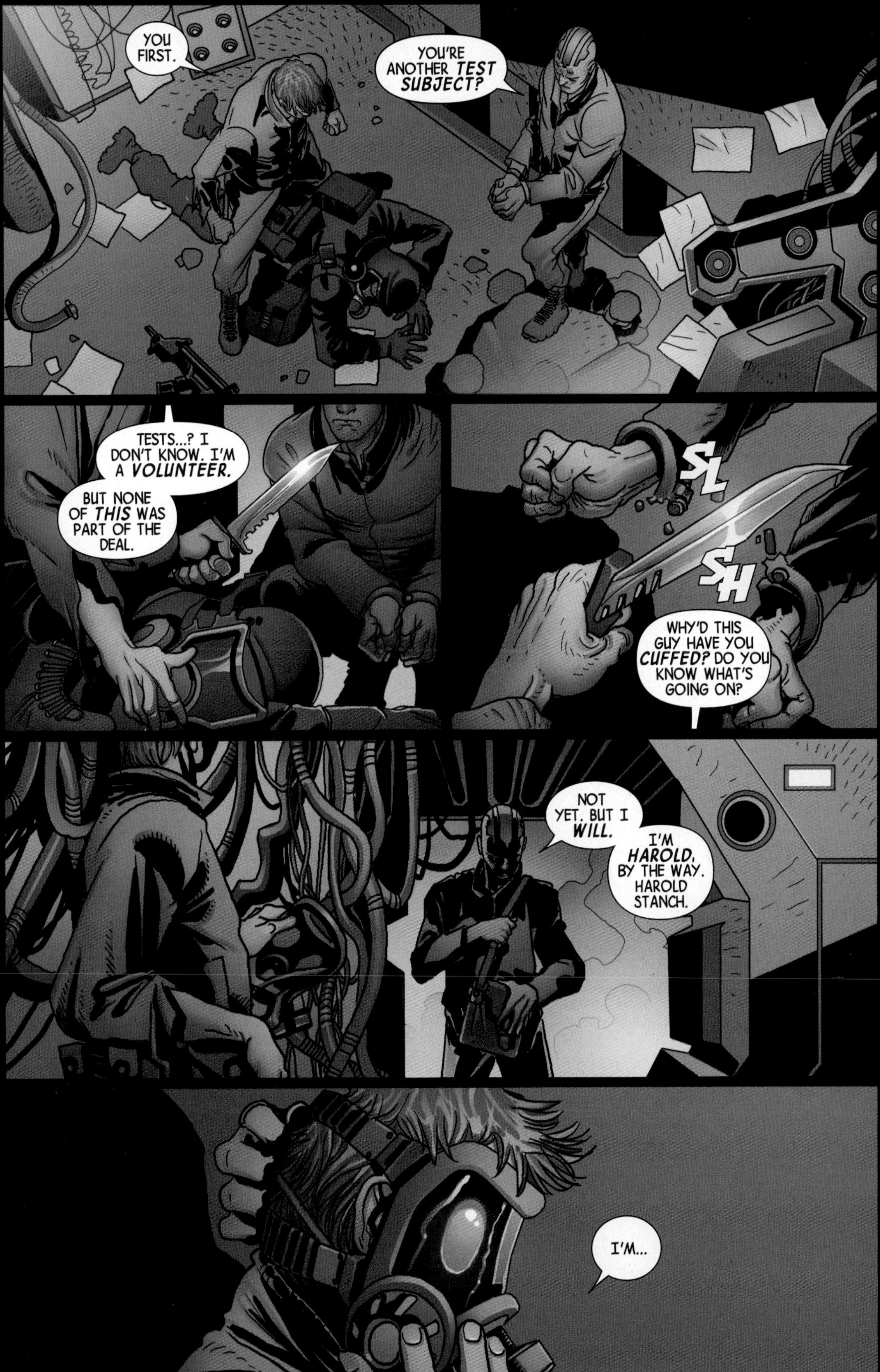
YOU FIRST.
YOU'RE ANOTHER TEST SUBJECT?
TESTS...? I DON'T KNOW. I'M A VOLUNTEER.
BUT NONE OF THIS WAS PART OF THE DEAL.
SLSH
WHY'D THIS GUY HAVE YOU CUFFED? DO YOU KNOW WHAT'S GOING ON?
NOT YET. BUT I WILL.
I'M HAROLD, BY THE WAY. HAROLD STANCH.
I'M...

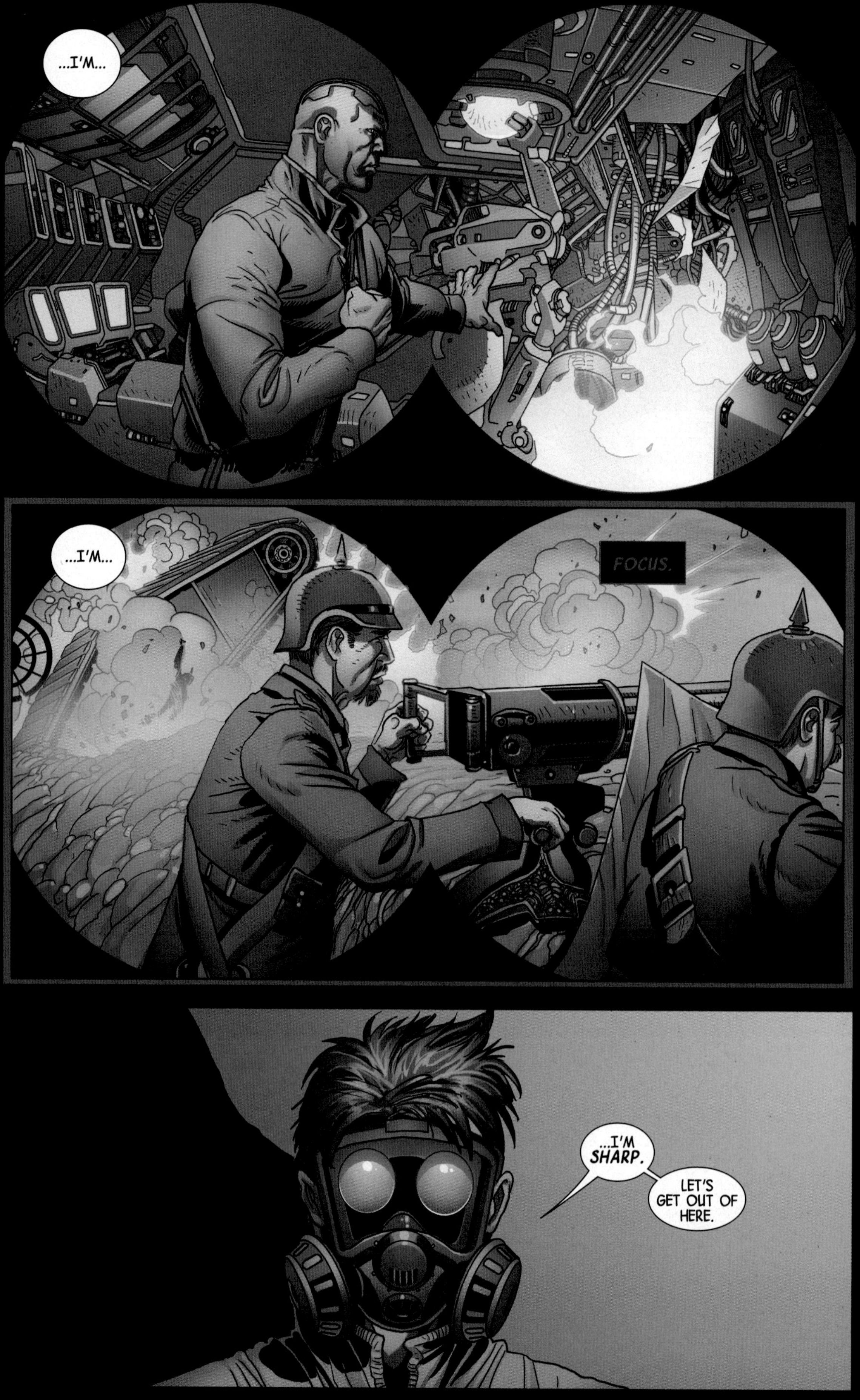
...I'M...
...I'M...
FOCUS.
...I'M SHARP.
LET'S GET OUT OF HERE.

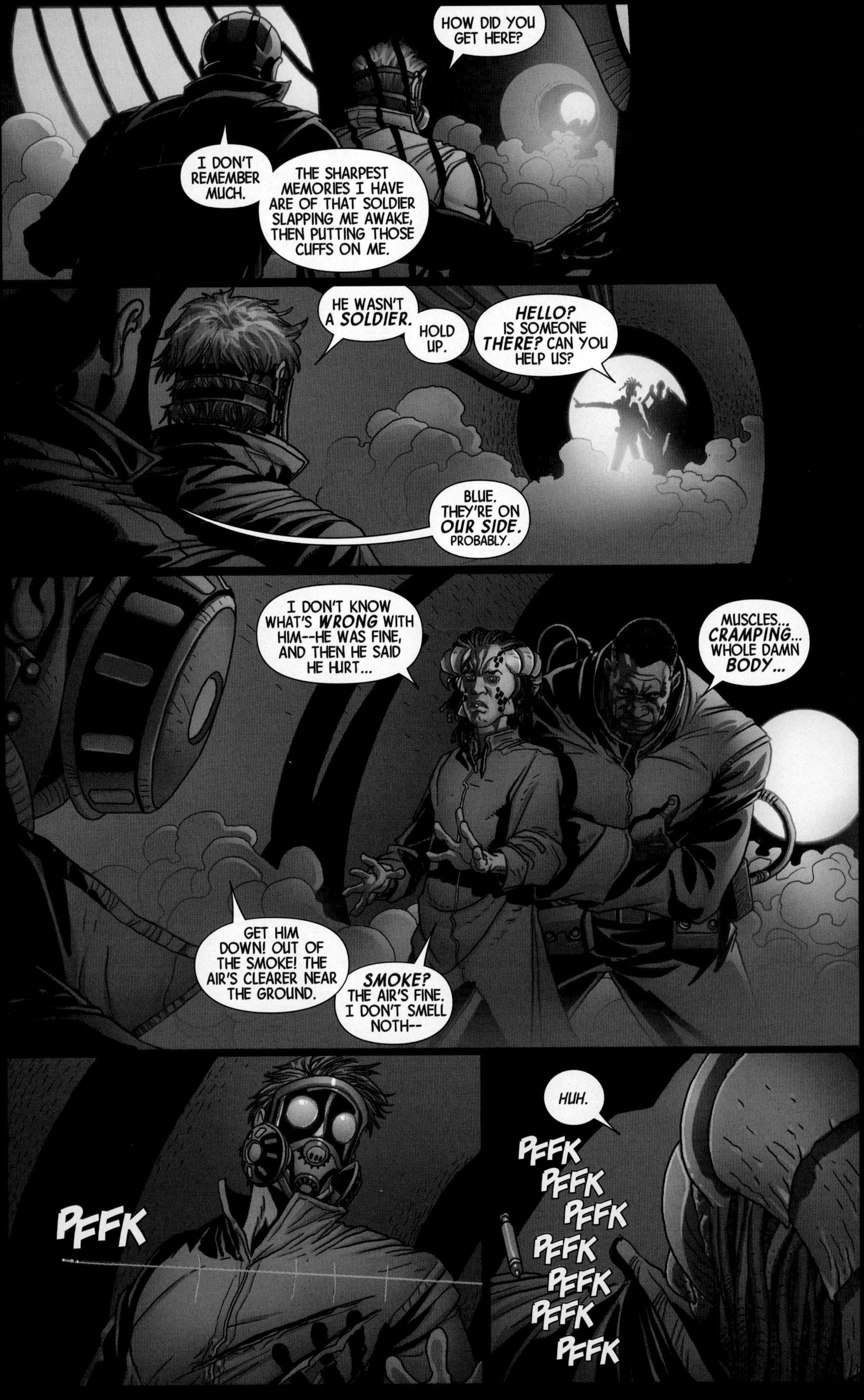
HOW DID YOU GET HERE?
I DON'T REMEMBER MUCH.
THE SHARPEST MEMORIES I HAVE ARE OF THAT SOLDIER SLAPPING ME AWAKE, THEN PUTTING THOSE CUFFS ON ME.
HE WASN'T A *SOLDIER.*
HOLD UP.
HELLO? IS SOMEONE *THERE?* CAN YOU HELP US?
BLUE. THEY'RE ON *OUR SIDE.* PROBABLY.
I DON'T KNOW WHAT'S *WRONG* WITH HIM--HE WAS FINE, AND THEN HE SAID HE HURT...
MUSCLES... *CRAMPING...* WHOLE DAMN *BODY...*
GET HIM DOWN! OUT OF THE SMOKE! THE AIR'S CLEARER NEAR THE GROUND.
SMOKE? THE AIR'S FINE. I DON'T SMELL NOTH--
PFFK
HUH.
PFFK
PFFK
PFFK
PFFK
PFFK
PFFK
PFFK

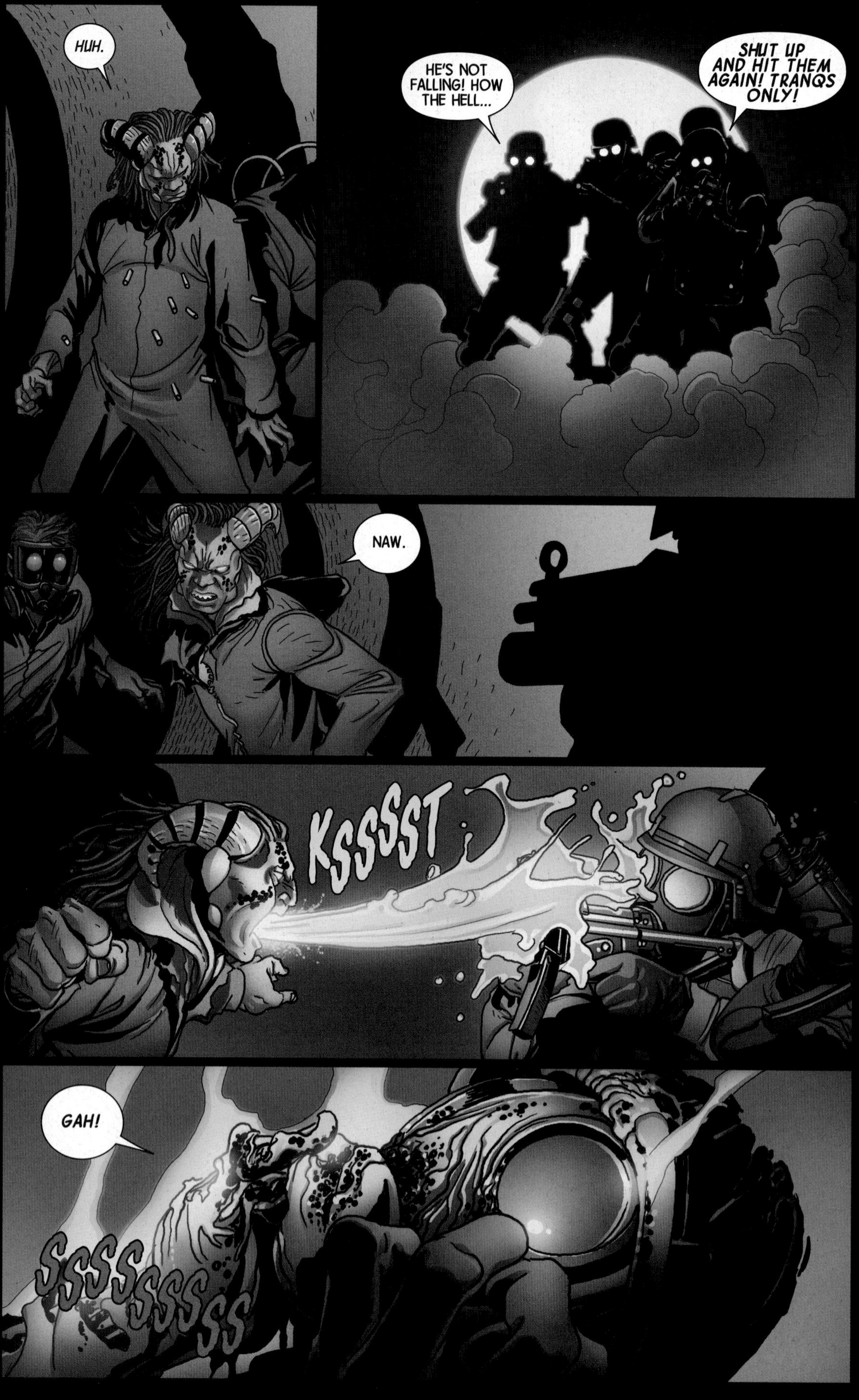
HUH.
HE'S NOT FALLING! HOW THE HELL...
SHUT UP AND HIT THEM AGAIN! TRANQS ONLY!
NAW.
KSSSST!
GAH!
SSSSSSSSSS

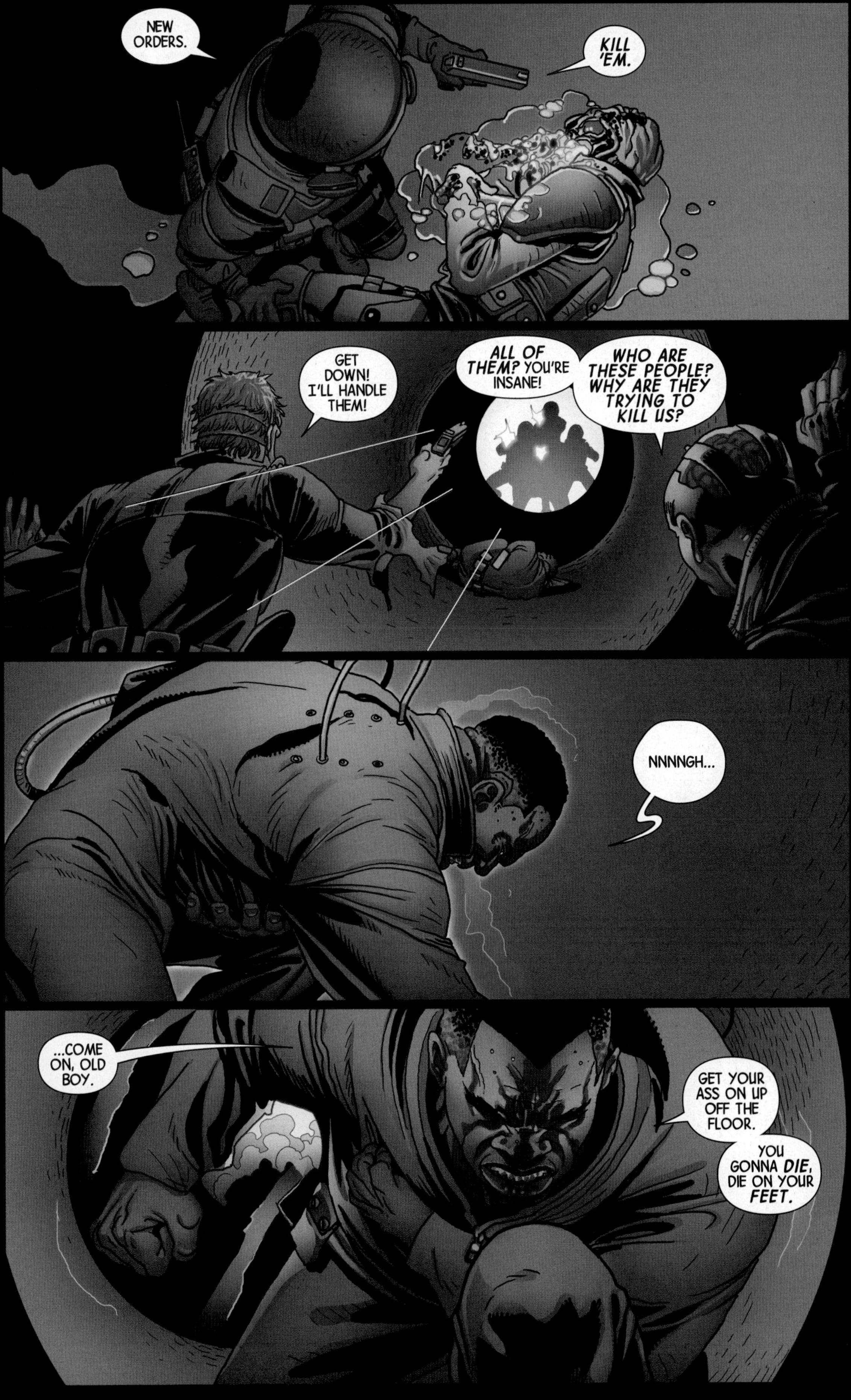
NEW ORDERS.
KILL 'EM.
GET DOWN! I'LL HANDLE THEM!
ALL OF THEM? YOU'RE INSANE!
WHO ARE THESE PEOPLE? WHY ARE THEY TRYING TO KILL US?
NNNNGH...
...COME ON, OLD BOY.
GET YOUR ASS ON UP OFF THE FLOOR.
YOU GONNA DIE, DIE ON YOUR FEET.

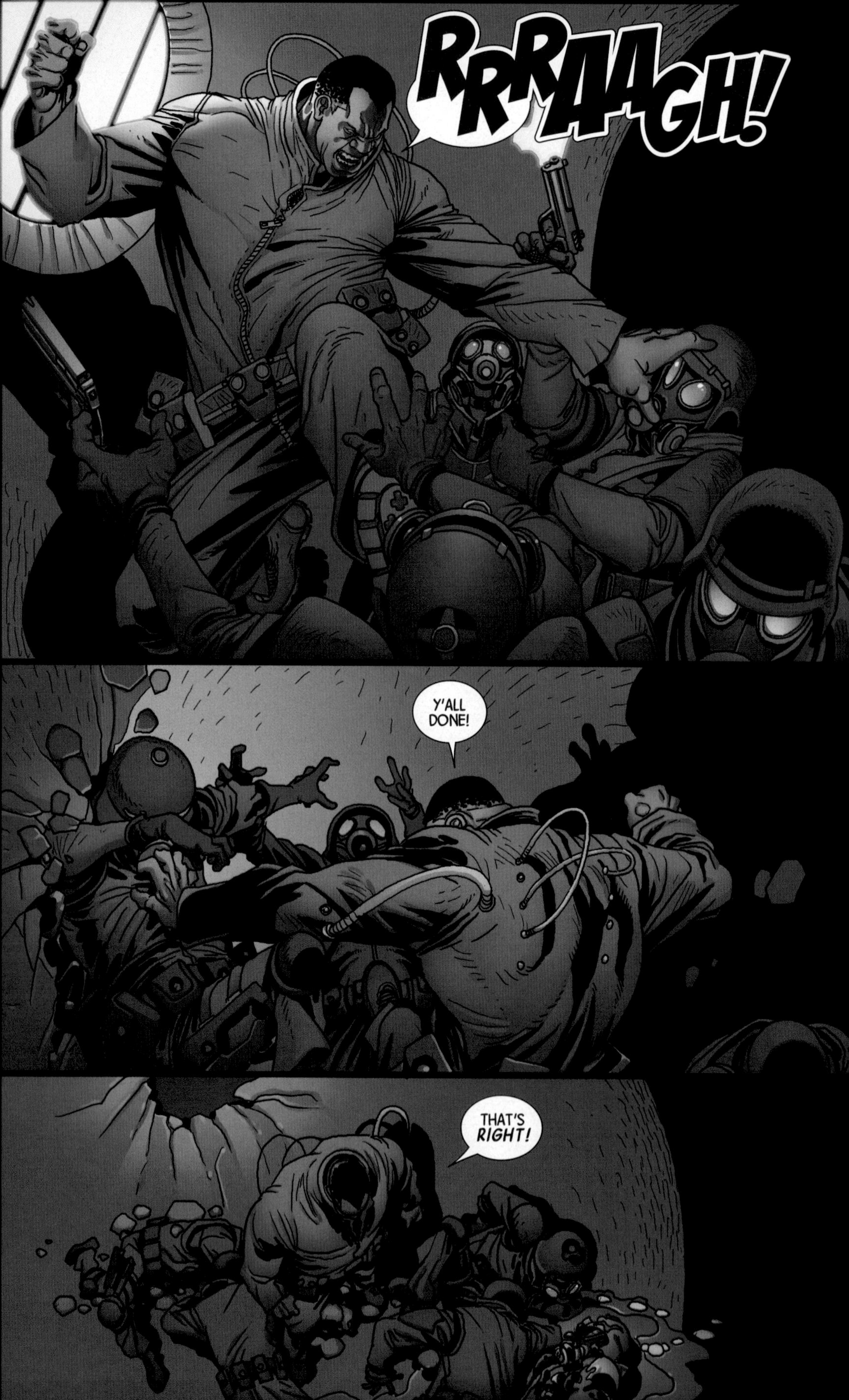
RRRAAAGH!
Y'ALL DONE!
THAT'S RIGHT!

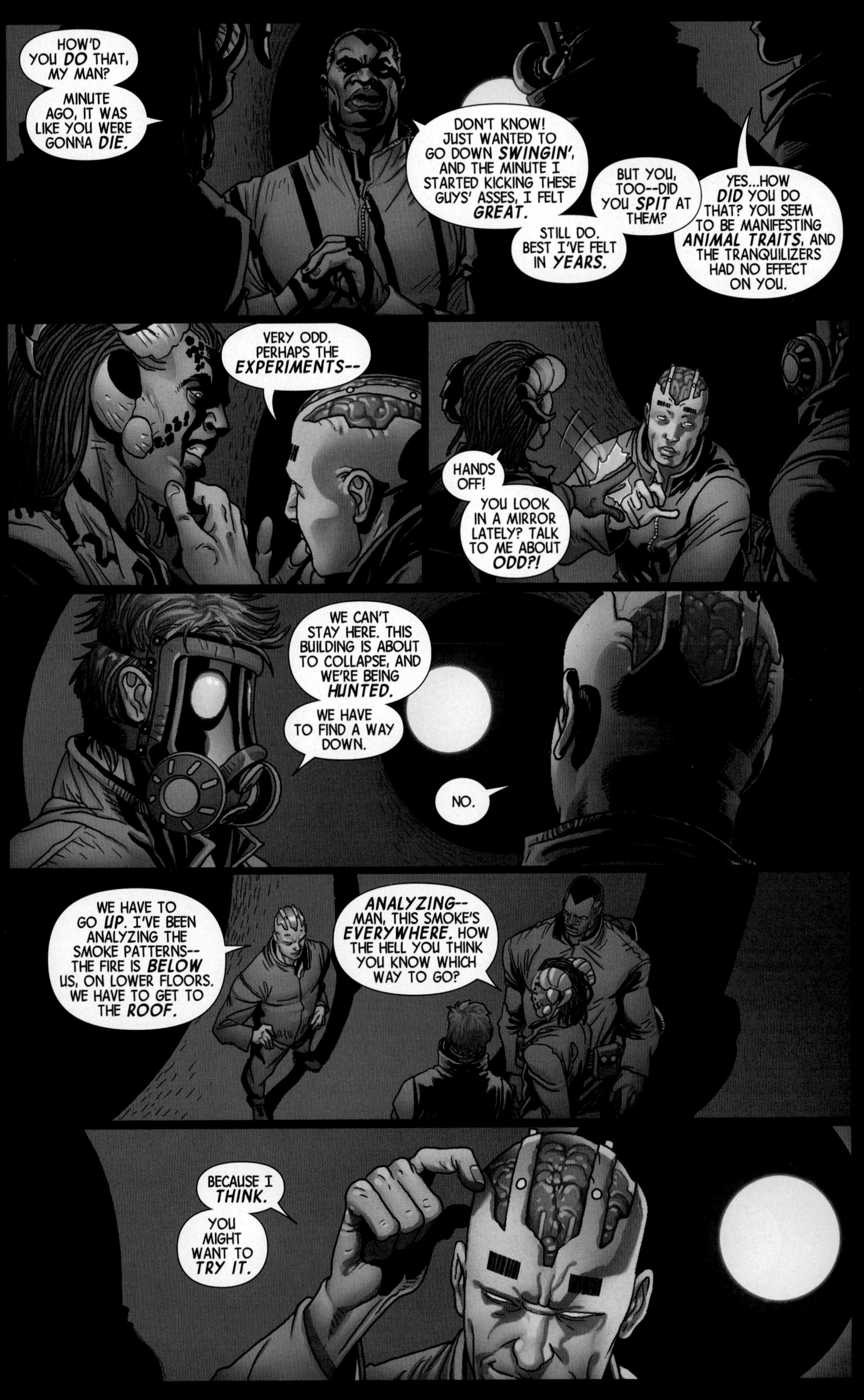
HOW'D YOU DO THAT, MY MAN?
MINUTE AGO, IT WAS LIKE YOU WERE GONNA DIE.
DON'T KNOW! JUST WANTED TO GO DOWN SWINGIN', AND THE MINUTE I STARTED KICKING THESE GUYS' ASSES, I FELT GREAT.
STILL DO. BEST I'VE FELT IN YEARS.
BUT YOU, TOO--DID YOU SPIT AT THEM?
YES...HOW DID YOU DO THAT? YOU SEEM TO BE MANIFESTING ANIMAL TRAITS, AND THE TRANQUILIZERS HAD NO EFFECT ON YOU.
VERY ODD. PERHAPS THE EXPERIMENTS--
HANDS OFF!
YOU LOOK IN A MIRROR LATELY? TALK TO ME ABOUT ODD?!
WE CAN'T STAY HERE. THIS BUILDING IS ABOUT TO COLLAPSE, AND WE'RE BEING HUNTED.
WE HAVE TO FIND A WAY DOWN.
NO.
WE HAVE TO GO UP. I'VE BEEN ANALYZING THE SMOKE PATTERNS-- THE FIRE IS BELOW US, ON LOWER FLOORS. WE HAVE TO GET TO THE ROOF.
ANALYZING-- MAN, THIS SMOKE'S EVERYWHERE. HOW THE HELL YOU THINK YOU KNOW WHICH WAY TO GO?
BECAUSE I THINK.
YOU MIGHT WANT TO TRY IT.

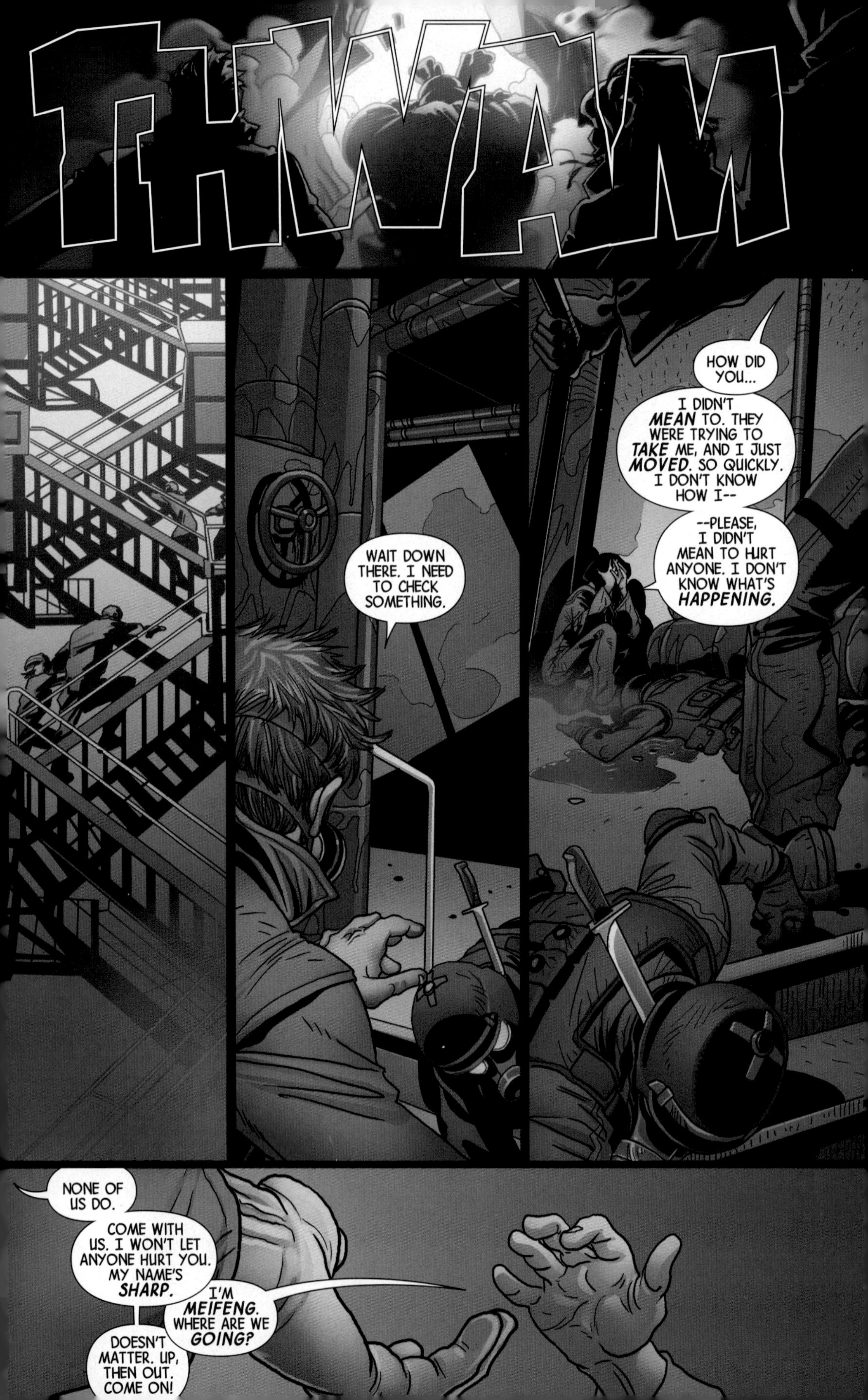
THWAM
WAIT DOWN THERE. I NEED TO CHECK SOMETHING.
HOW DID YOU...
I DIDN'T MEAN TO. THEY WERE TRYING TO TAKE ME, AND I JUST MOVED. SO QUICKLY. I DON'T KNOW HOW I--
--PLEASE, I DIDN'T MEAN TO HURT ANYONE. I DON'T KNOW WHAT'S HAPPENING.
NONE OF US DO.
COME WITH US. I WON'T LET ANYONE HURT YOU. MY NAME'S SHARP.
I'M MEIFENG. WHERE ARE WE GOING?
DOESN'T MATTER. UP, THEN OUT. COME ON!

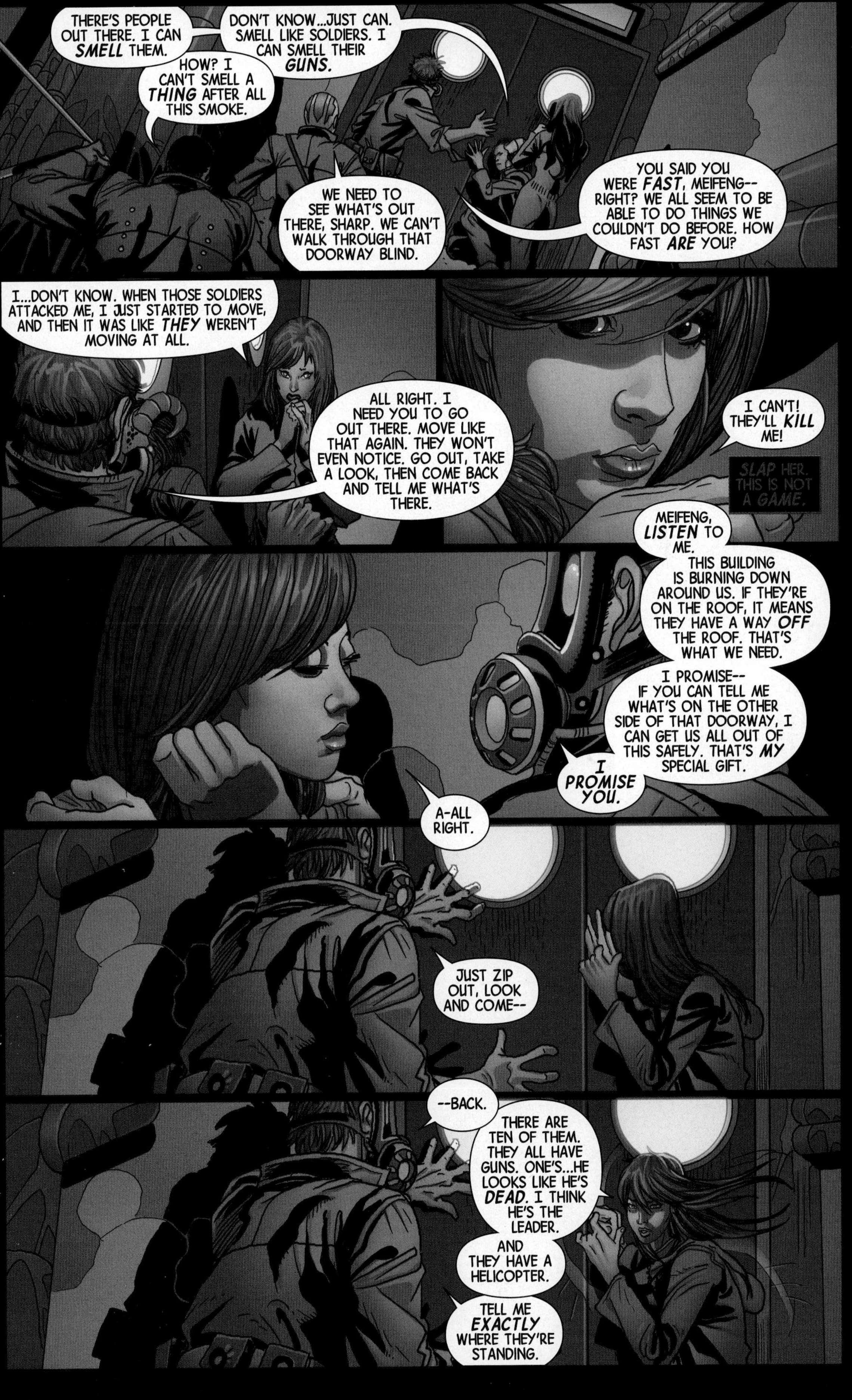

THERE'S PEOPLE OUT THERE. I CAN SMELL THEM.
HOW? I CAN'T SMELL A THING AFTER ALL THIS SMOKE.
DON'T KNOW...JUST CAN. SMELL LIKE SOLDIERS. I CAN SMELL THEIR GUNS.
WE NEED TO SEE WHAT'S OUT THERE, SHARP. WE CAN'T WALK THROUGH THAT DOORWAY BLIND.
YOU SAID YOU WERE FAST, MEIFENG-- RIGHT? WE ALL SEEM TO BE ABLE TO DO THINGS WE COULDN'T DO BEFORE. HOW FAST ARE YOU?
I...DON'T KNOW. WHEN THOSE SOLDIERS ATTACKED ME, I JUST STARTED TO MOVE, AND THEN IT WAS LIKE THEY WEREN'T MOVING AT ALL.
ALL RIGHT. I NEED YOU TO GO OUT THERE. MOVE LIKE THAT AGAIN. THEY WON'T EVEN NOTICE. GO OUT, TAKE A LOOK, THEN COME BACK AND TELL ME WHAT'S THERE.
I CAN'T! THEY'LL KILL ME!
SLAP HER. THIS IS NOT A GAME.
MEIFENG, LISTEN TO ME.
THIS BUILDING IS BURNING DOWN AROUND US. IF THEY'RE ON THE ROOF, IT MEANS THEY HAVE A WAY OFF THE ROOF. THAT'S WHAT WE NEED.
I PROMISE-- IF YOU CAN TELL ME WHAT'S ON THE OTHER SIDE OF THAT DOORWAY, I CAN GET US ALL OUT OF THIS SAFELY. THAT'S MY SPECIAL GIFT.
I PROMISE YOU.
A-ALL RIGHT.
JUST ZIP OUT, LOOK AND COME--
--BACK.
THERE ARE TEN OF THEM. THEY ALL HAVE GUNS. ONE'S...HE LOOKS LIKE HE'S DEAD. I THINK HE'S THE LEADER.
AND THEY HAVE A HELICOPTER.
TELL ME EXACTLY WHERE THEY'RE STANDING.

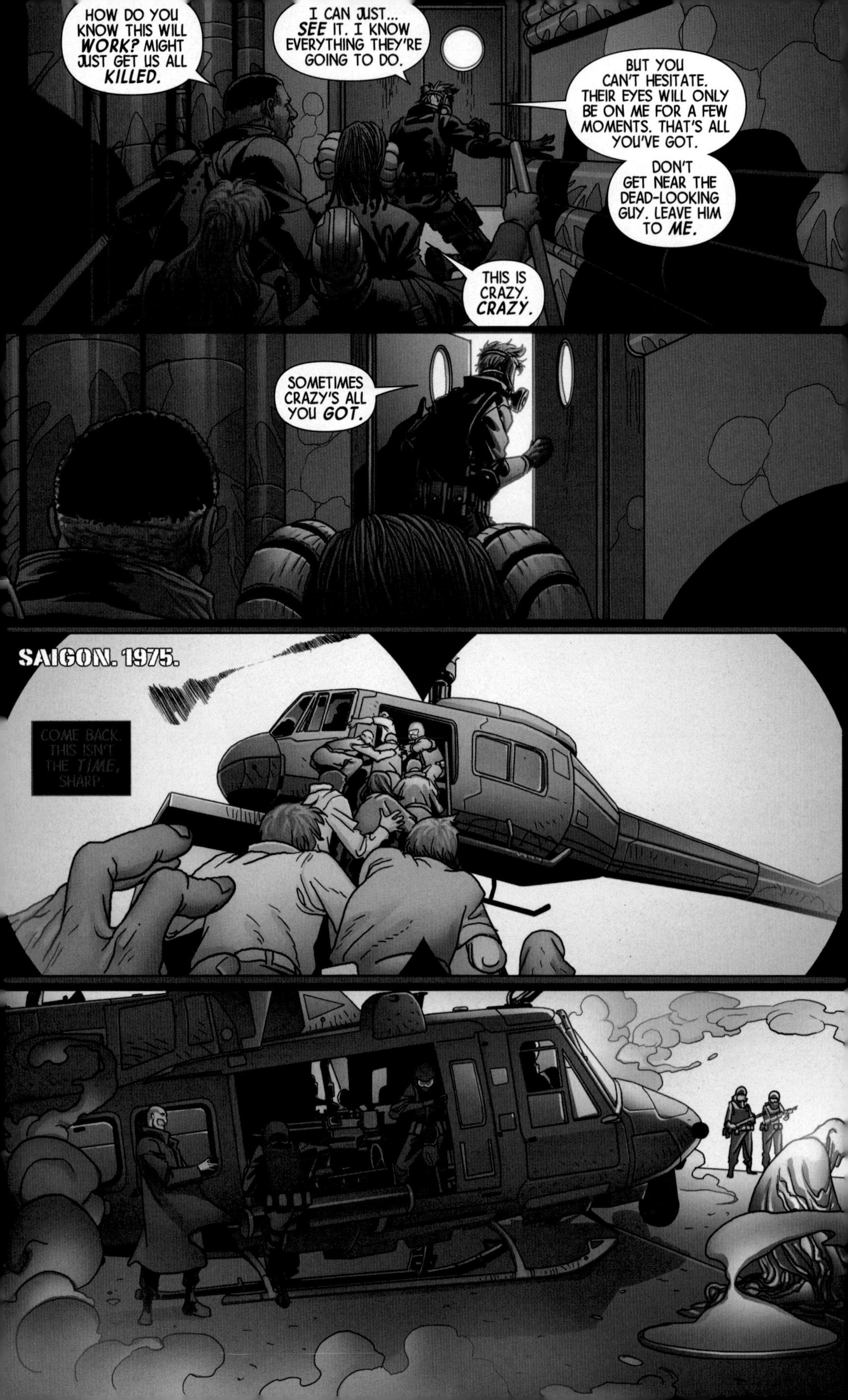
HOW DO YOU KNOW THIS WILL WORK? MIGHT JUST GET US ALL KILLED.
I CAN JUST... SEE IT. I KNOW EVERYTHING THEY'RE GOING TO DO.
BUT YOU CAN'T HESITATE. THEIR EYES WILL ONLY BE ON ME FOR A FEW MOMENTS. THAT'S ALL YOU'VE GOT.
DON'T GET NEAR THE DEAD-LOOKING GUY. LEAVE HIM TO ME.
THIS IS CRAZY. CRAZY.
SOMETIMES CRAZY'S ALL YOU GOT.
SAIGON. 1975.
COME BACK. THIS ISN'T THE TIME, SHARP.

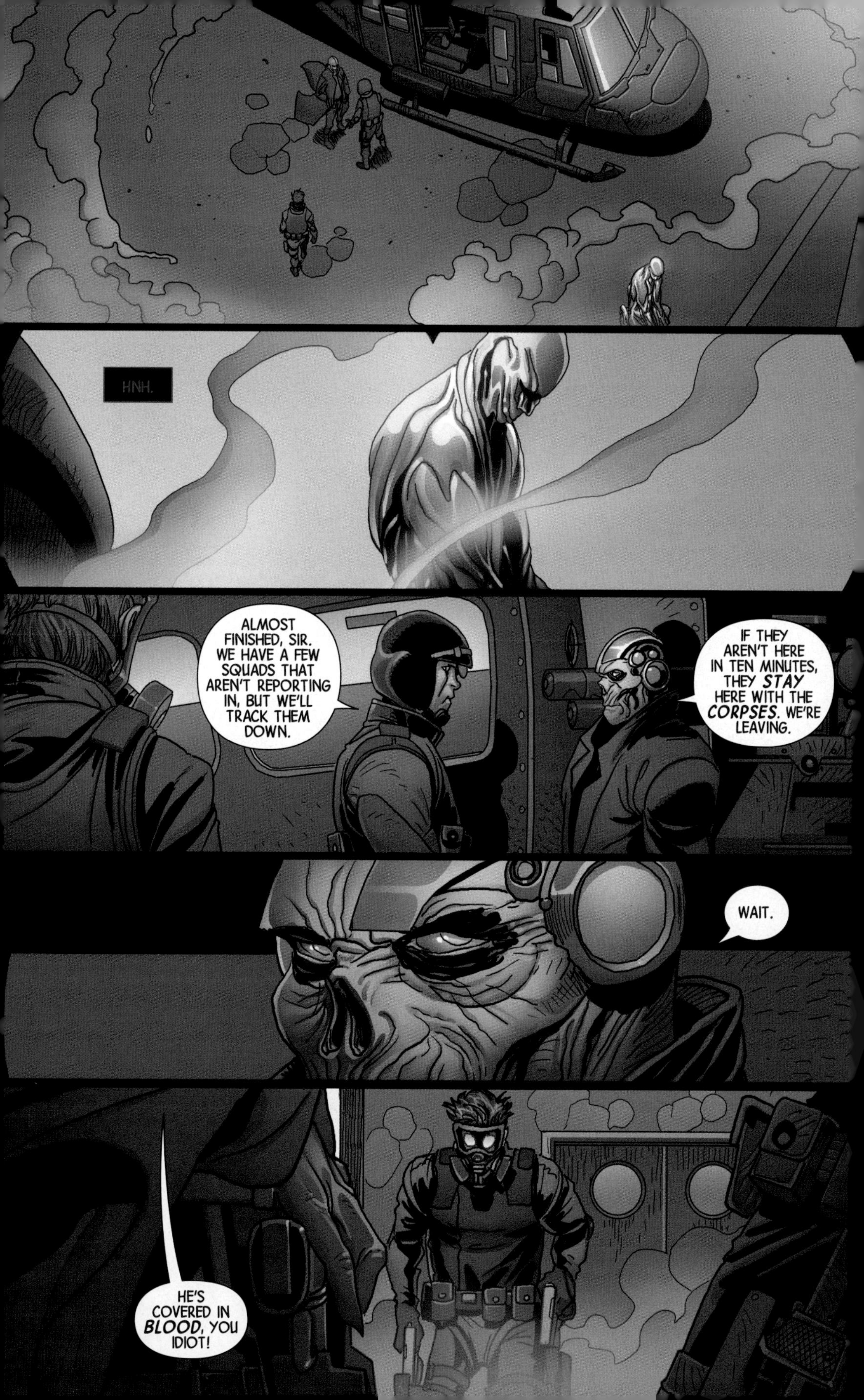
HNH.
ALMOST FINISHED, SIR. WE HAVE A FEW SQUADS THAT AREN'T REPORTING IN, BUT WE'LL TRACK THEM DOWN.
IF THEY AREN'T HERE IN TEN MINUTES, THEY STAY HERE WITH THE CORPSES. WE'RE LEAVING.
WAIT.
HE'S COVERED IN BLOOD, YOU IDIOT!

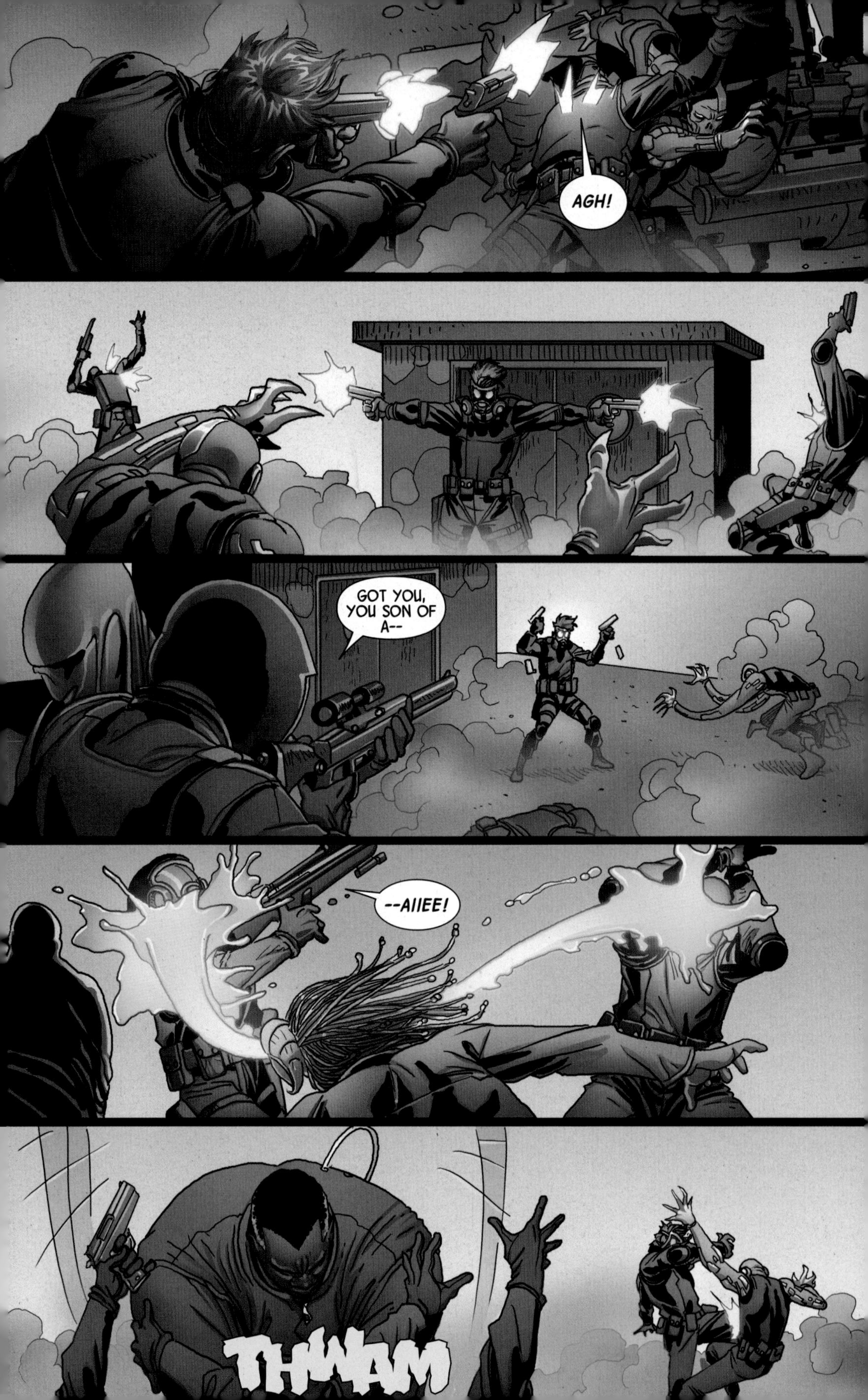
AGH!
GOT YOU, YOU SON OF A--
--AIIEE!
THWAM

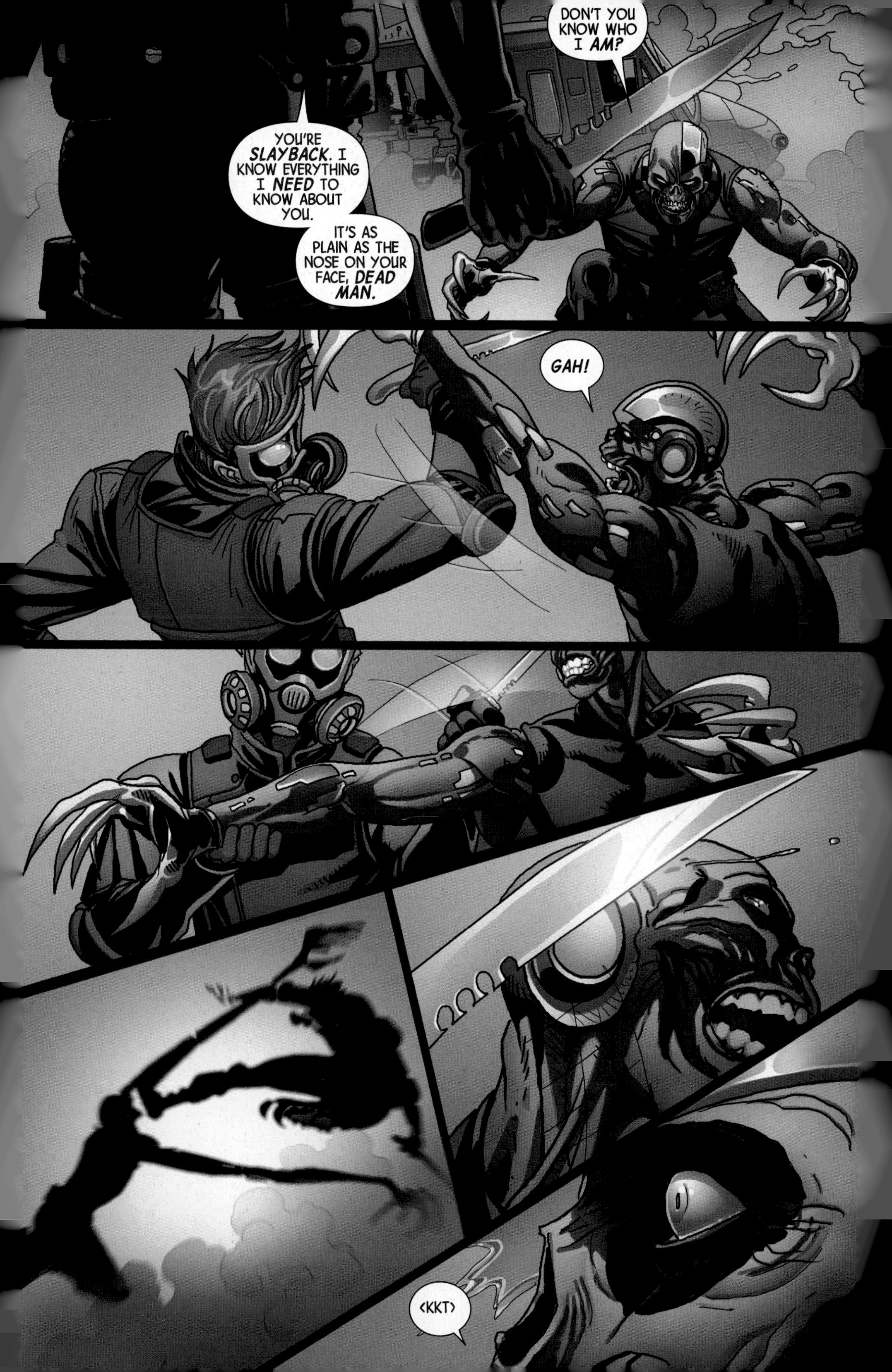
DON'T YOU KNOW WHO I AM?
YOU'RE SLAYBACK. I KNOW EVERYTHING I NEED TO KNOW ABOUT YOU.
IT'S AS PLAIN AS THE NOSE ON YOUR FACE, DEAD MAN.
GAH!
<KKT>

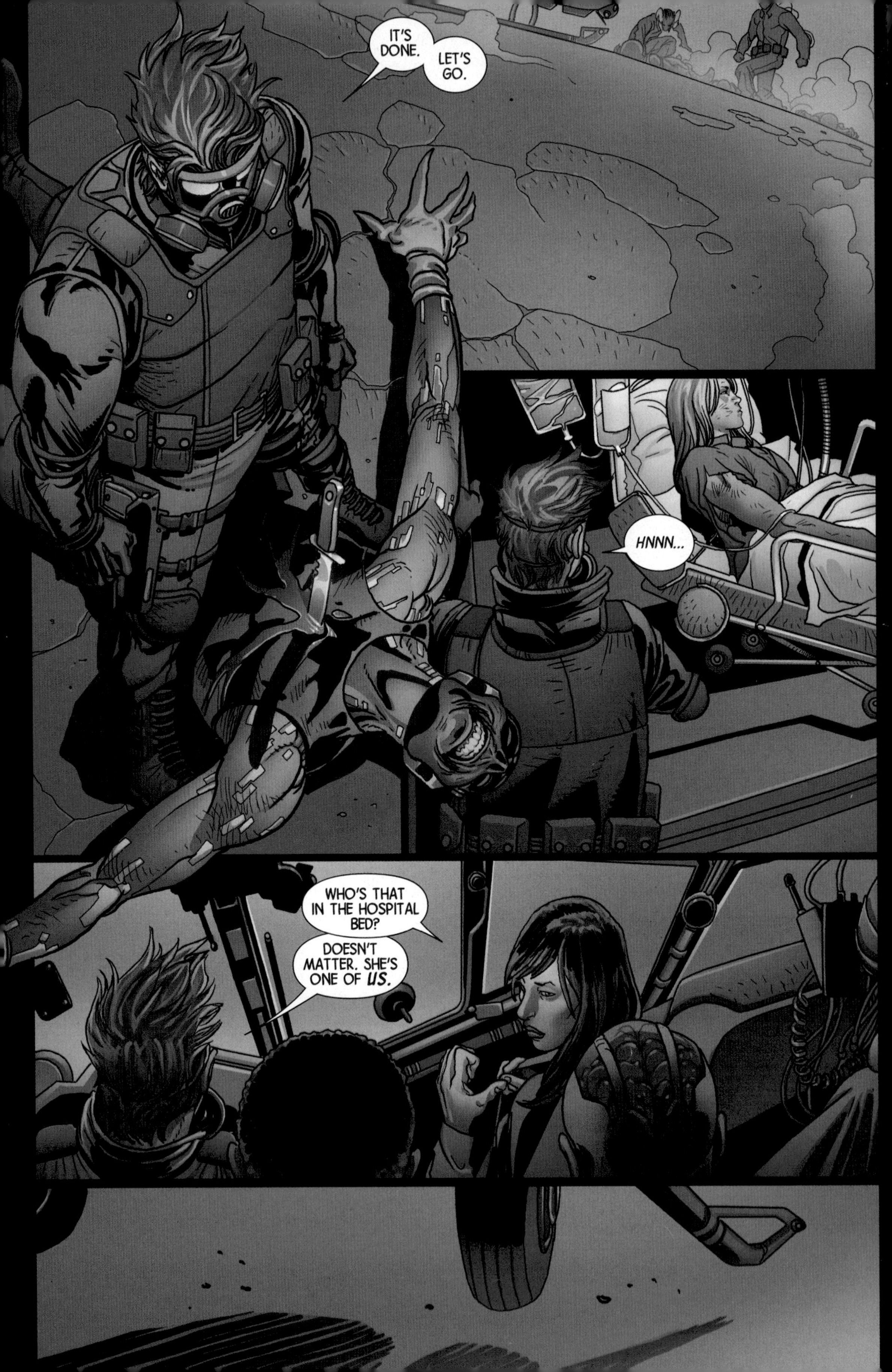
IT'S DONE.
LET'S GO.
HNNN...
WHO'S THAT IN THE HOSPITAL BED?
DOESN'T MATTER. SHE'S ONE OF US.

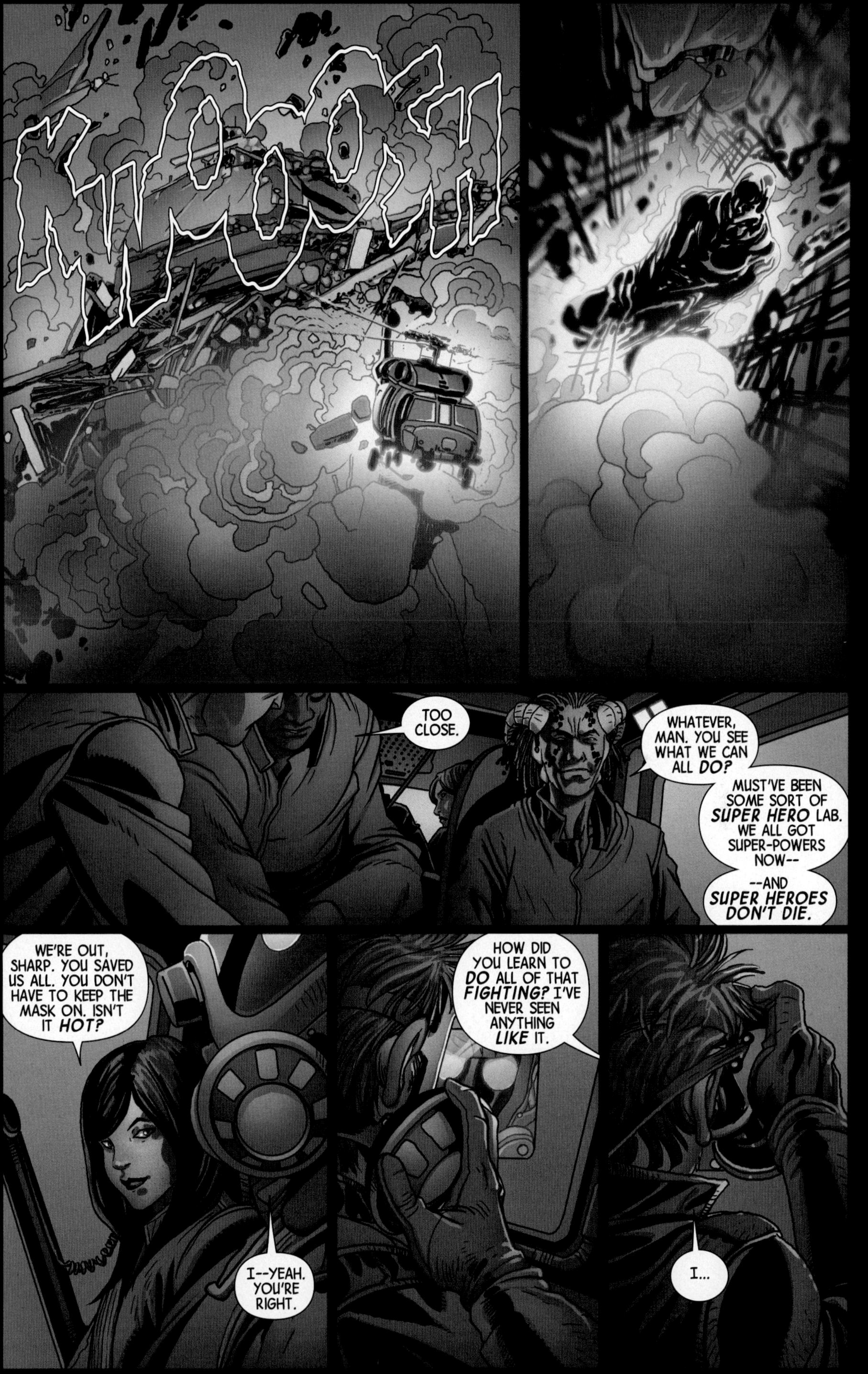
KRROOOOM
TOO CLOSE.
WHATEVER, MAN. YOU SEE WHAT WE CAN ALL DO?
MUST'VE BEEN SOME SORT OF SUPER HERO LAB. WE ALL GOT SUPER-POWERS NOW--
--AND SUPER HEROES DON'T DIE.
WE'RE OUT, SHARP. YOU SAVED US ALL. YOU DON'T HAVE TO KEEP THE MASK ON. ISN'T IT HOT?
I--YEAH. YOU'RE RIGHT.
HOW DID YOU LEARN TO DO ALL OF THAT FIGHTING? I'VE NEVER SEEN ANYTHING LIKE IT.
I...

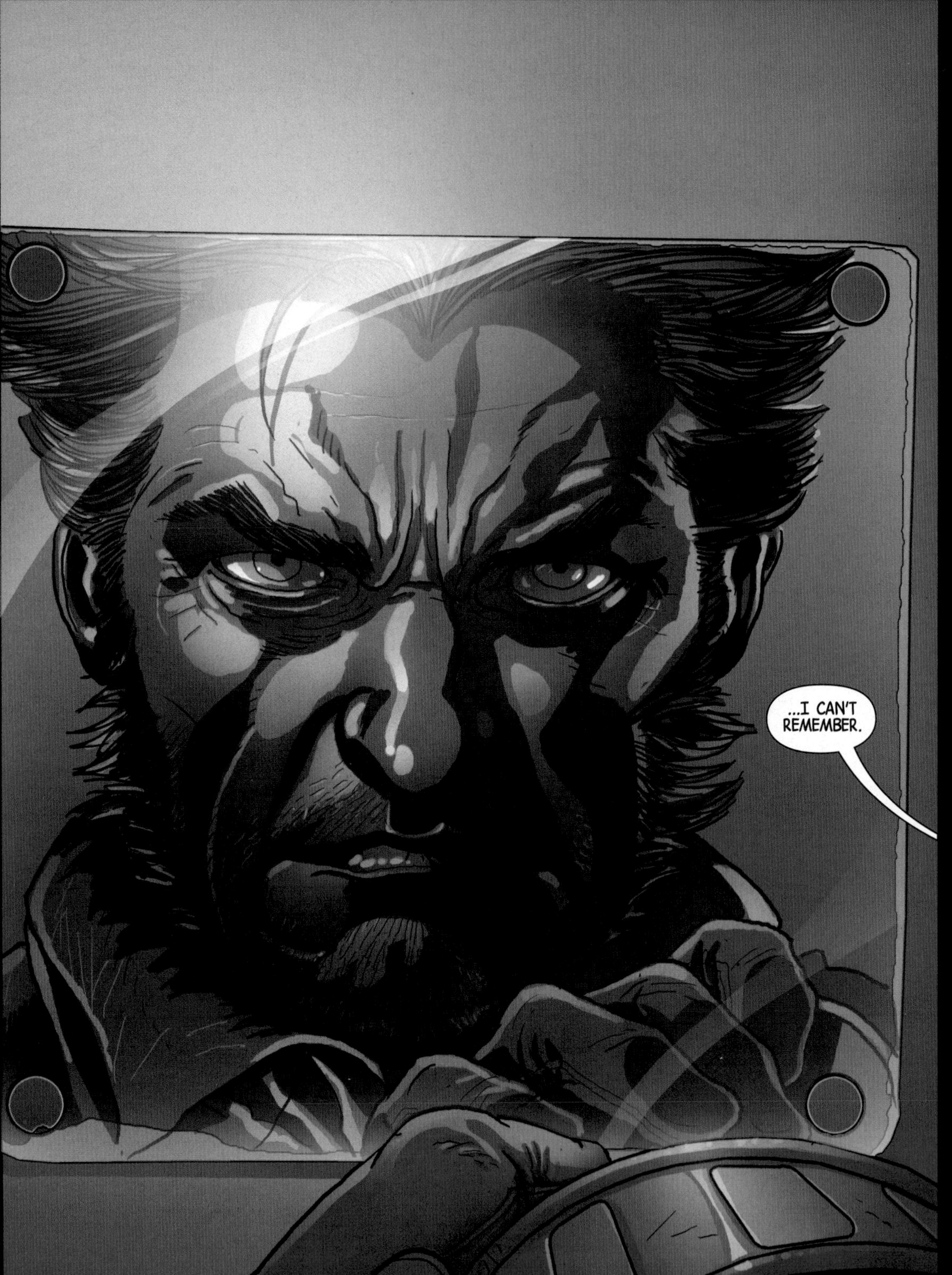
...I CAN'T REMEMBER.

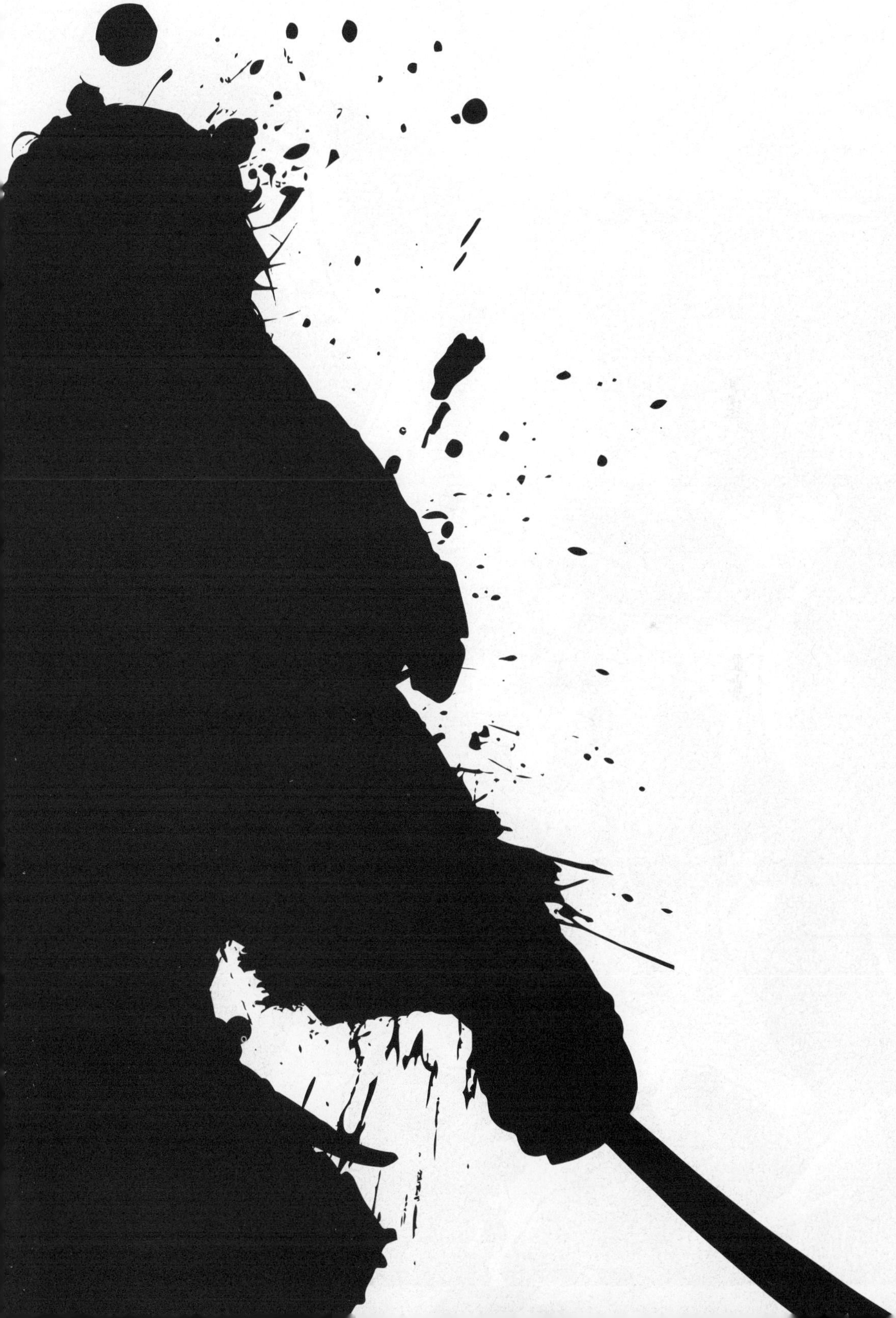

2 HYPOTHESIS

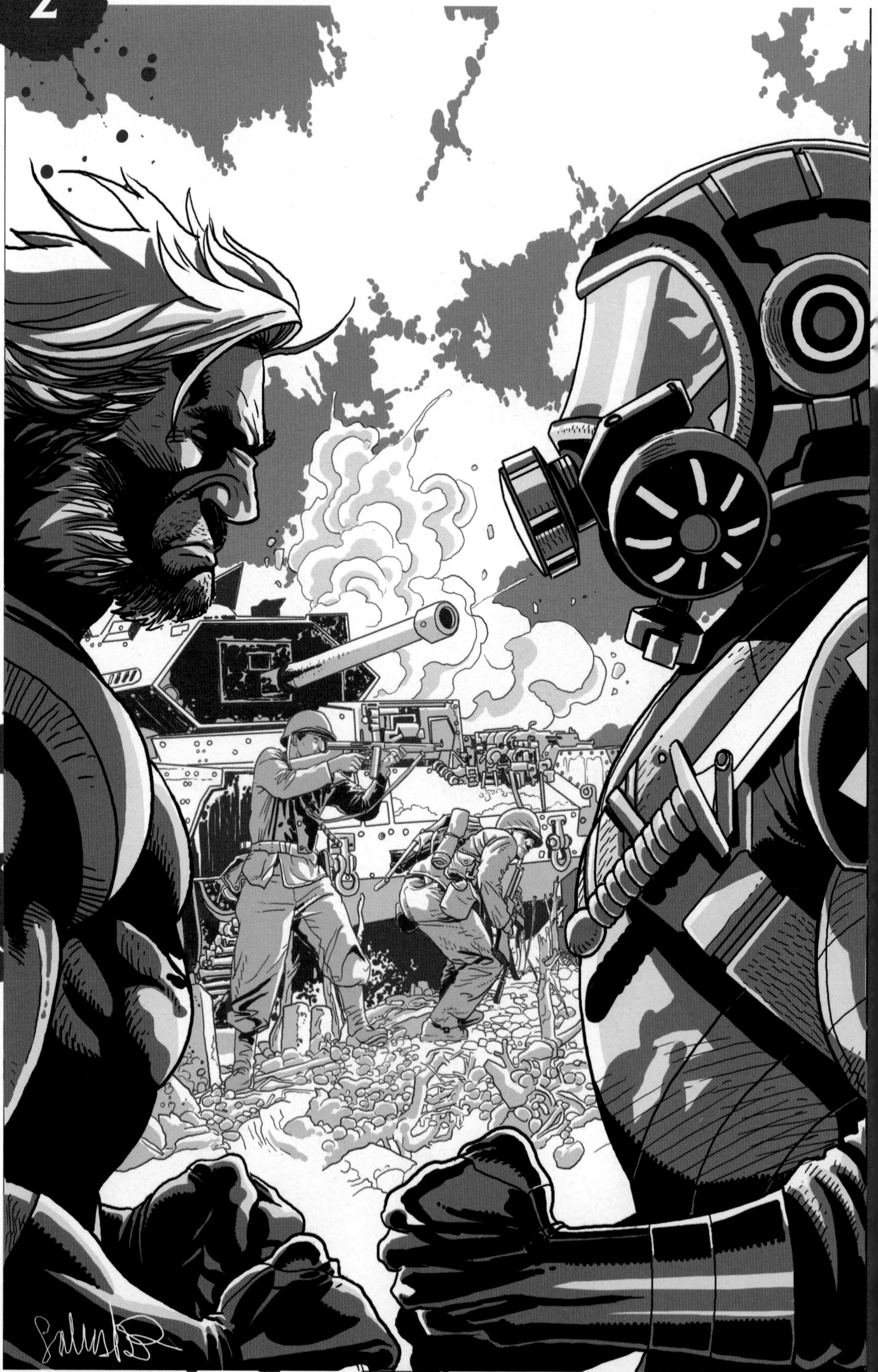

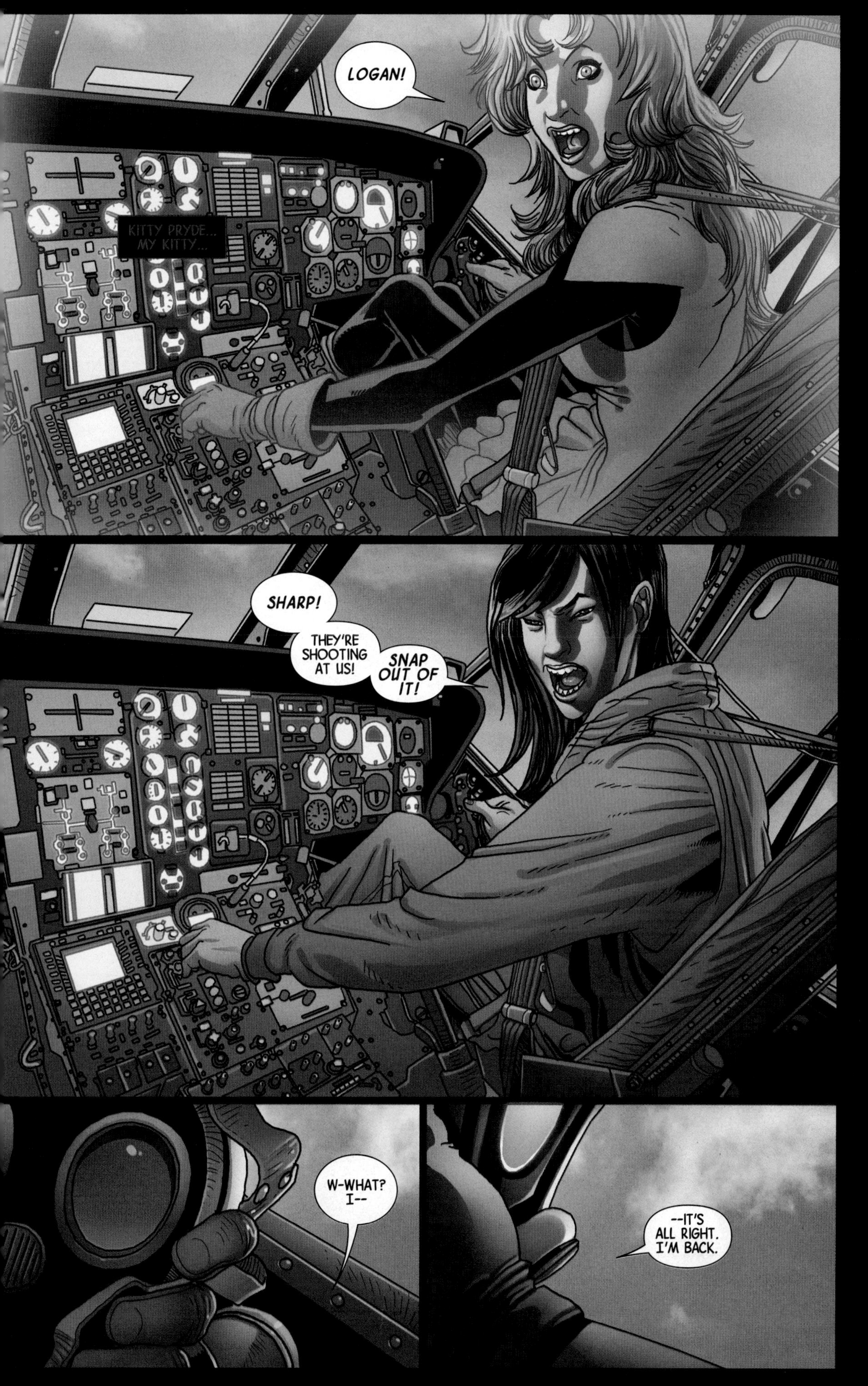
LOGAN!
KITTY PRYDE... MY KITTY...
SHARP!
THEY'RE SHOOTING AT US!
SNAP OUT OF IT!
W-WHAT? I--
--IT'S ALL RIGHT. I'M BACK.

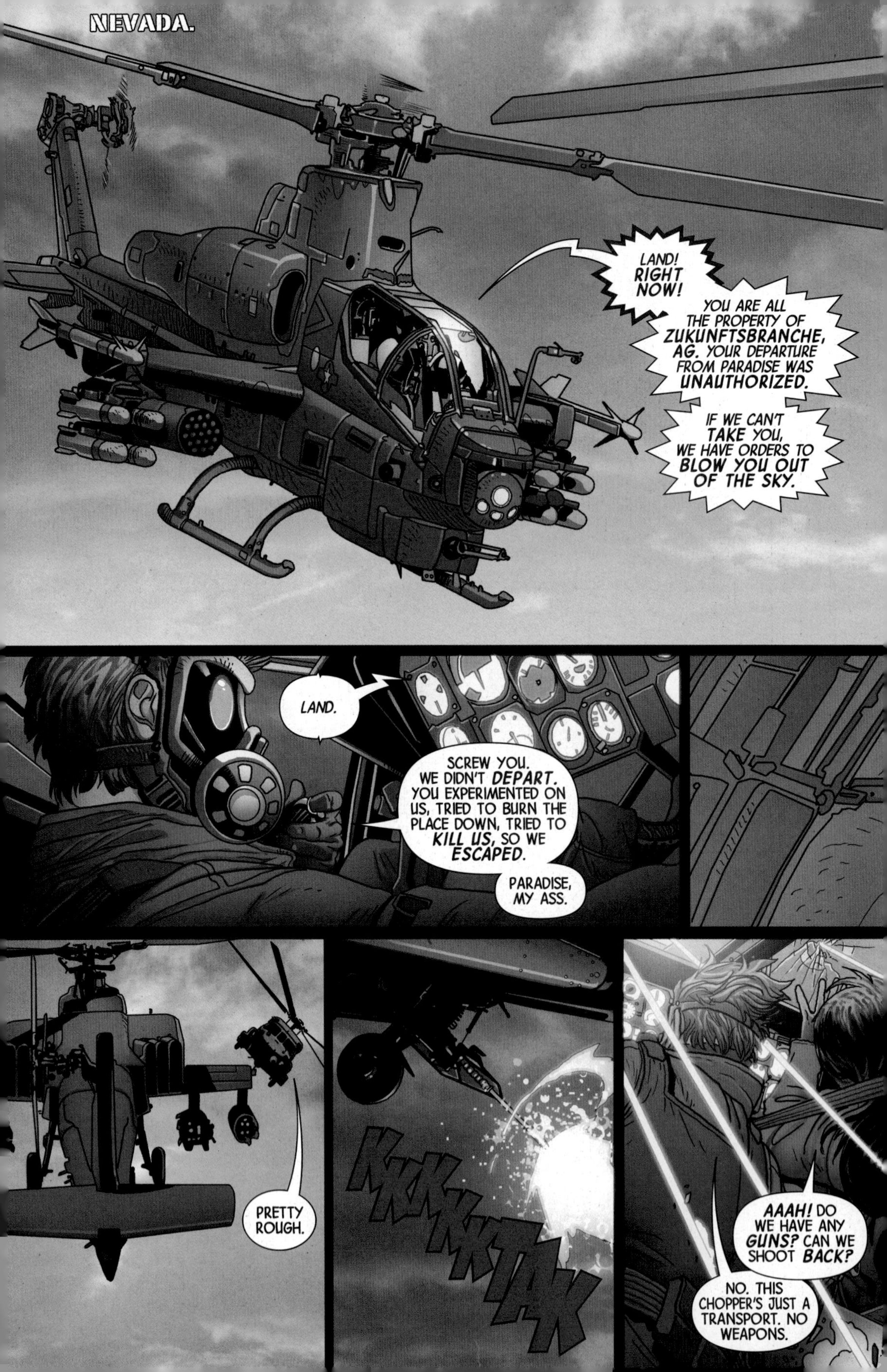
NEVADA.
LAND! RIGHT NOW!
YOU ARE ALL THE PROPERTY OF ZUKUNFTSBRANCHE, AG. YOUR DEPARTURE FROM PARADISE WAS UNAUTHORIZED.
IF WE CAN'T TAKE YOU, WE HAVE ORDERS TO BLOW YOU OUT OF THE SKY.
LAND.
SCREW YOU. WE DIDN'T DEPART. YOU EXPERIMENTED ON US, TRIED TO BURN THE PLACE DOWN, TRIED TO KILL US, SO WE ESCAPED.
PARADISE, MY ASS.
PRETTY ROUGH.
KKKKKTAK
AAAH! DO WE HAVE ANY GUNS? CAN WE SHOOT BACK?
NO. THIS CHOPPER'S JUST A TRANSPORT. NO WEAPONS.

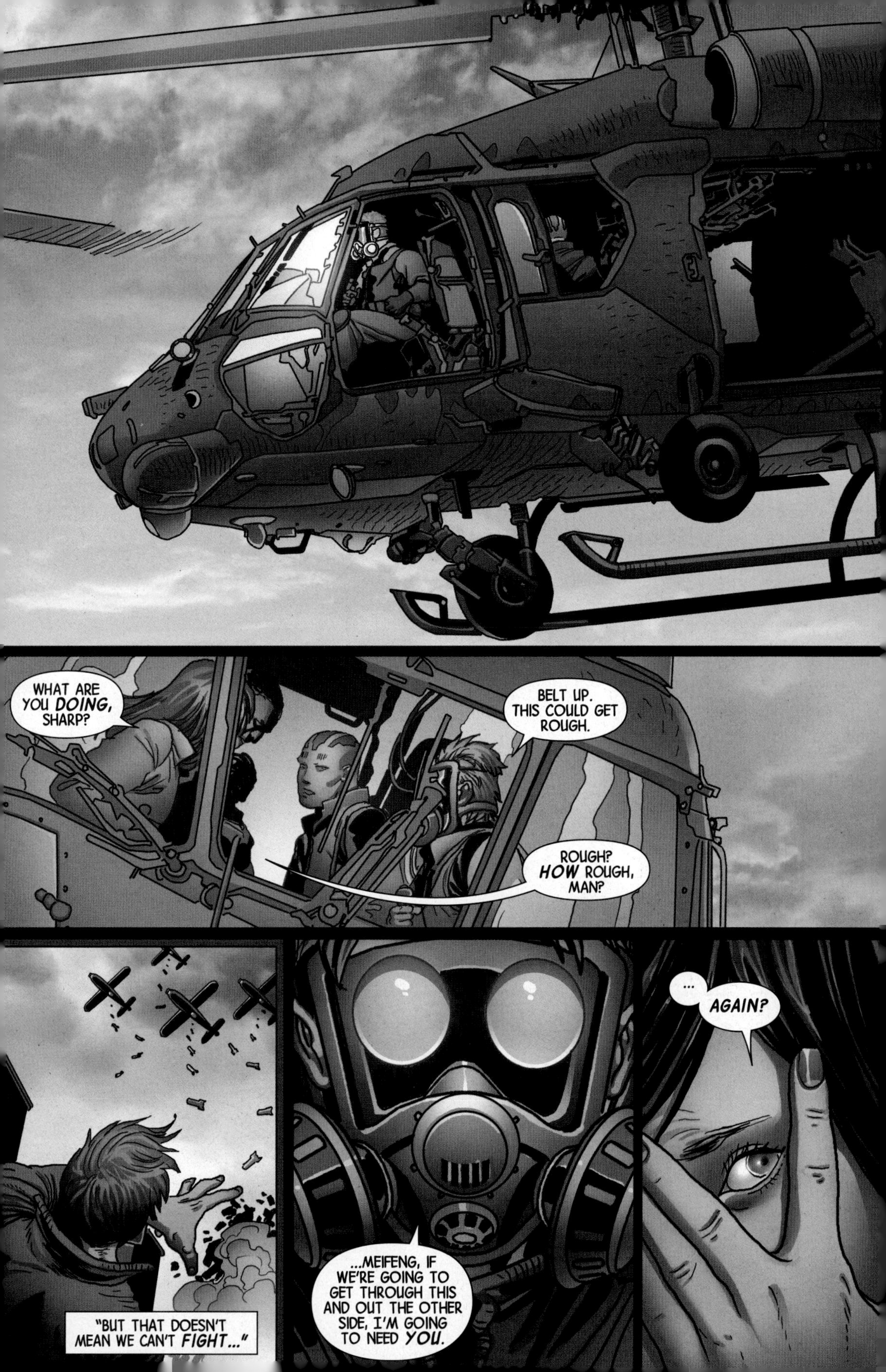
WHAT ARE YOU DOING, SHARP?
BELT UP. THIS COULD GET ROUGH.
ROUGH? HOW ROUGH, MAN?
"BUT THAT DOESN'T MEAN WE CAN'T FIGHT..."
...MEIFENG, IF WE'RE GOING TO GET THROUGH THIS AND OUT THE OTHER SIDE, I'M GOING TO NEED YOU.
... AGAIN?

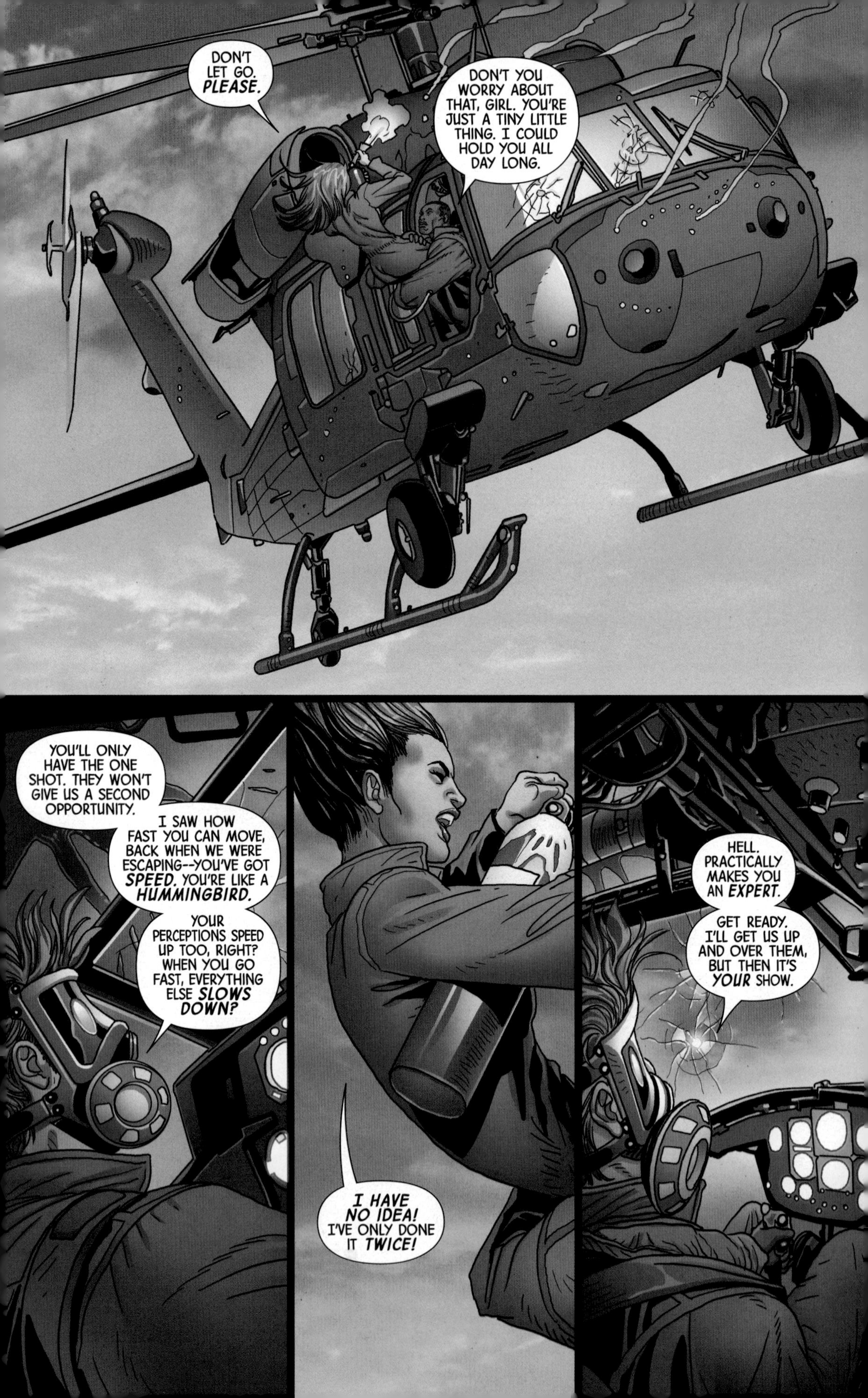
DON'T LET GO. PLEASE.
DON'T YOU WORRY ABOUT THAT, GIRL. YOU'RE JUST A TINY LITTLE THING. I COULD HOLD YOU ALL DAY LONG.
YOU'LL ONLY HAVE THE ONE SHOT. THEY WON'T GIVE US A SECOND OPPORTUNITY.
I SAW HOW FAST YOU CAN MOVE, BACK WHEN WE WERE ESCAPING--YOU'VE GOT SPEED. YOU'RE LIKE A HUMMINGBIRD.
YOUR PERCEPTIONS SPEED UP TOO, RIGHT? WHEN YOU GO FAST, EVERYTHING ELSE SLOWS DOWN?
I HAVE NO IDEA! I'VE ONLY DONE IT TWICE!
HELL. PRACTICALLY MAKES YOU AN EXPERT.
GET READY. I'LL GET US UP AND OVER THEM, BUT THEN IT'S YOUR SHOW.

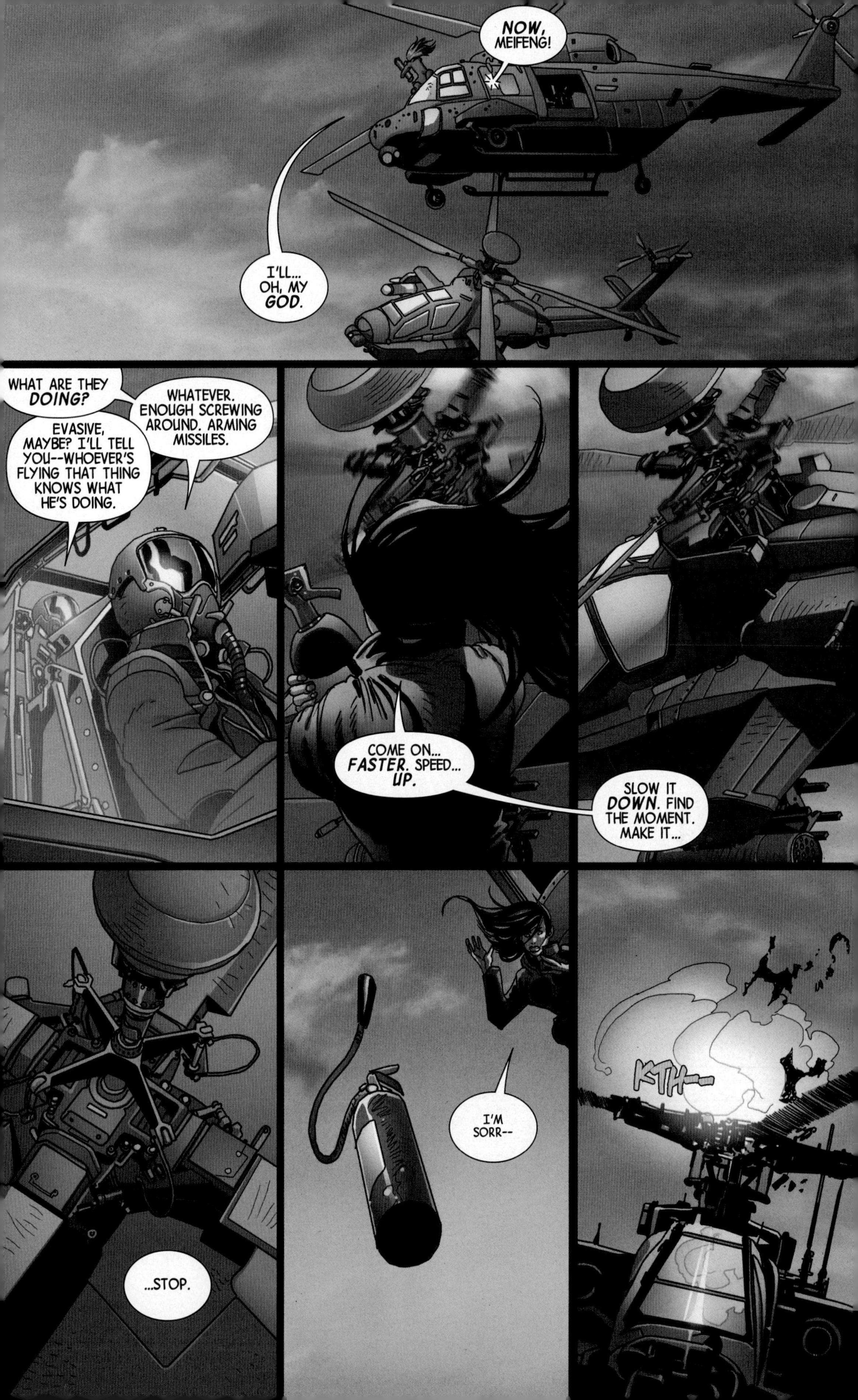
NOW, MEIFENG!
I'LL... OH, MY GOD.
WHAT ARE THEY DOING?
EVASIVE, MAYBE? I'LL TELL YOU--WHOEVER'S FLYING THAT THING KNOWS WHAT HE'S DOING.
WHATEVER. ENOUGH SCREWING AROUND. ARMING MISSILES.
COME ON... FASTER. SPEED... UP.
SLOW IT DOWN. FIND THE MOMENT. MAKE IT...
...STOP.
I'M SORR--
KTH--

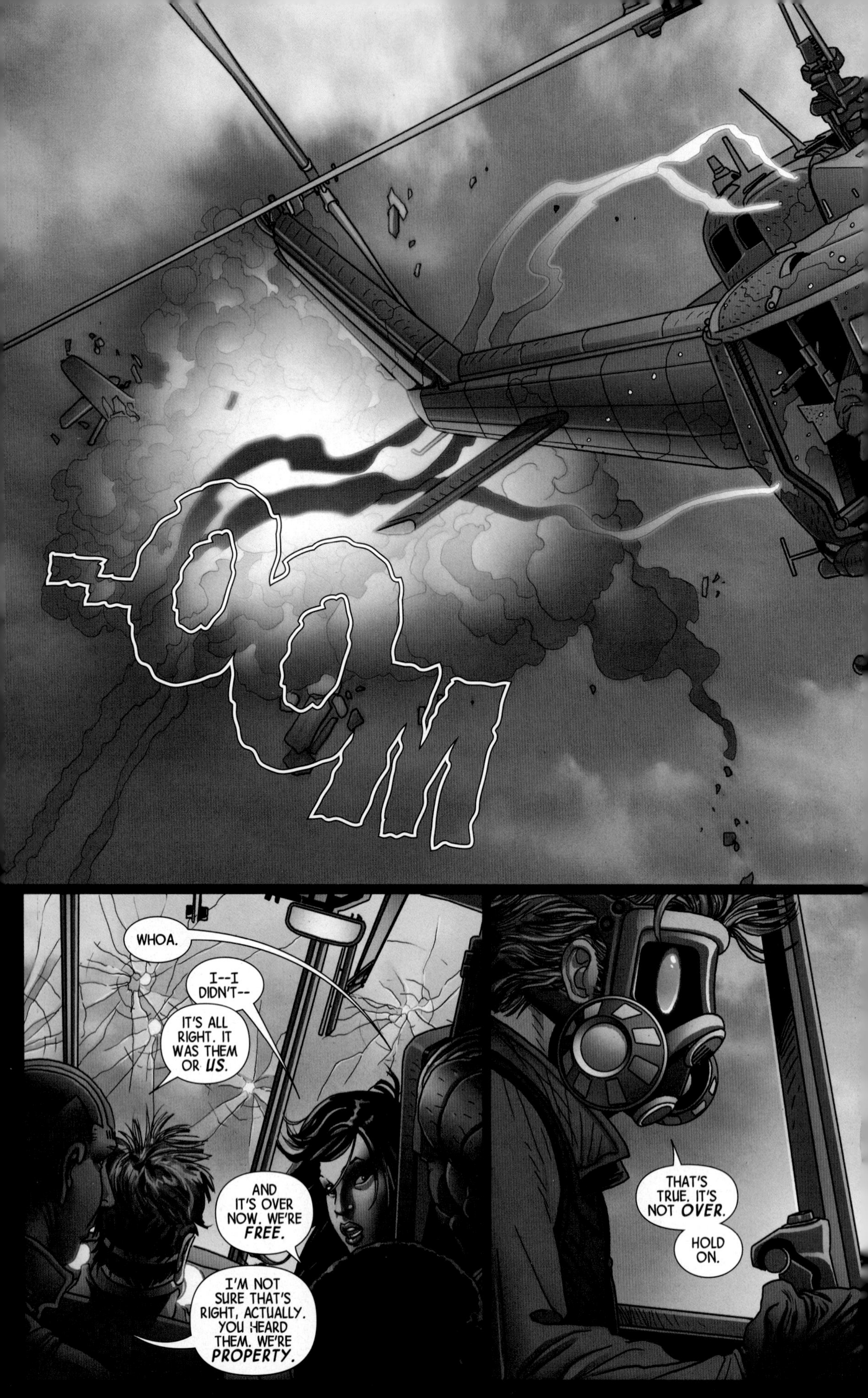

WHOA.
I--I DIDN'T--
IT'S ALL RIGHT. IT WAS THEM OR *US*.
AND IT'S OVER NOW. WE'RE *FREE*.
I'M NOT SURE THAT'S RIGHT, ACTUALLY. YOU HEARD THEM. WE'RE *PROPERTY*.
THAT'S TRUE. IT'S NOT *OVER*.
HOLD ON.

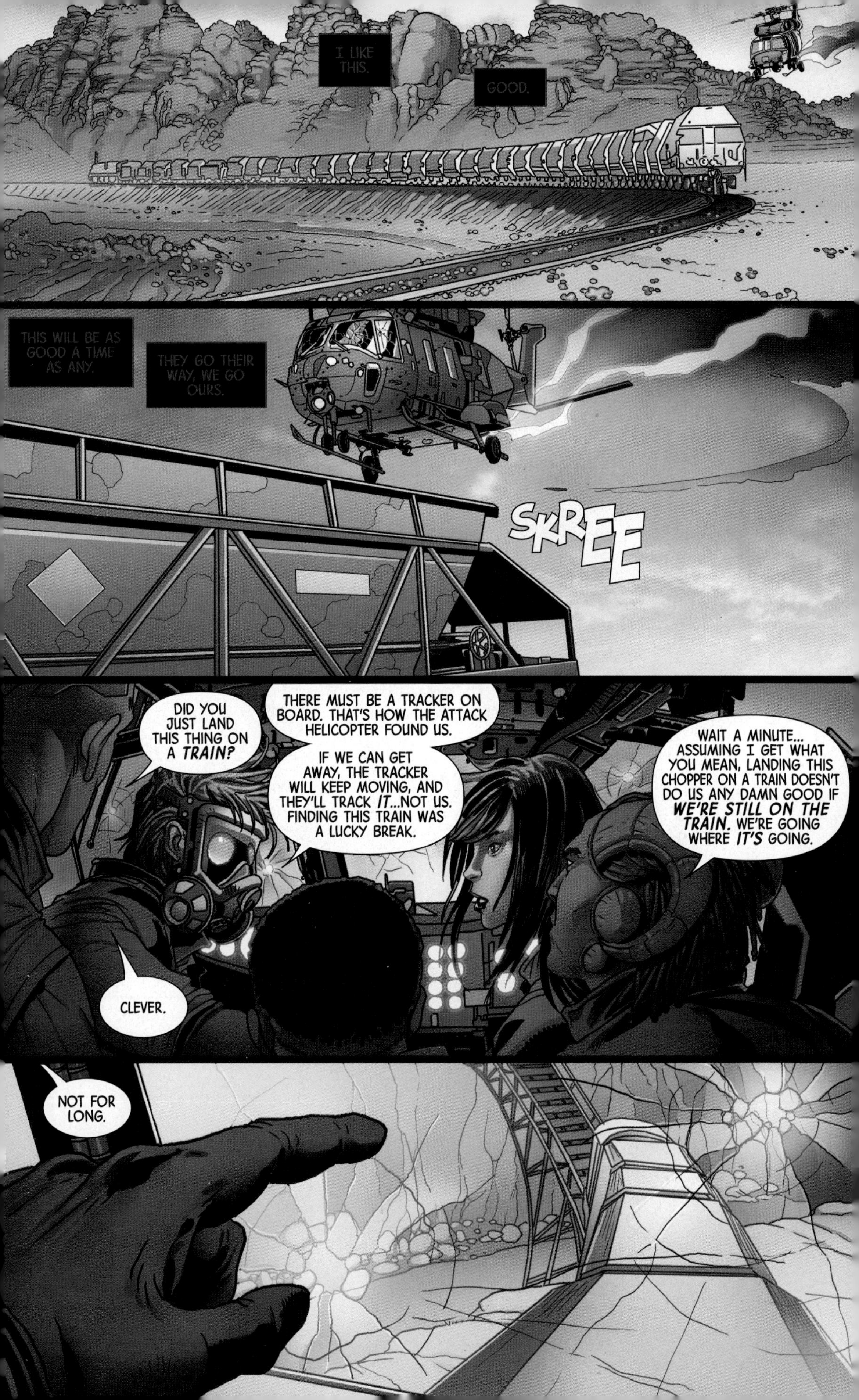
I LIKE THIS.
GOOD.
THIS WILL BE AS GOOD A TIME AS ANY.
THEY GO THEIR WAY, WE GO OURS.
SKREEE
DID YOU JUST LAND THIS THING ON A *TRAIN?*
THERE MUST BE A TRACKER ON BOARD. THAT'S HOW THE ATTACK HELICOPTER FOUND US.
IF WE CAN GET AWAY, THE TRACKER WILL KEEP MOVING, AND THEY'LL TRACK *IT*...NOT US. FINDING THIS TRAIN WAS A LUCKY BREAK.
WAIT A MINUTE... ASSUMING I GET WHAT YOU MEAN, LANDING THIS CHOPPER ON A TRAIN DOESN'T DO US ANY DAMN GOOD IF *WE'RE STILL ON THE TRAIN.* WE'RE GOING WHERE *IT'S* GOING.
CLEVER.
NOT FOR LONG.

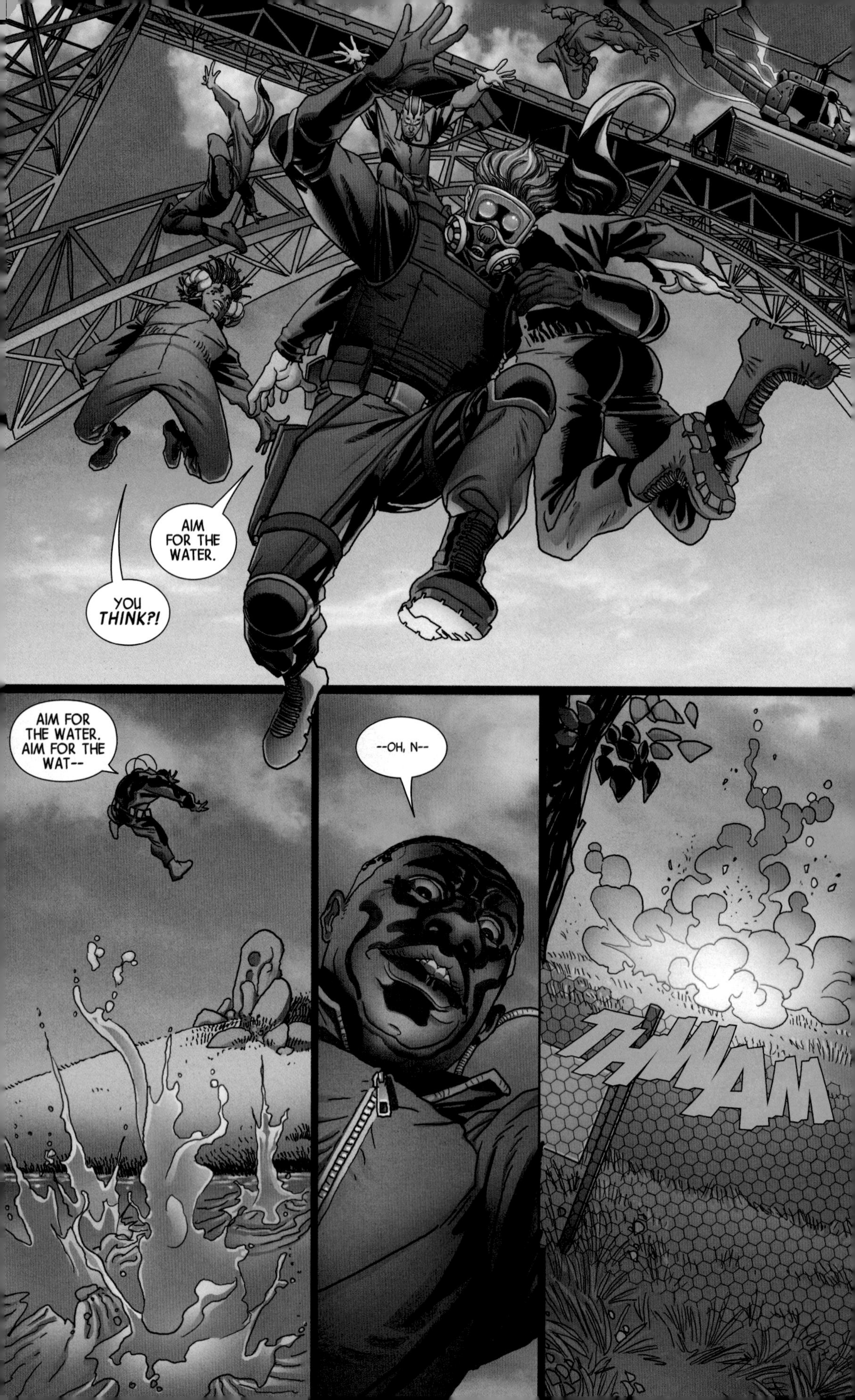
AIM FOR THE WATER.
YOU THINK?!
AIM FOR THE WATER. AIM FOR THE WAT--
--OH, N--
THWAM

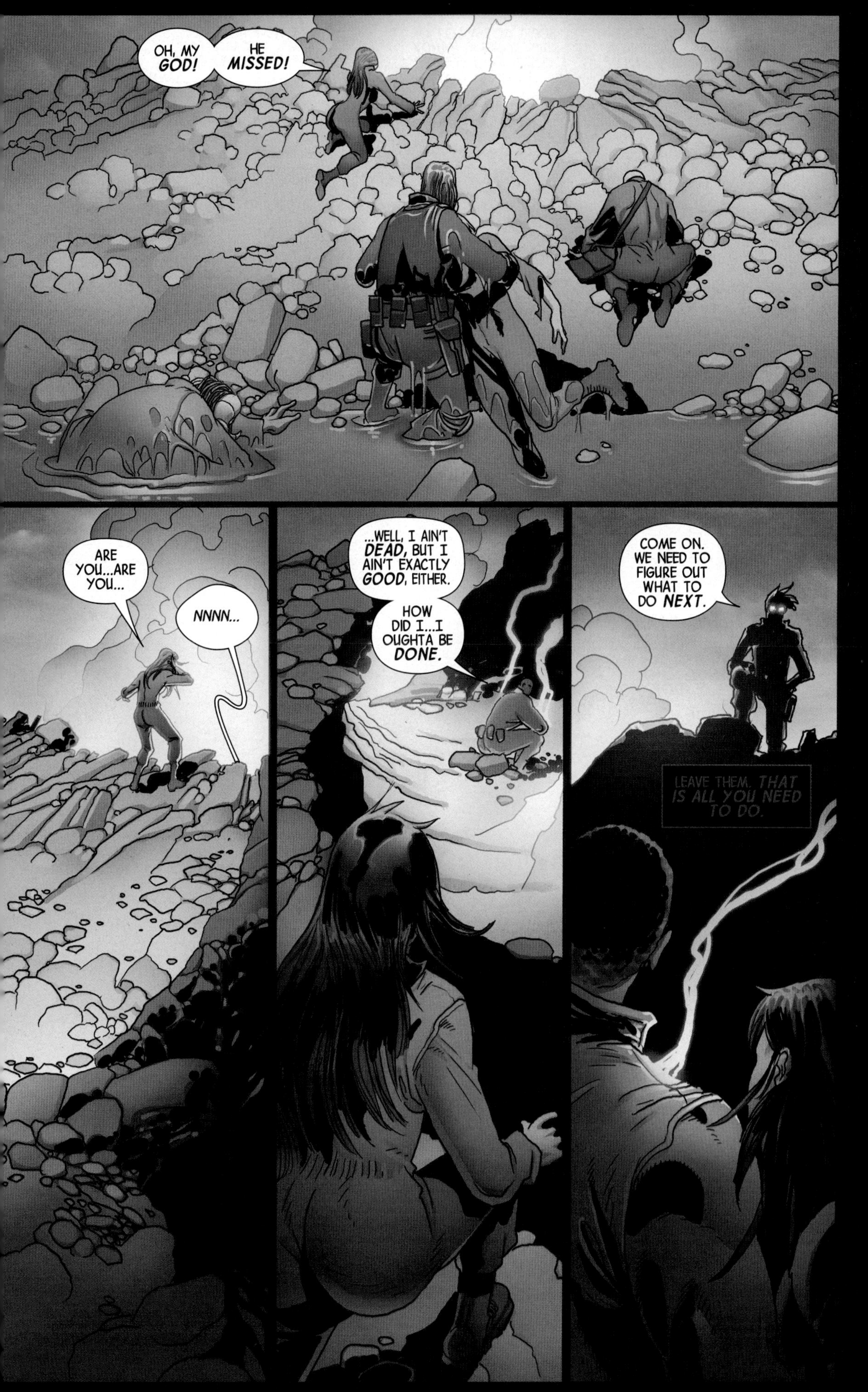
OH, MY GOD!
HE MISSED!
ARE YOU...ARE YOU...
NNNN...
...WELL, I AIN'T DEAD, BUT I AIN'T EXACTLY GOOD, EITHER.
HOW DID I...I OUGHTA BE DONE.
COME ON. WE NEED TO FIGURE OUT WHAT TO DO NEXT.
LEAVE THEM. THAT IS ALL YOU NEED TO DO.

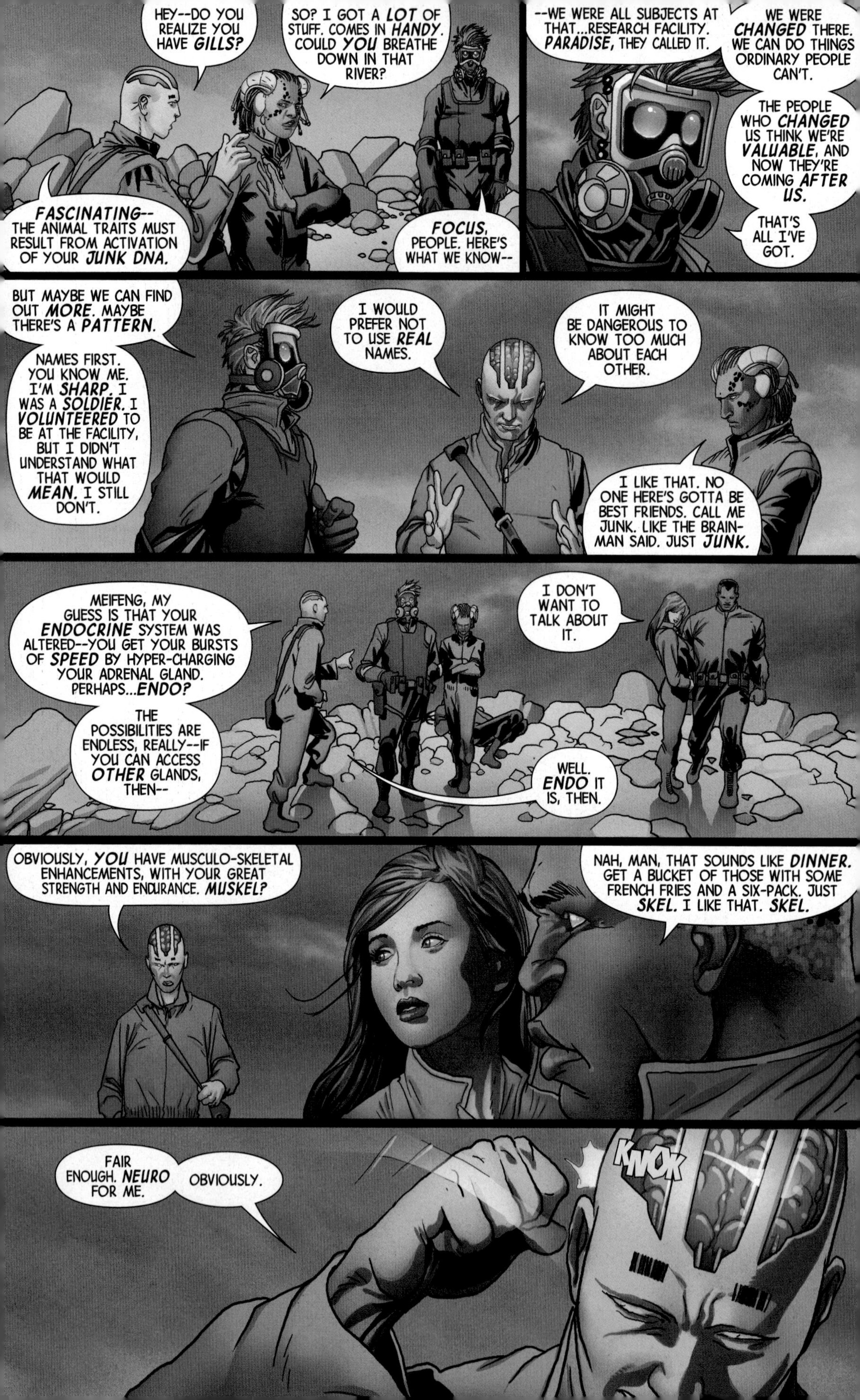
HEY--DO YOU REALIZE YOU HAVE GILLS?
SO? I GOT A LOT OF STUFF. COMES IN HANDY. COULD YOU BREATHE DOWN IN THAT RIVER?
FASCINATING-- THE ANIMAL TRAITS MUST RESULT FROM ACTIVATION OF YOUR JUNK DNA.
FOCUS, PEOPLE. HERE'S WHAT WE KNOW--
--WE WERE ALL SUBJECTS AT THAT...RESEARCH FACILITY. PARADISE, THEY CALLED IT.
WE WERE CHANGED THERE. WE CAN DO THINGS ORDINARY PEOPLE CAN'T.
THE PEOPLE WHO CHANGED US THINK WE'RE VALUABLE, AND NOW THEY'RE COMING AFTER US.
THAT'S ALL I'VE GOT.
BUT MAYBE WE CAN FIND OUT MORE. MAYBE THERE'S A PATTERN.
NAMES FIRST. YOU KNOW ME. I'M SHARP. I WAS A SOLDIER. I VOLUNTEERED TO BE AT THE FACILITY, BUT I DIDN'T UNDERSTAND WHAT THAT WOULD MEAN. I STILL DON'T.
I WOULD PREFER NOT TO USE REAL NAMES.
IT MIGHT BE DANGEROUS TO KNOW TOO MUCH ABOUT EACH OTHER.
I LIKE THAT. NO ONE HERE'S GOTTA BE BEST FRIENDS. CALL ME JUNK. LIKE THE BRAIN-MAN SAID. JUST JUNK.
MEIFENG, MY GUESS IS THAT YOUR ENDOCRINE SYSTEM WAS ALTERED--YOU GET YOUR BURSTS OF SPEED BY HYPER-CHARGING YOUR ADRENAL GLAND. PERHAPS...ENDO?
THE POSSIBILITIES ARE ENDLESS, REALLY--IF YOU CAN ACCESS OTHER GLANDS, THEN--
I DON'T WANT TO TALK ABOUT IT.
WELL. ENDO IT IS, THEN.
OBVIOUSLY, YOU HAVE MUSCULO-SKELETAL ENHANCEMENTS, WITH YOUR GREAT STRENGTH AND ENDURANCE. MUSKEL?
NAH, MAN, THAT SOUNDS LIKE DINNER. GET A BUCKET OF THOSE WITH SOME FRENCH FRIES AND A SIX-PACK. JUST SKEL. I LIKE THAT. SKEL.
FAIR ENOUGH. NEURO FOR ME.
OBVIOUSLY.
KNOK

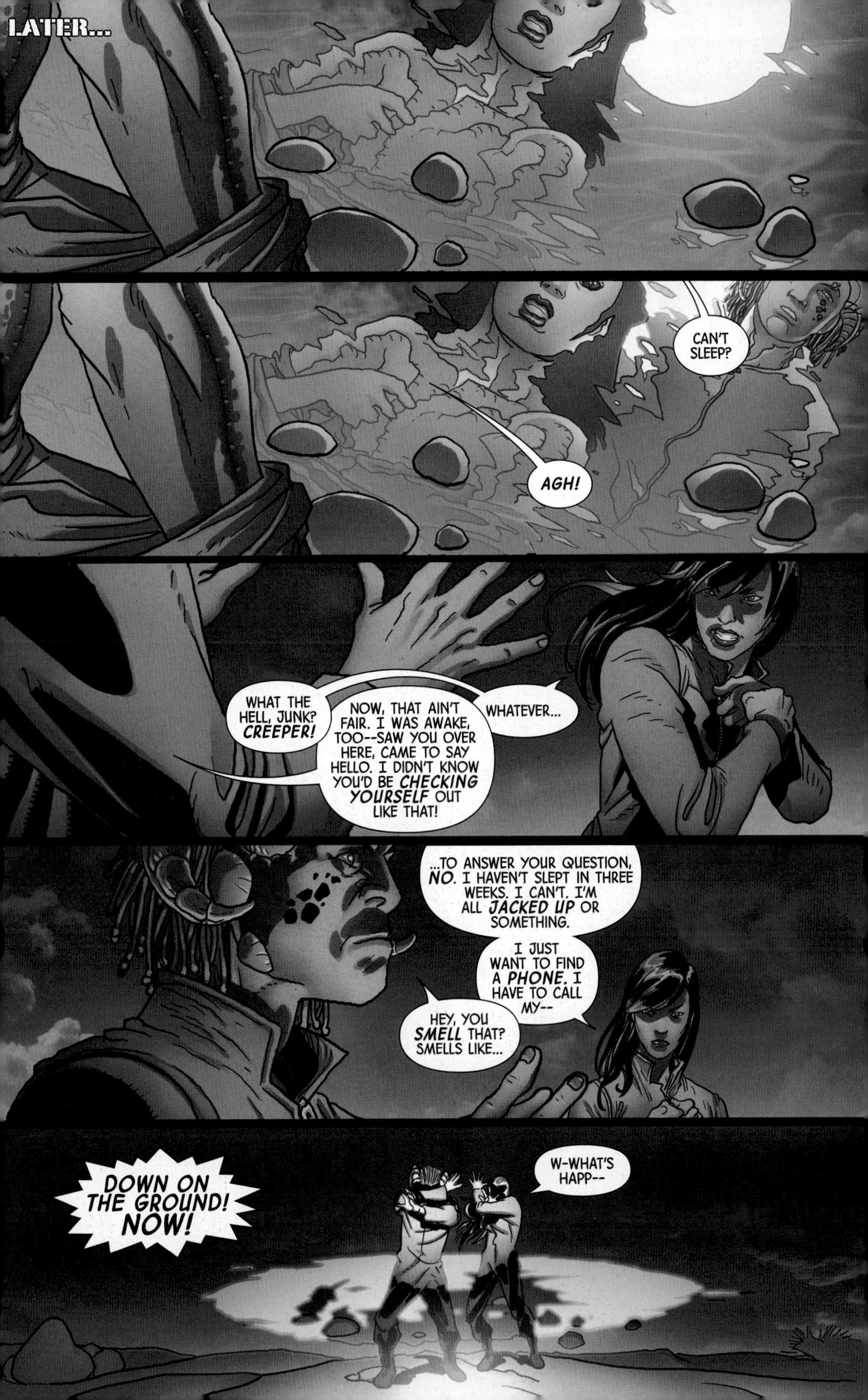
LATER...
CAN'T SLEEP?
AGH!
WHAT THE HELL, JUNK? CREEPER!
NOW, THAT AIN'T FAIR. I WAS AWAKE, TOO--SAW YOU OVER HERE, CAME TO SAY HELLO. I DIDN'T KNOW YOU'D BE CHECKING YOURSELF OUT LIKE THAT!
WHATEVER...
...TO ANSWER YOUR QUESTION, NO. I HAVEN'T SLEPT IN THREE WEEKS. I CAN'T. I'M ALL JACKED UP OR SOMETHING.
I JUST WANT TO FIND A PHONE. I HAVE TO CALL MY--
HEY, YOU SMELL THAT? SMELLS LIKE...
DOWN ON THE GROUND! NOW!
W-WHAT'S HAPP--

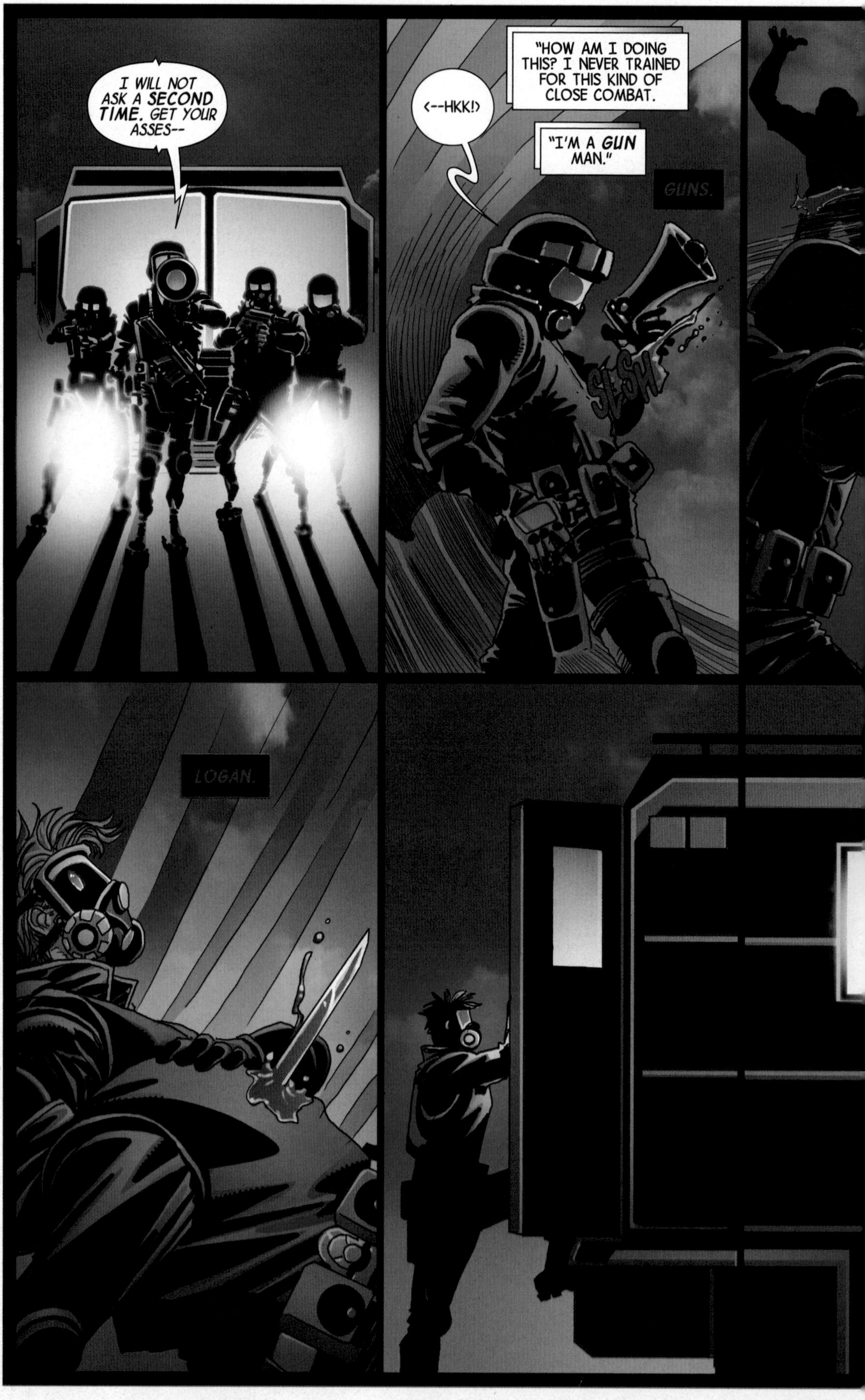
I WILL NOT ASK A SECOND TIME. GET YOUR ASSES--
"HOW AM I DOING THIS? I NEVER TRAINED FOR THIS KIND OF CLOSE COMBAT.
<--HKK!>
"I'M A GUN MAN."
GUNS.
SLSH
LOGAN.

SEE HOW MUCH GOOD GUNS DO THESE FOOLS.
DID *CORNELIUS* GIVE ME THIS? IS THAT HOW I'M DOING IT?
ANOTHER FOOL.
DO IT LIKE *THIS.*
"ARE YOU THE FACE I SAW IN THE MIRROR? THAT'S NOT MY FACE.
"NOT THE FACE I *REMEMBER,* ANYWAY. MAYBE THAT CHANGED, TOO."
KRRACK
WHO *IS* THIS GUY?

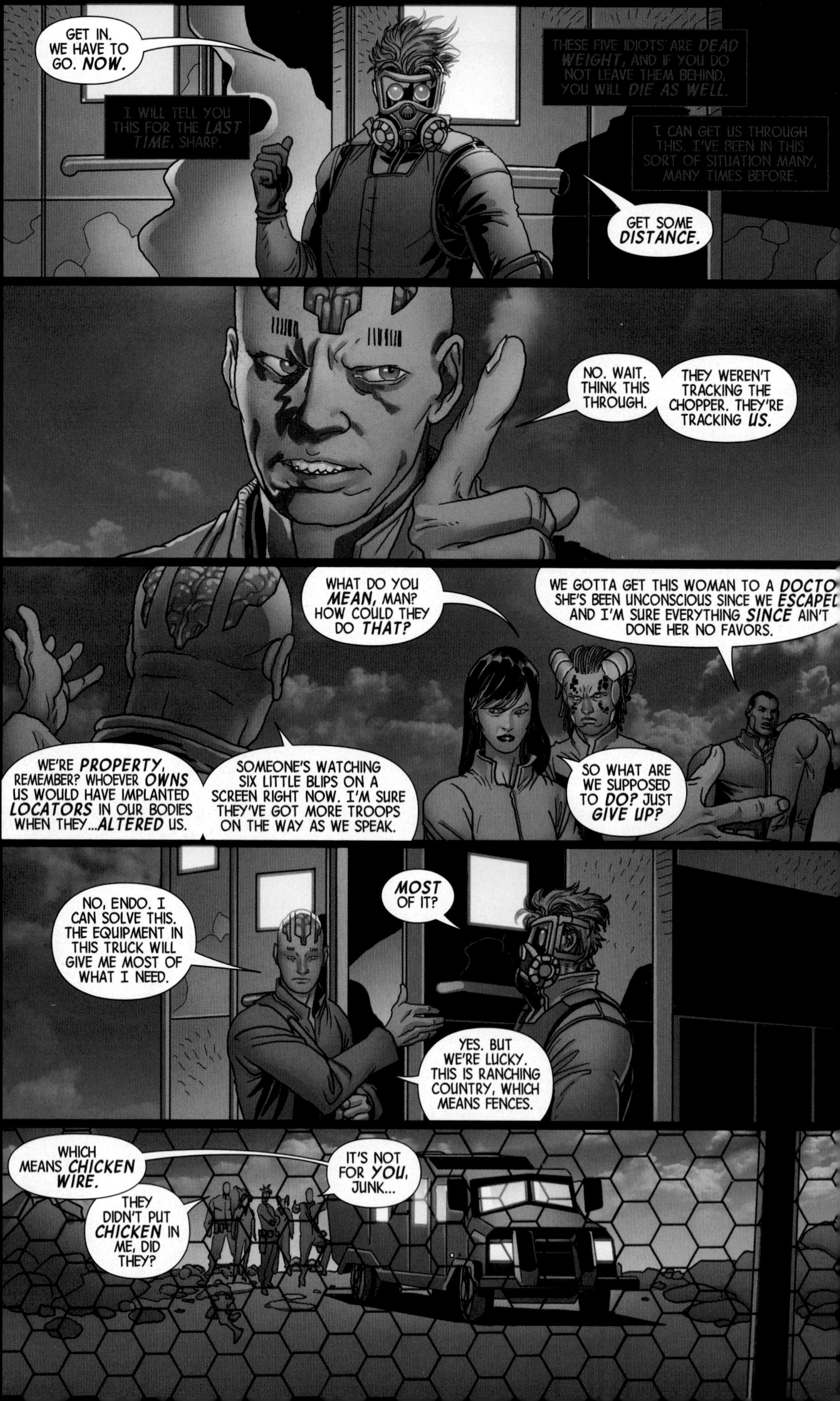
GET IN. WE HAVE TO GO. NOW.
I WILL TELL YOU THIS FOR THE LAST TIME, SHARP.
THESE FIVE IDIOTS ARE DEAD WEIGHT, AND IF YOU DO NOT LEAVE THEM BEHIND, YOU WILL DIE AS WELL.
I CAN GET US THROUGH THIS. I'VE BEEN IN THIS SORT OF SITUATION MANY, MANY TIMES BEFORE.
GET SOME DISTANCE.
NO. WAIT. THINK THIS THROUGH.
THEY WEREN'T TRACKING THE CHOPPER. THEY'RE TRACKING US.
WHAT DO YOU MEAN, MAN? HOW COULD THEY DO THAT?
WE GOTTA GET THIS WOMAN TO A DOCTO
SHE'S BEEN UNCONSCIOUS SINCE WE ESCAPEI
AND I'M SURE EVERYTHING SINCE AIN'T DONE HER NO FAVORS.
WE'RE PROPERTY, REMEMBER? WHOEVER OWNS US WOULD HAVE IMPLANTED LOCATORS IN OUR BODIES WHEN THEY...ALTERED US.
SOMEONE'S WATCHING SIX LITTLE BLIPS ON A SCREEN RIGHT NOW. I'M SURE THEY'VE GOT MORE TROOPS ON THE WAY AS WE SPEAK.
SO WHAT ARE WE SUPPOSED TO DO? JUST GIVE UP?
NO, ENDO. I CAN SOLVE THIS. THE EQUIPMENT IN THIS TRUCK WILL GIVE ME MOST OF WHAT I NEED.
MOST OF IT?
YES. BUT WE'RE LUCKY. THIS IS RANCHING COUNTRY, WHICH MEANS FENCES.
WHICH MEANS CHICKEN WIRE.
IT'S NOT FOR YOU, JUNK...
THEY DIDN'T PUT CHICKEN IN ME, DID THEY?

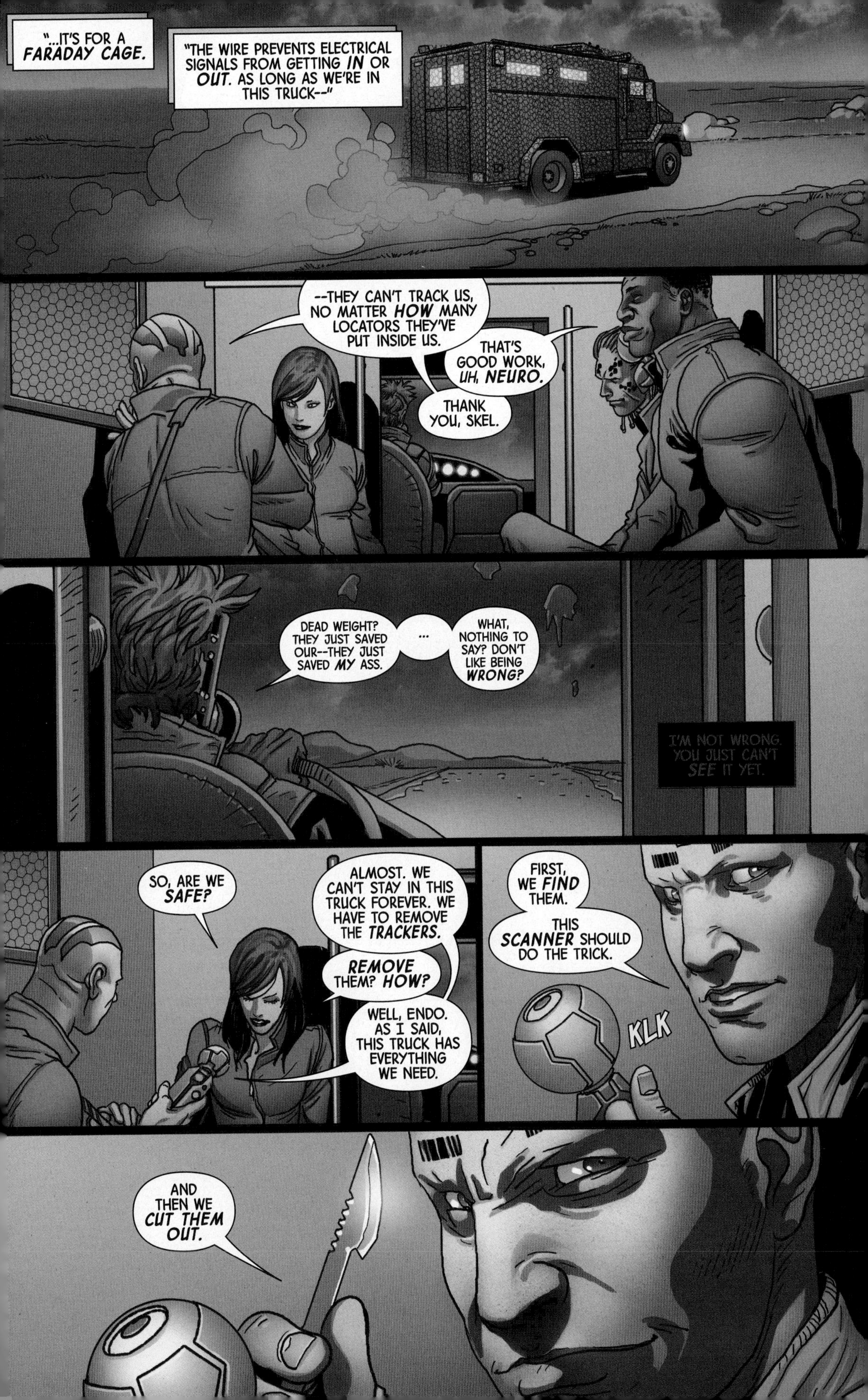
"...IT'S FOR A FARADAY CAGE.
"THE WIRE PREVENTS ELECTRICAL SIGNALS FROM GETTING IN OR OUT. AS LONG AS WE'RE IN THIS TRUCK--"
--THEY CAN'T TRACK US, NO MATTER HOW MANY LOCATORS THEY'VE PUT INSIDE US.
THAT'S GOOD WORK, UH, NEURO.
THANK YOU, SKEL.
DEAD WEIGHT? THEY JUST SAVED OUR--THEY JUST SAVED MY ASS.
...
WHAT, NOTHING TO SAY? DON'T LIKE BEING WRONG?
I'M NOT WRONG. YOU JUST CAN'T SEE IT YET.
SO, ARE WE SAFE?
ALMOST. WE CAN'T STAY IN THIS TRUCK FOREVER. WE HAVE TO REMOVE THE TRACKERS.
REMOVE THEM? HOW?
WELL, ENDO. AS I SAID, THIS TRUCK HAS EVERYTHING WE NEED.
FIRST, WE FIND THEM.
THIS SCANNER SHOULD DO THE TRICK.
KLK
AND THEN WE CUT THEM OUT.

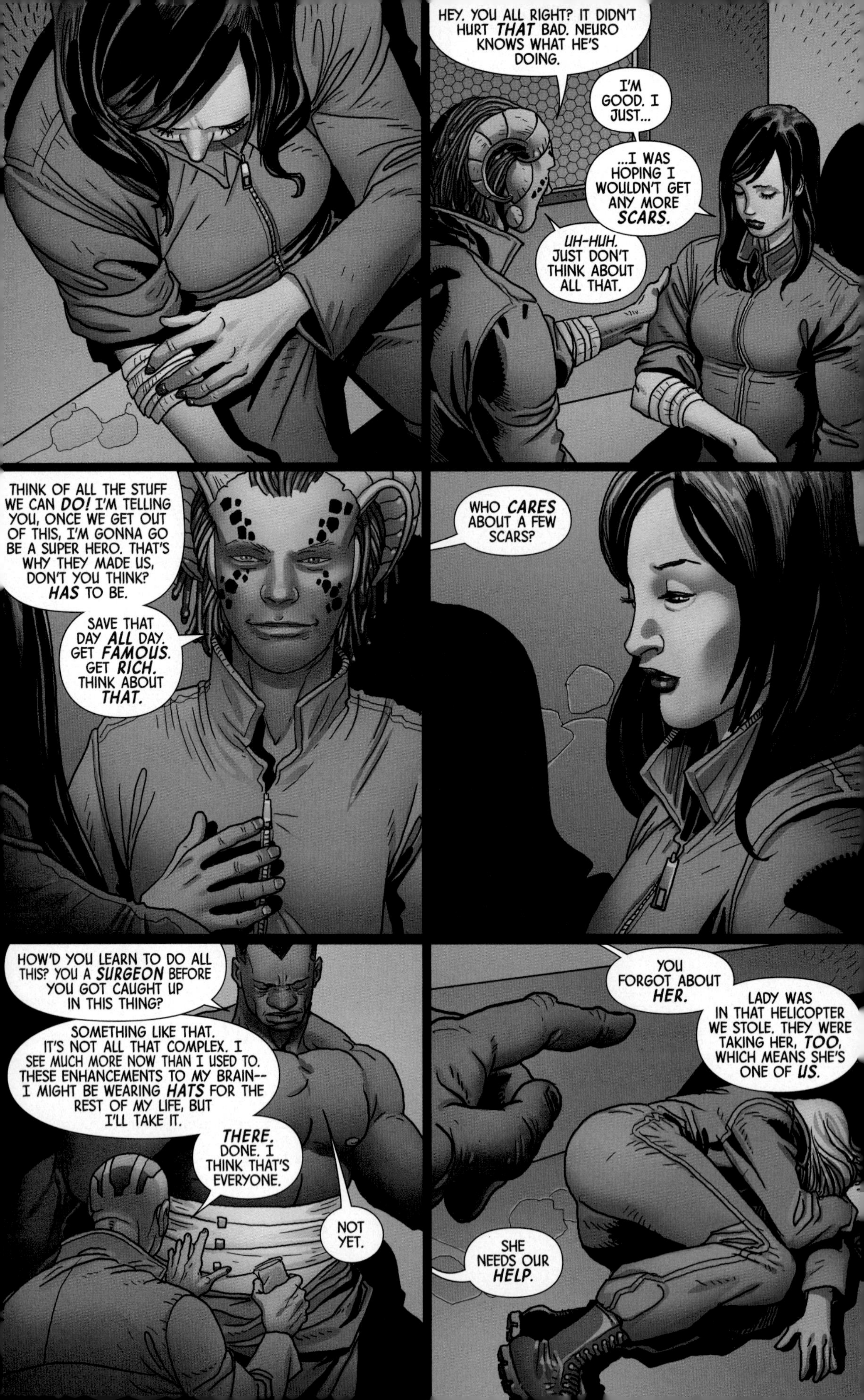
HEY. YOU ALL RIGHT? IT DIDN'T HURT THAT BAD. NEURO KNOWS WHAT HE'S DOING.
I'M GOOD. I JUST...
...I WAS HOPING I WOULDN'T GET ANY MORE SCARS.
UH-HUH. JUST DON'T THINK ABOUT ALL THAT.
THINK OF ALL THE STUFF WE CAN DO! I'M TELLING YOU, ONCE WE GET OUT OF THIS, I'M GONNA GO BE A SUPER HERO. THAT'S WHY THEY MADE US, DON'T YOU THINK? HAS TO BE.
SAVE THAT DAY ALL DAY. GET FAMOUS. GET RICH. THINK ABOUT THAT.
WHO CARES ABOUT A FEW SCARS?
HOW'D YOU LEARN TO DO ALL THIS? YOU A SURGEON BEFORE YOU GOT CAUGHT UP IN THIS THING?
SOMETHING LIKE THAT. IT'S NOT ALL THAT COMPLEX. I SEE MUCH MORE NOW THAN I USED TO. THESE ENHANCEMENTS TO MY BRAIN-- I MIGHT BE WEARING HATS FOR THE REST OF MY LIFE, BUT I'LL TAKE IT.
THERE. DONE. I THINK THAT'S EVERYONE.
NOT YET.
YOU FORGOT ABOUT HER.
LADY WAS IN THAT HELICOPTER WE STOLE. THEY WERE TAKING HER, TOO, WHICH MEANS SHE'S ONE OF US.
SHE NEEDS OUR HELP.

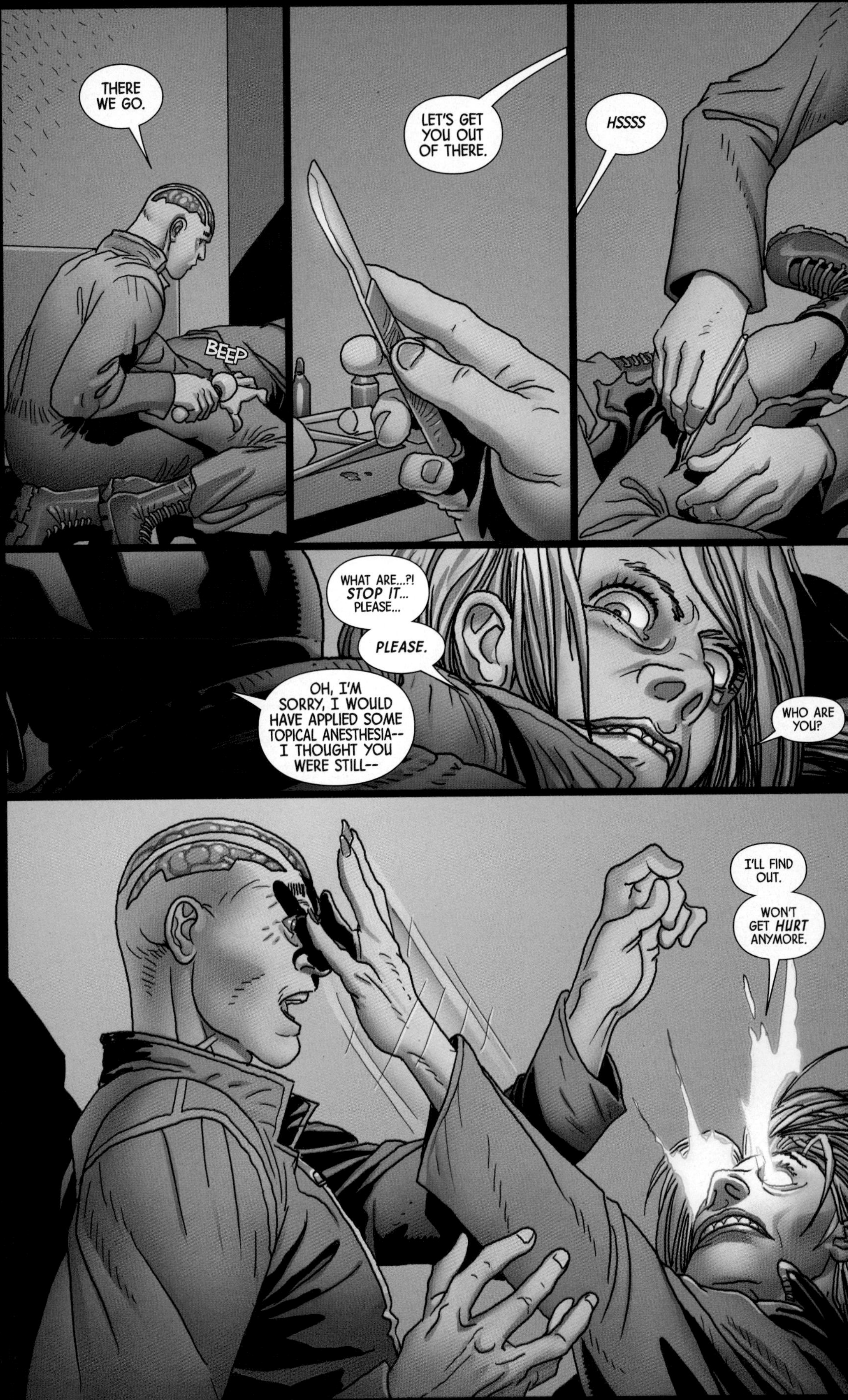
THERE WE GO.
BEEP
LET'S GET YOU OUT OF THERE.
HSSSS
WHAT ARE...?! STOP IT... PLEASE...
PLEASE.
OH, I'M SORRY, I WOULD HAVE APPLIED SOME TOPICAL ANESTHESIA-- I THOUGHT YOU WERE STILL--
WHO ARE YOU?
I'LL FIND OUT.
WON'T GET HURT ANYMORE.

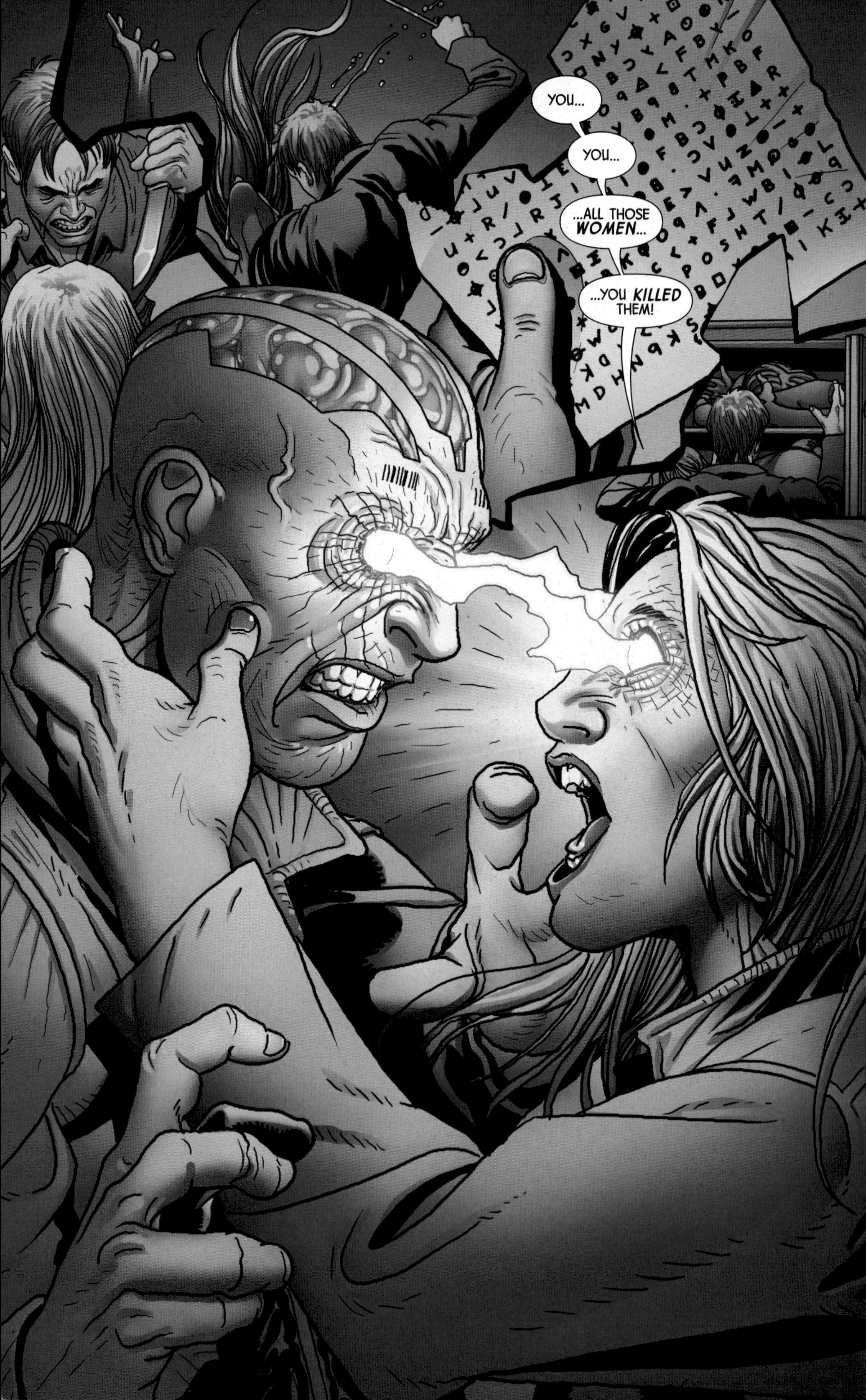
YOU...
YOU...
...ALL THOSE WOMEN...
...YOU KILLED THEM!

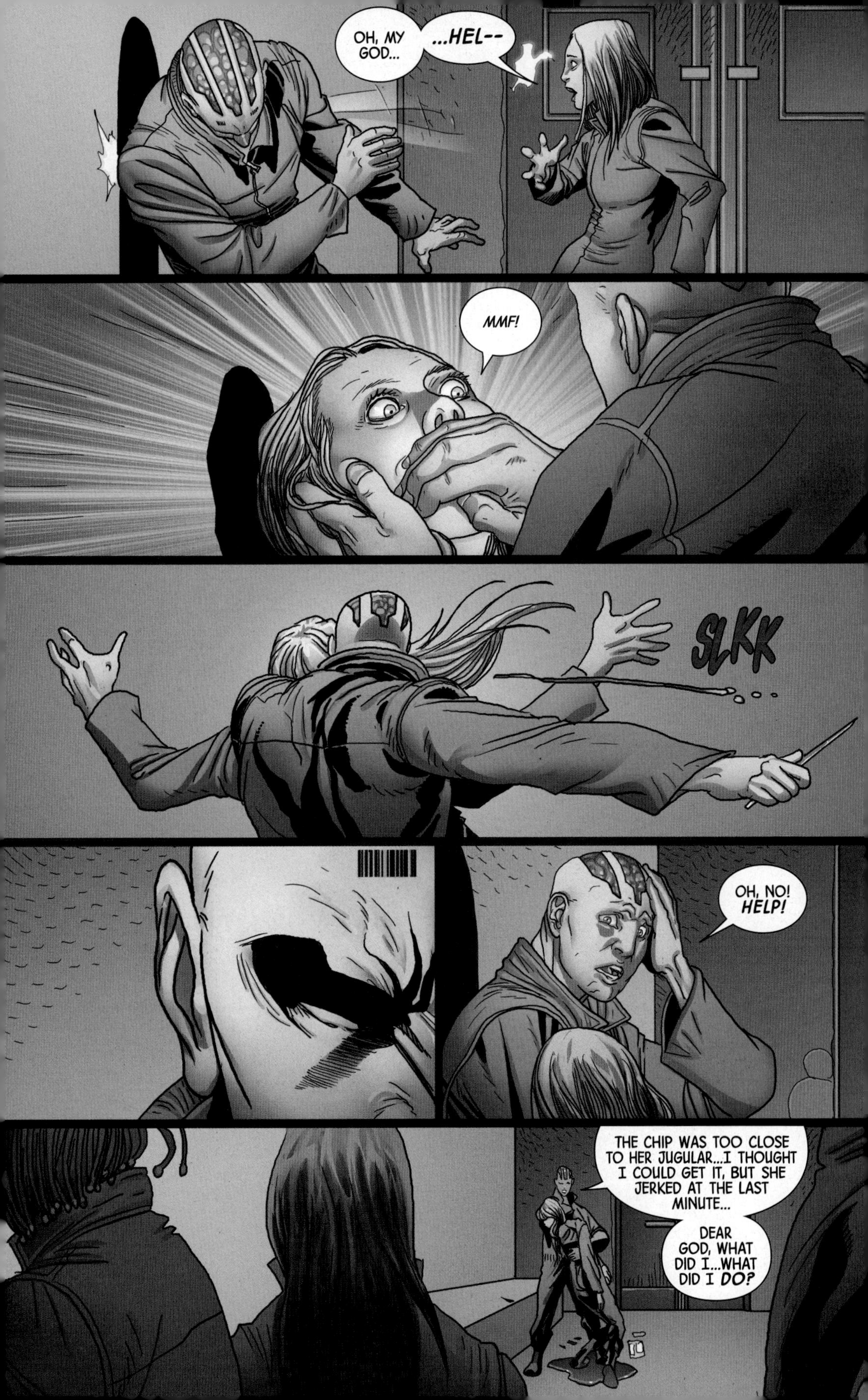
OH, MY GOD...
...HEL--
MMF!
SLKK
OH, NO! HELP!
THE CHIP WAS TOO CLOSE TO HER JUGULAR...I THOUGHT I COULD GET IT, BUT SHE JERKED AT THE LAST MINUTE...
DEAR GOD, WHAT DID I...WHAT DID I DO?

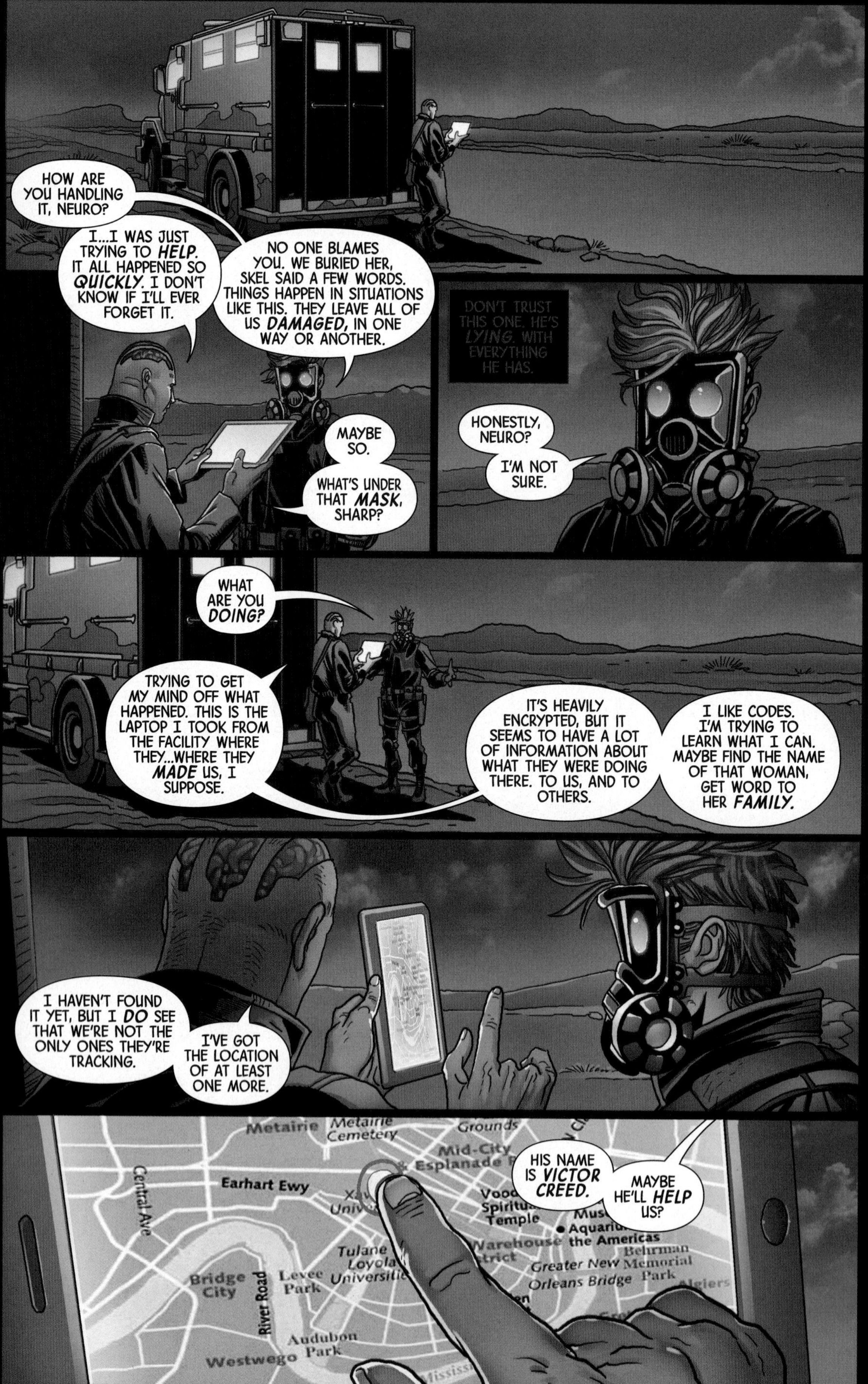
HOW ARE YOU HANDLING IT, NEURO?
I...I WAS JUST TRYING TO HELP. IT ALL HAPPENED SO QUICKLY. I DON'T KNOW IF I'LL EVER FORGET IT.
NO ONE BLAMES YOU. WE BURIED HER, SKEL SAID A FEW WORDS. THINGS HAPPEN IN SITUATIONS LIKE THIS. THEY LEAVE ALL OF US DAMAGED, IN ONE WAY OR ANOTHER.
MAYBE SO.
WHAT'S UNDER THAT MASK, SHARP?
DON'T TRUST THIS ONE. HE'S LYING. WITH EVERYTHING HE HAS.
HONESTLY, NEURO?
I'M NOT SURE.
WHAT ARE YOU DOING?
TRYING TO GET MY MIND OFF WHAT HAPPENED. THIS IS THE LAPTOP I TOOK FROM THE FACILITY WHERE THEY...WHERE THEY MADE US, I SUPPOSE.
IT'S HEAVILY ENCRYPTED, BUT IT SEEMS TO HAVE A LOT OF INFORMATION ABOUT WHAT THEY WERE DOING THERE. TO US, AND TO OTHERS.
I LIKE CODES. I'M TRYING TO LEARN WHAT I CAN. MAYBE FIND THE NAME OF THAT WOMAN, GET WORD TO HER FAMILY.
I HAVEN'T FOUND IT YET, BUT I DO SEE THAT WE'RE NOT THE ONLY ONES THEY'RE TRACKING.
I'VE GOT THE LOCATION OF AT LEAST ONE MORE.
Metairie
Metairie Cemetery
Grounds
Mid-City
Earhart Ewy
Central Ave
Spiritual Temple
Warehouse
the Americas
Greater New Orleans Bridge
Tulane
Loyola
Bridge City
River Road
Levee Park
Audubon Park
Westwego
HIS NAME IS VICTOR CREED.
MAYBE HE'LL HELP US?

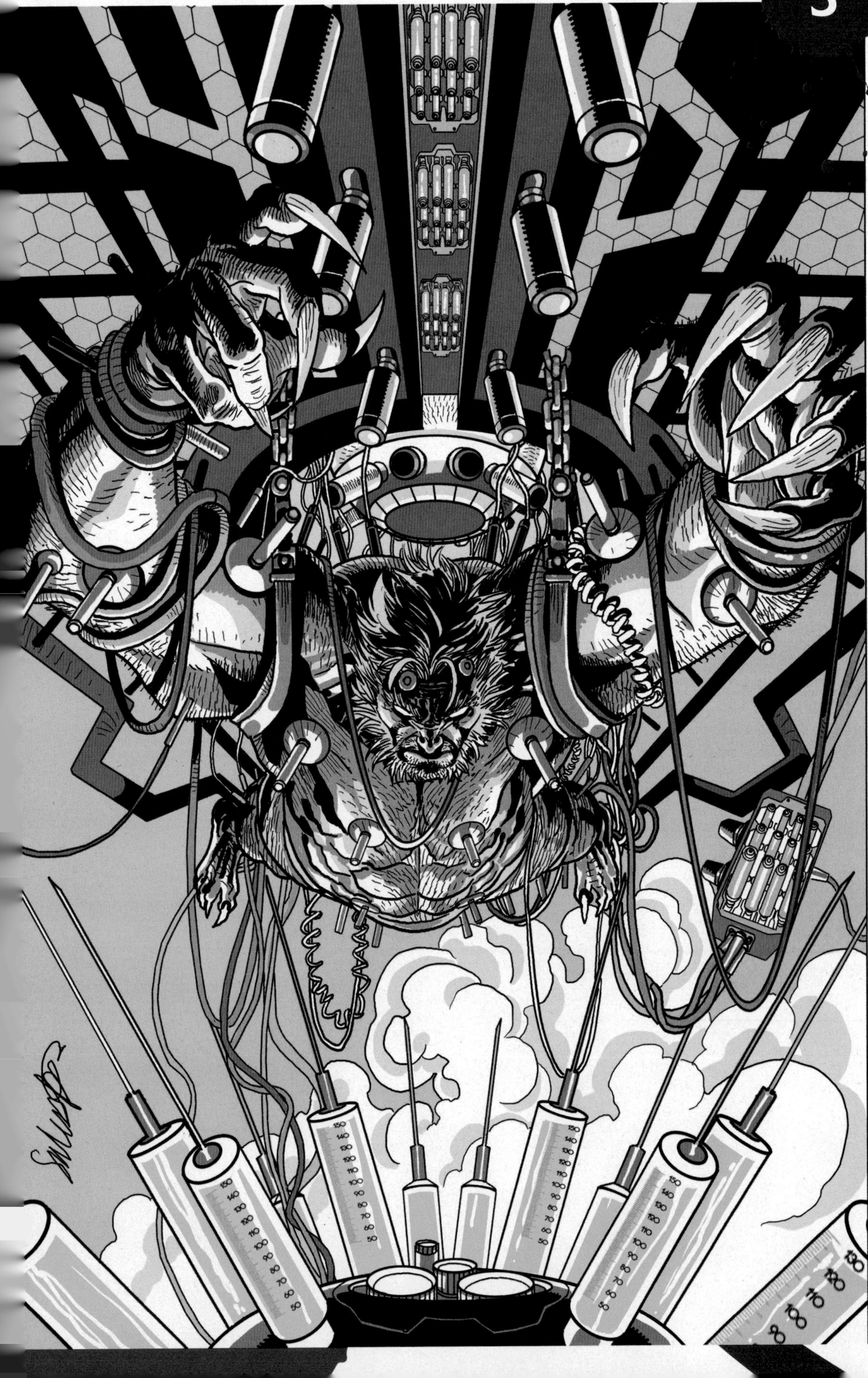

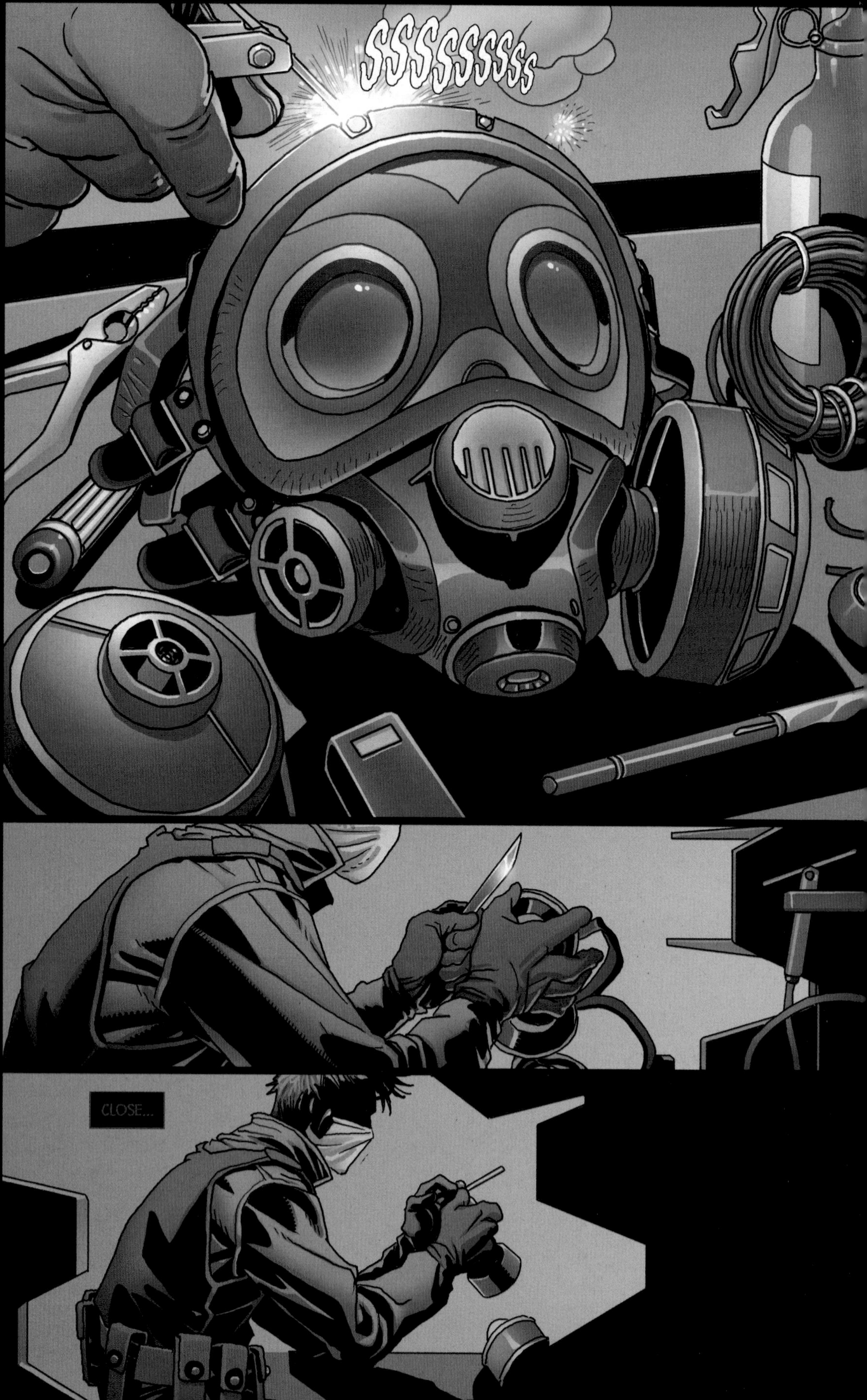
SSSSSSSSs
CLOSE...

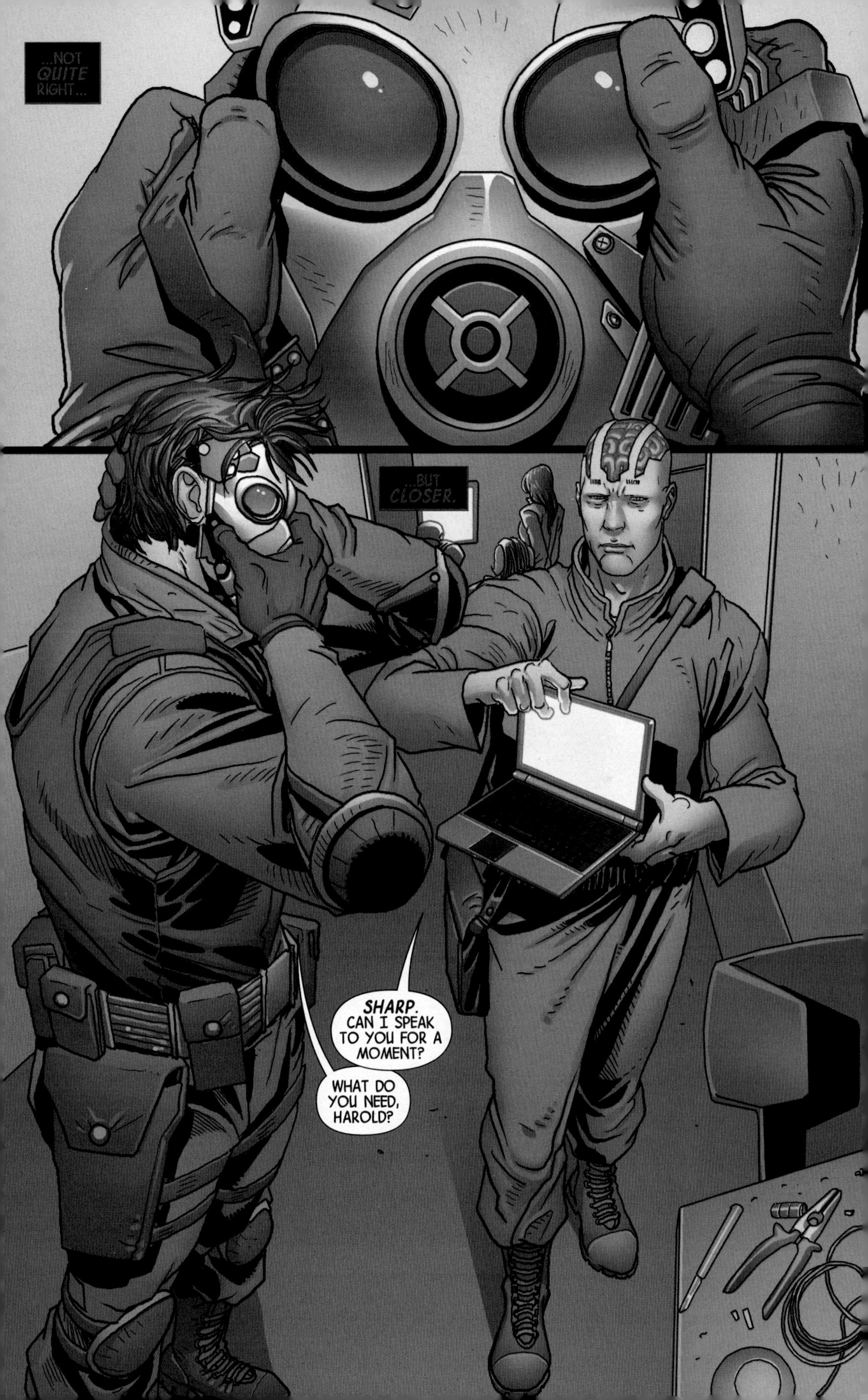
...NOT QUITE RIGHT...
...BUT CLOSER.
SHARP. CAN I SPEAK TO YOU FOR A MOMENT?
WHAT DO YOU NEED, HAROLD?

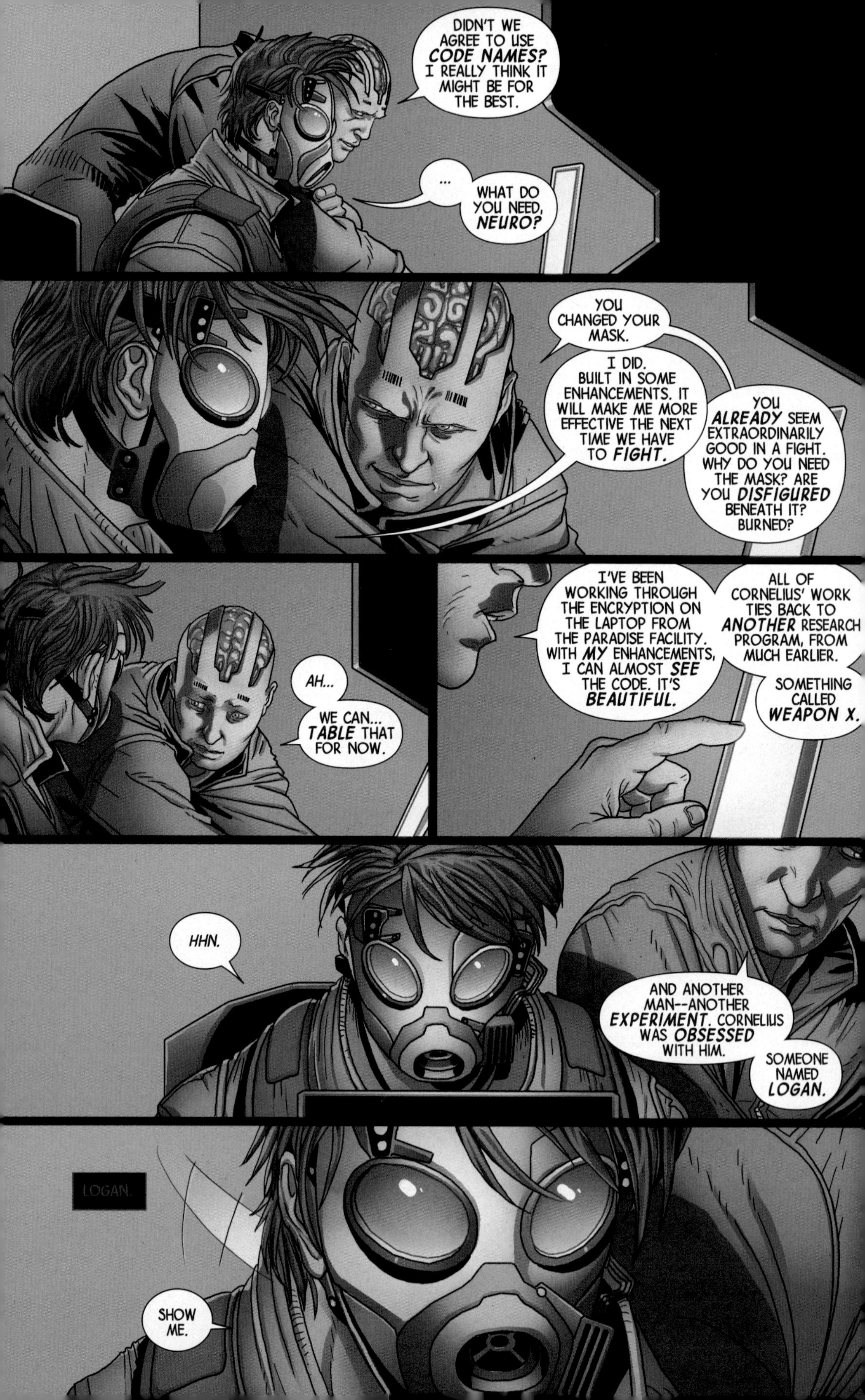

DIDN'T WE AGREE TO USE CODE NAMES? I REALLY THINK IT MIGHT BE FOR THE BEST.
...
WHAT DO YOU NEED, NEURO?
YOU CHANGED YOUR MASK.
I DID. BUILT IN SOME ENHANCEMENTS. IT WILL MAKE ME MORE EFFECTIVE THE NEXT TIME WE HAVE TO FIGHT.
YOU ALREADY SEEM EXTRAORDINARILY GOOD IN A FIGHT. WHY DO YOU NEED THE MASK? ARE YOU DISFIGURED BENEATH IT? BURNED?
AH...
WE CAN... TABLE THAT FOR NOW.
I'VE BEEN WORKING THROUGH THE ENCRYPTION ON THE LAPTOP FROM THE PARADISE FACILITY. WITH MY ENHANCEMENTS, I CAN ALMOST SEE THE CODE. IT'S BEAUTIFUL.
ALL OF CORNELIUS' WORK TIES BACK TO ANOTHER RESEARCH PROGRAM, FROM MUCH EARLIER.
SOMETHING CALLED WEAPON X.
HHN.
AND ANOTHER MAN--ANOTHER EXPERIMENT. CORNELIUS WAS OBSESSED WITH HIM.
SOMEONE NAMED LOGAN.
LOGAN.
SHOW ME.

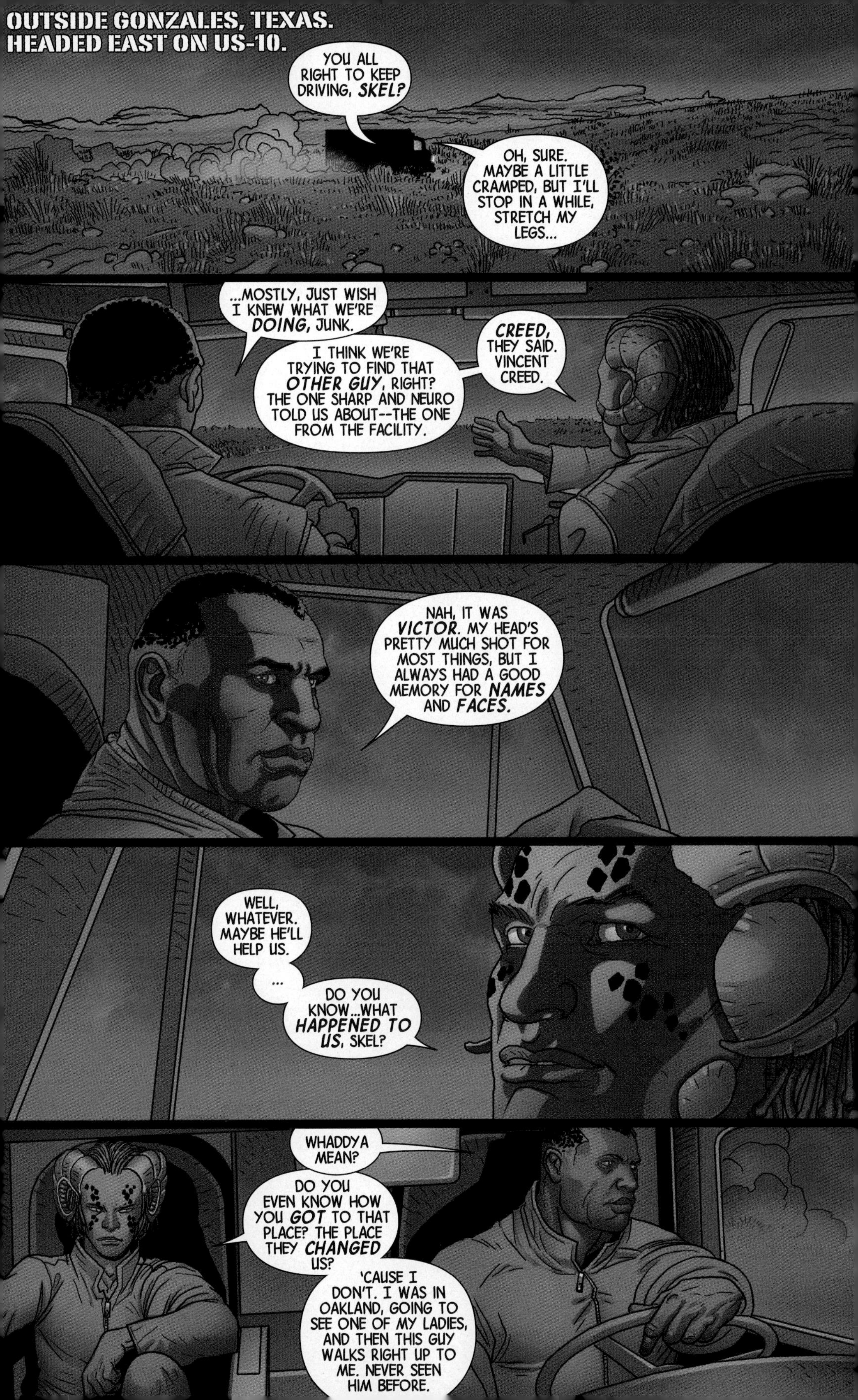
OUTSIDE GONZALES, TEXAS. HEADED EAST ON US-10.
YOU ALL RIGHT TO KEEP DRIVING, SKEL?
OH, SURE. MAYBE A LITTLE CRAMPED, BUT I'LL STOP IN A WHILE, STRETCH MY LEGS...
...MOSTLY, JUST WISH I KNEW WHAT WE'RE DOING, JUNK.
I THINK WE'RE TRYING TO FIND THAT OTHER GUY, RIGHT? THE ONE SHARP AND NEURO TOLD US ABOUT--THE ONE FROM THE FACILITY.
CREED, THEY SAID. VINCENT CREED.
NAH, IT WAS VICTOR. MY HEAD'S PRETTY MUCH SHOT FOR MOST THINGS, BUT I ALWAYS HAD A GOOD MEMORY FOR NAMES AND FACES.
WELL, WHATEVER. MAYBE HE'LL HELP US.
...
DO YOU KNOW...WHAT HAPPENED TO US, SKEL?
WHADDYA MEAN?
DO YOU EVEN KNOW HOW YOU GOT TO THAT PLACE? THE PLACE THEY CHANGED US?
'CAUSE I DON'T. I WAS IN OAKLAND, GOING TO SEE ONE OF MY LADIES, AND THEN THIS GUY WALKS RIGHT UP TO ME. NEVER SEEN HIM BEFORE.

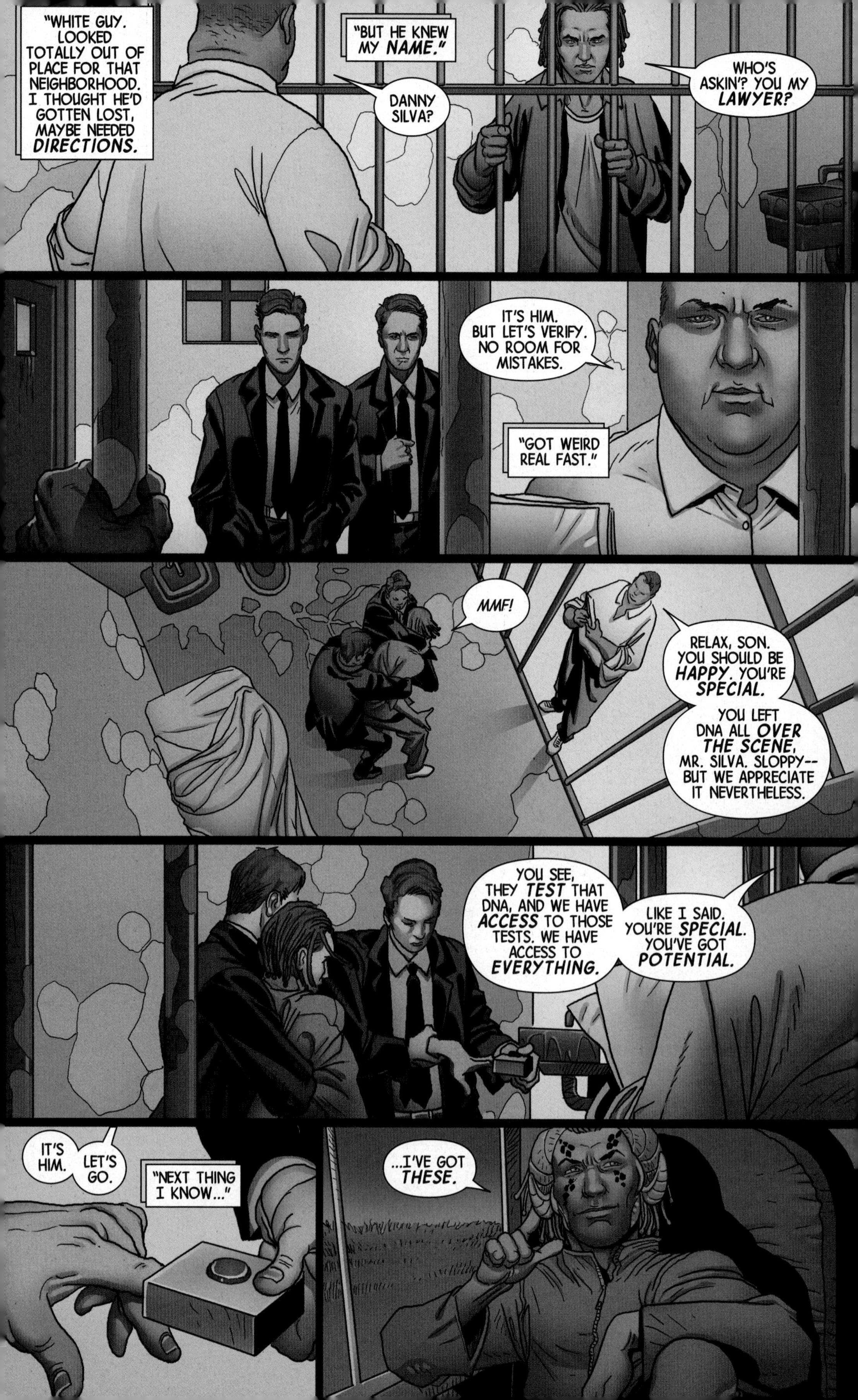
"WHITE GUY. LOOKED TOTALLY OUT OF PLACE FOR THAT NEIGHBORHOOD. I THOUGHT HE'D GOTTEN LOST, MAYBE NEEDED DIRECTIONS.
"BUT HE KNEW MY NAME."
DANNY SILVA?
WHO'S ASKIN'? YOU MY LAWYER?
IT'S HIM. BUT LET'S VERIFY. NO ROOM FOR MISTAKES.
"GOT WEIRD REAL FAST."
MMF!
RELAX, SON. YOU SHOULD BE HAPPY. YOU'RE SPECIAL.
YOU LEFT DNA ALL OVER THE SCENE, MR. SILVA. SLOPPY-- BUT WE APPRECIATE IT NEVERTHELESS.
YOU SEE, THEY TEST THAT DNA, AND WE HAVE ACCESS TO THOSE TESTS. WE HAVE ACCESS TO EVERYTHING.
LIKE I SAID. YOU'RE SPECIAL. YOU'VE GOT POTENTIAL.
IT'S HIM.
LET'S GO.
"NEXT THING I KNOW..."
...I'VE GOT THESE.

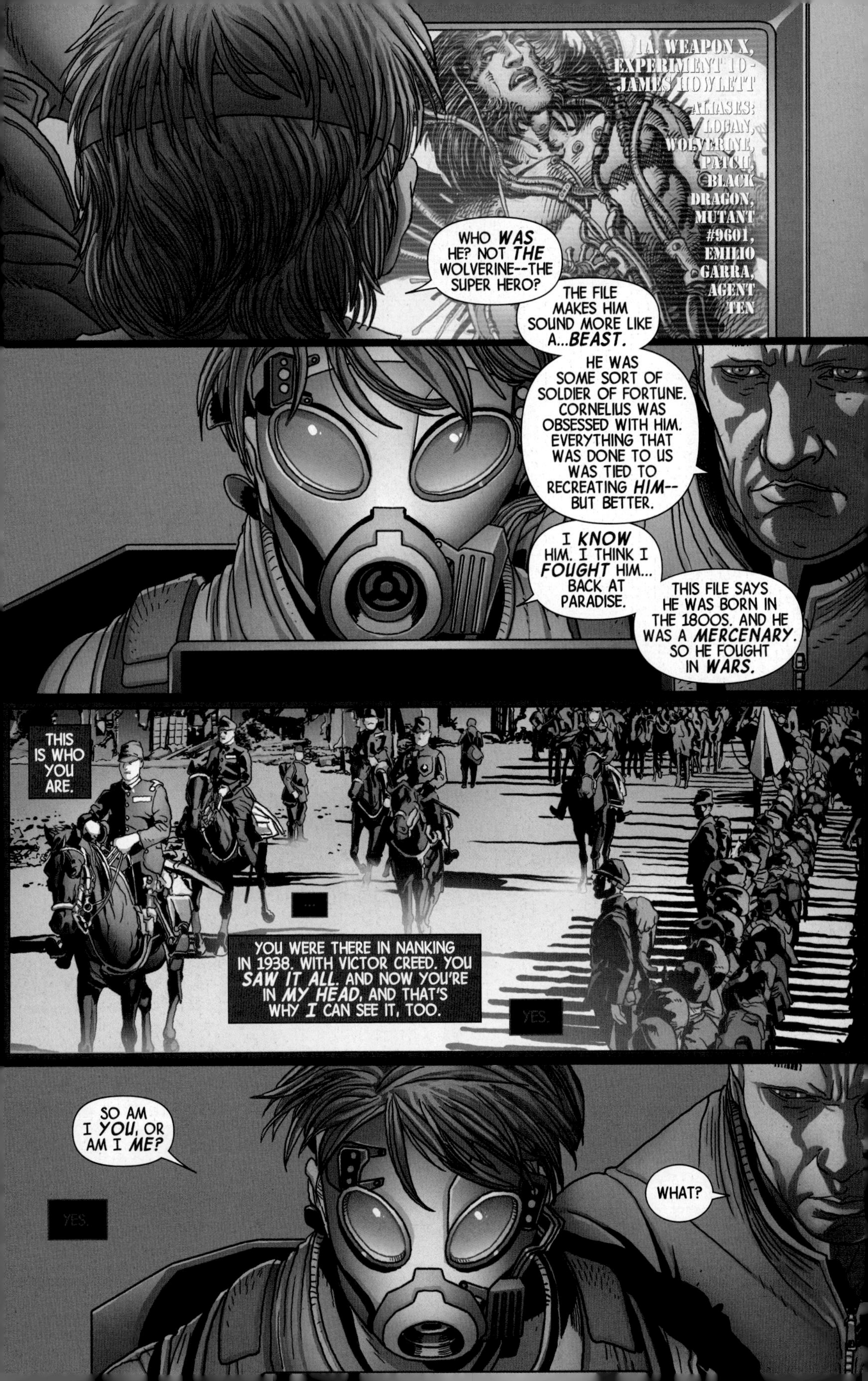
1A. WEAPON X, EXPERIMENT 10 - JAMES HOWLETT
ALIASES: LOGAN, WOLVERINE, PATCH, BLACK DRAGON, MUTANT #9601, EMILIO GARRA, AGENT TEN
WHO *WAS* HE? NOT *THE* WOLVERINE--THE SUPER HERO?
THE FILE MAKES HIM SOUND MORE LIKE A...*BEAST*.
HE WAS SOME SORT OF SOLDIER OF FORTUNE. CORNELIUS WAS OBSESSED WITH HIM. EVERYTHING THAT WAS DONE TO US WAS TIED TO RECREATING *HIM*--BUT BETTER.
I *KNOW* HIM. I THINK I *FOUGHT* HIM... BACK AT PARADISE.
THIS FILE SAYS HE WAS BORN IN THE 1800S. AND HE WAS A *MERCENARY*. SO HE FOUGHT IN *WARS*.
THIS IS WHO YOU ARE.
...
YOU WERE THERE IN NANKING IN 1938. WITH VICTOR CREED. YOU *SAW IT ALL*. AND NOW YOU'RE IN *MY HEAD*, AND THAT'S WHY *I* CAN SEE IT, TOO.
YES.
SO AM I *YOU*, OR AM I *ME*?
YES.
WHAT?

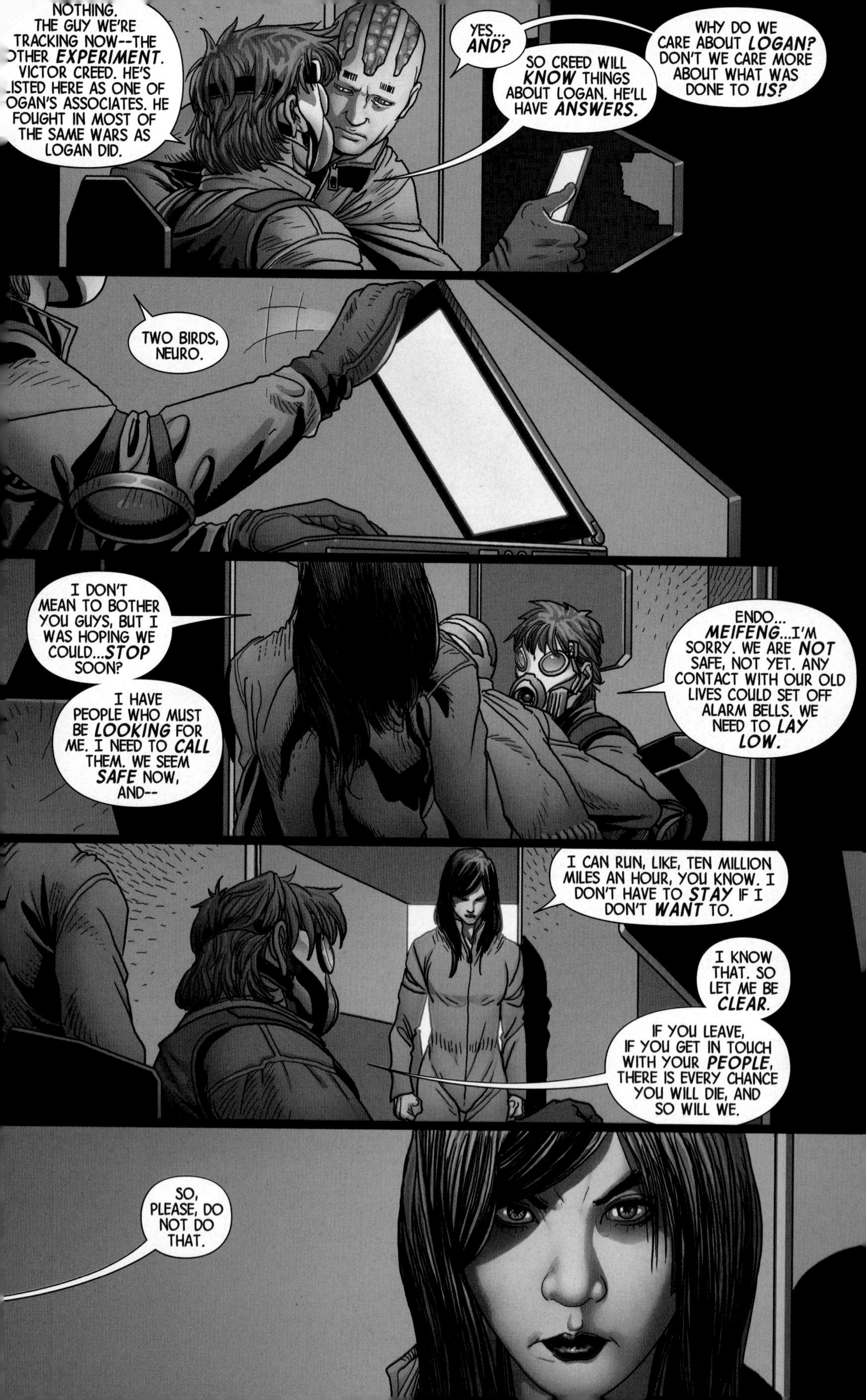
NOTHING. THE GUY WE'RE TRACKING NOW--THE OTHER EXPERIMENT. VICTOR CREED. HE'S LISTED HERE AS ONE OF LOGAN'S ASSOCIATES. HE FOUGHT IN MOST OF THE SAME WARS AS LOGAN DID.
YES... AND?
SO CREED WILL KNOW THINGS ABOUT LOGAN. HE'LL HAVE ANSWERS.
WHY DO WE CARE ABOUT LOGAN? DON'T WE CARE MORE ABOUT WHAT WAS DONE TO US?
TWO BIRDS, NEURO.
I DON'T MEAN TO BOTHER YOU GUYS, BUT I WAS HOPING WE COULD...STOP SOON?
I HAVE PEOPLE WHO MUST BE LOOKING FOR ME. I NEED TO CALL THEM. WE SEEM SAFE NOW, AND--
ENDO... MEIFENG...I'M SORRY. WE ARE NOT SAFE, NOT YET. ANY CONTACT WITH OUR OLD LIVES COULD SET OFF ALARM BELLS. WE NEED TO LAY LOW.
I CAN RUN, LIKE, TEN MILLION MILES AN HOUR, YOU KNOW. I DON'T HAVE TO STAY IF I DON'T WANT TO.
I KNOW THAT. SO LET ME BE CLEAR.
IF YOU LEAVE, IF YOU GET IN TOUCH WITH YOUR PEOPLE, THERE IS EVERY CHANCE YOU WILL DIE, AND SO WILL WE.
SO, PLEASE, DO NOT DO THAT.

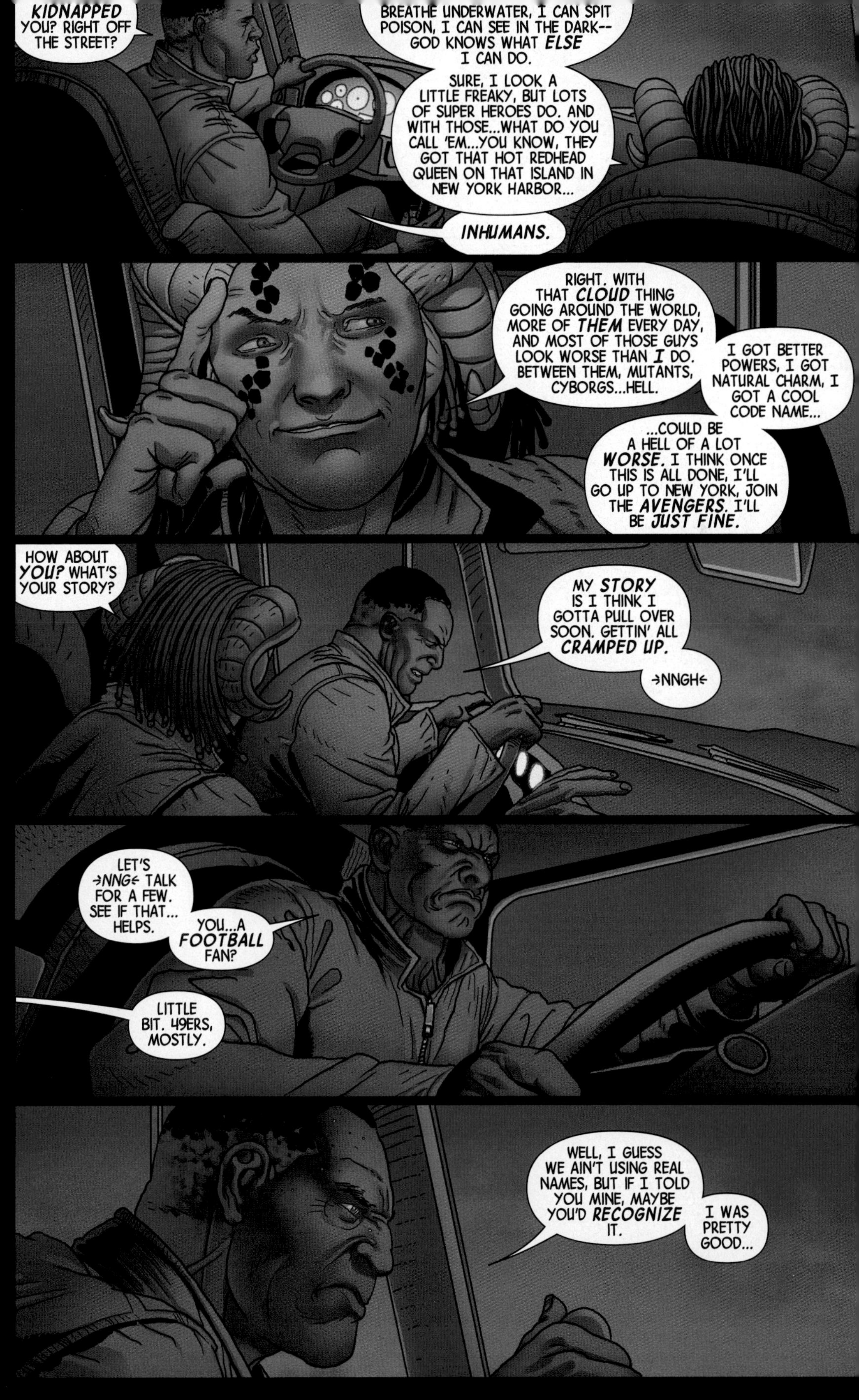
KIDNAPPED YOU? RIGHT OFF THE STREET?
BREATHE UNDERWATER, I CAN SPIT POISON, I CAN SEE IN THE DARK-- GOD KNOWS WHAT ELSE I CAN DO.
SURE, I LOOK A LITTLE FREAKY, BUT LOTS OF SUPER HEROES DO. AND WITH THOSE...WHAT DO YOU CALL 'EM...YOU KNOW, THEY GOT THAT HOT REDHEAD QUEEN ON THAT ISLAND IN NEW YORK HARBOR...
INHUMANS.
RIGHT. WITH THAT CLOUD THING GOING AROUND THE WORLD, MORE OF THEM EVERY DAY, AND MOST OF THOSE GUYS LOOK WORSE THAN I DO. BETWEEN THEM, MUTANTS, CYBORGS...HELL.
I GOT BETTER POWERS, I GOT NATURAL CHARM, I GOT A COOL CODE NAME...
...COULD BE A HELL OF A LOT WORSE. I THINK ONCE THIS IS ALL DONE, I'LL GO UP TO NEW YORK, JOIN THE AVENGERS. I'LL BE JUST FINE.
HOW ABOUT YOU? WHAT'S YOUR STORY?
MY STORY IS I THINK I GOTTA PULL OVER SOON. GETTIN' ALL CRAMPED UP.
→NNGH←
LET'S →NNG← TALK FOR A FEW. SEE IF THAT... HELPS.
YOU...A FOOTBALL FAN?
LITTLE BIT. 49ERS, MOSTLY.
WELL, I GUESS WE AIN'T USING REAL NAMES, BUT IF I TOLD YOU MINE, MAYBE YOU'D RECOGNIZE IT.
I WAS PRETTY GOOD...

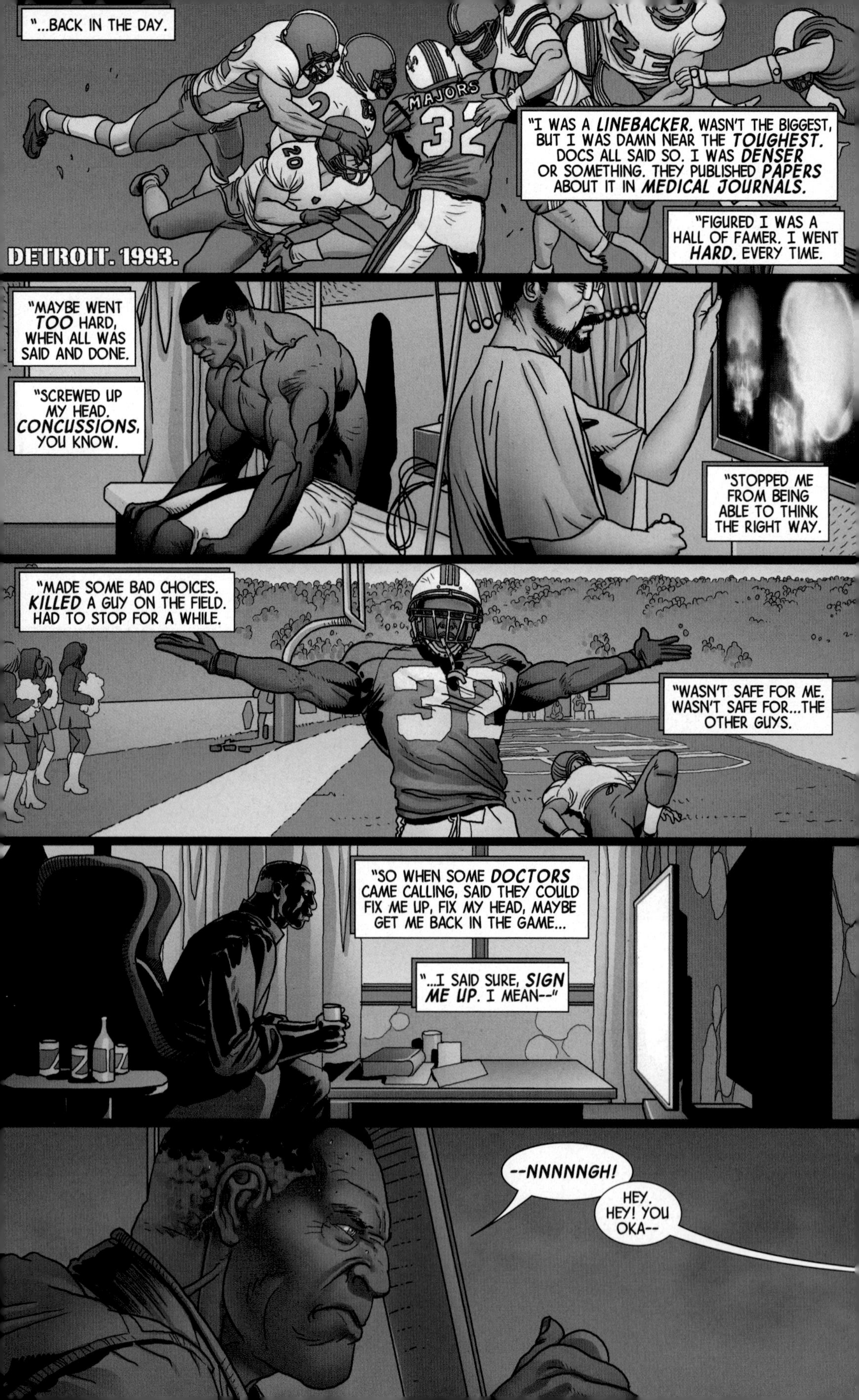
"...BACK IN THE DAY.
MAJORS 32
20
DETROIT. 1993.
"I WAS A LINEBACKER. WASN'T THE BIGGEST, BUT I WAS DAMN NEAR THE TOUGHEST. DOCS ALL SAID SO. I WAS DENSER OR SOMETHING. THEY PUBLISHED PAPERS ABOUT IT IN MEDICAL JOURNALS.
"FIGURED I WAS A HALL OF FAMER. I WENT HARD. EVERY TIME.
"MAYBE WENT TOO HARD, WHEN ALL WAS SAID AND DONE.
"SCREWED UP MY HEAD. CONCUSSIONS, YOU KNOW.
"STOPPED ME FROM BEING ABLE TO THINK THE RIGHT WAY.
"MADE SOME BAD CHOICES. KILLED A GUY ON THE FIELD. HAD TO STOP FOR A WHILE.
"WASN'T SAFE FOR ME. WASN'T SAFE FOR...THE OTHER GUYS.
"SO WHEN SOME DOCTORS CAME CALLING, SAID THEY COULD FIX ME UP, FIX MY HEAD, MAYBE GET ME BACK IN THE GAME...
"...I SAID SURE, SIGN ME UP. I MEAN--"
--NNNNNGH!
HEY. HEY! YOU OKA--

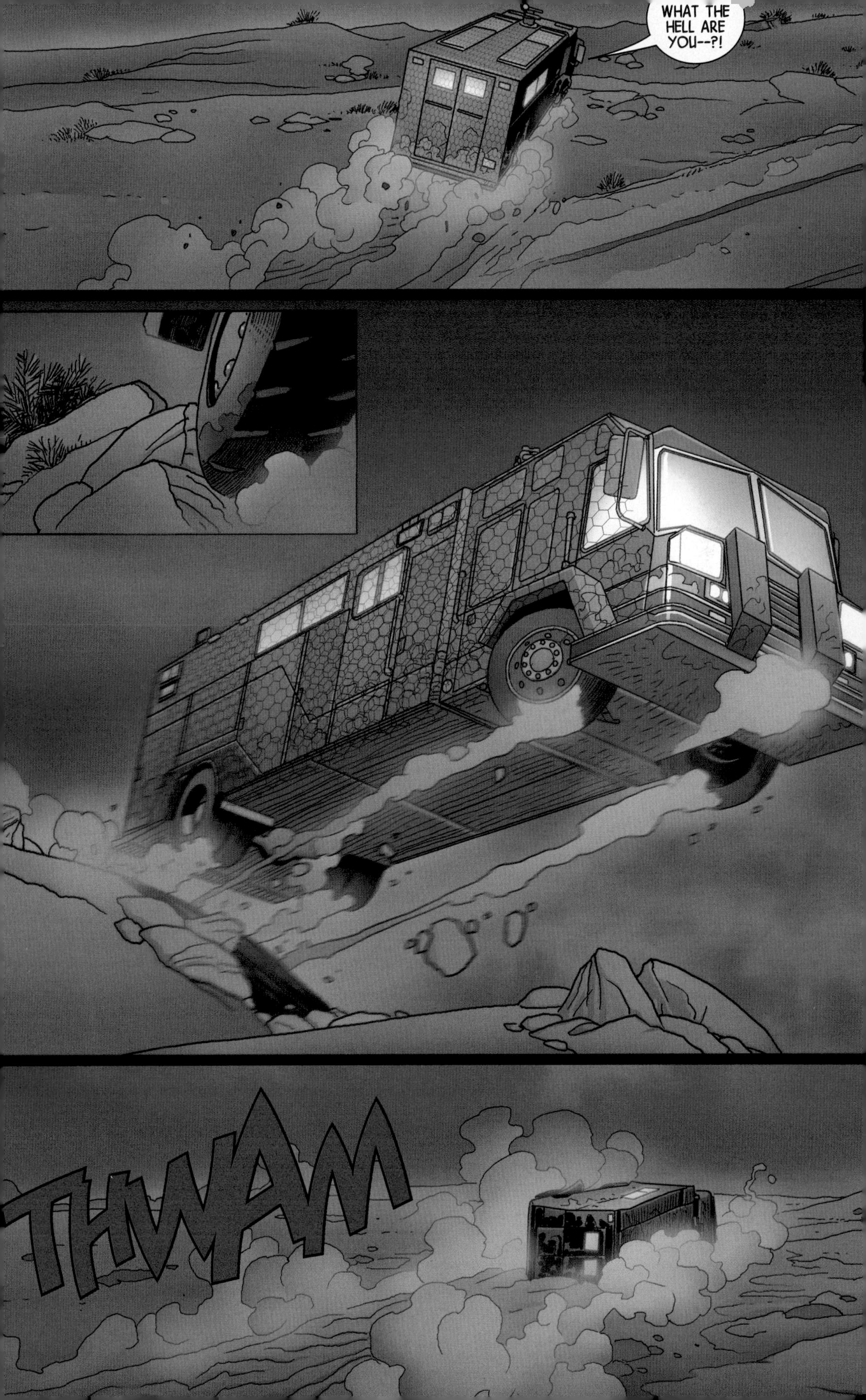
WHAT THE HELL ARE YOU--?!
THWAM

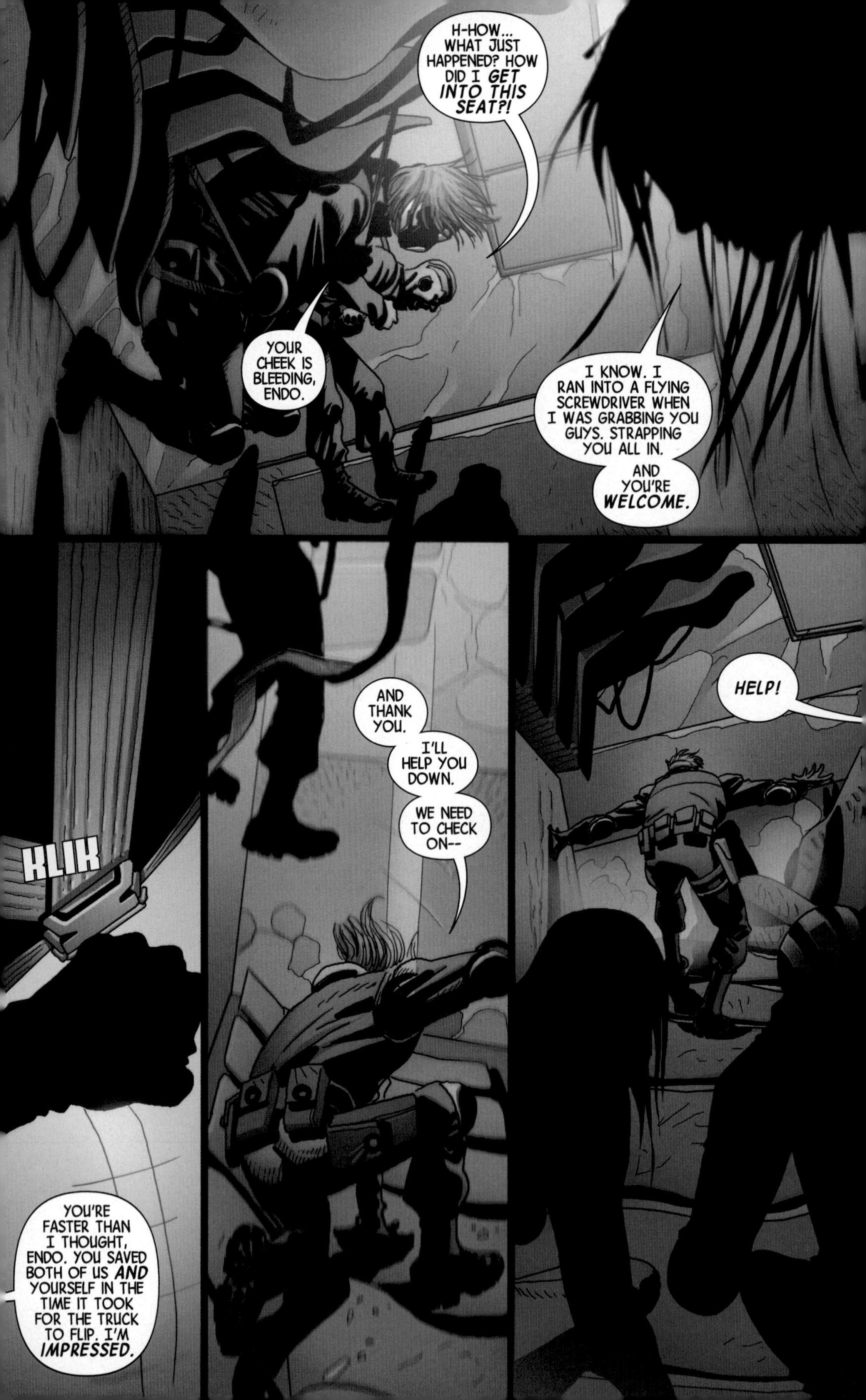
H-HOW... WHAT JUST HAPPENED? HOW DID I GET INTO THIS SEAT?!
YOUR CHEEK IS BLEEDING, ENDO.
I KNOW. I RAN INTO A FLYING SCREWDRIVER WHEN I WAS GRABBING YOU GUYS. STRAPPING YOU ALL IN.
AND YOU'RE WELCOME.
KLIK
YOU'RE FASTER THAN I THOUGHT, ENDO. YOU SAVED BOTH OF US AND YOURSELF IN THE TIME IT TOOK FOR THE TRUCK TO FLIP. I'M IMPRESSED.
AND THANK YOU.
I'LL HELP YOU DOWN.
WE NEED TO CHECK ON--
HELP!

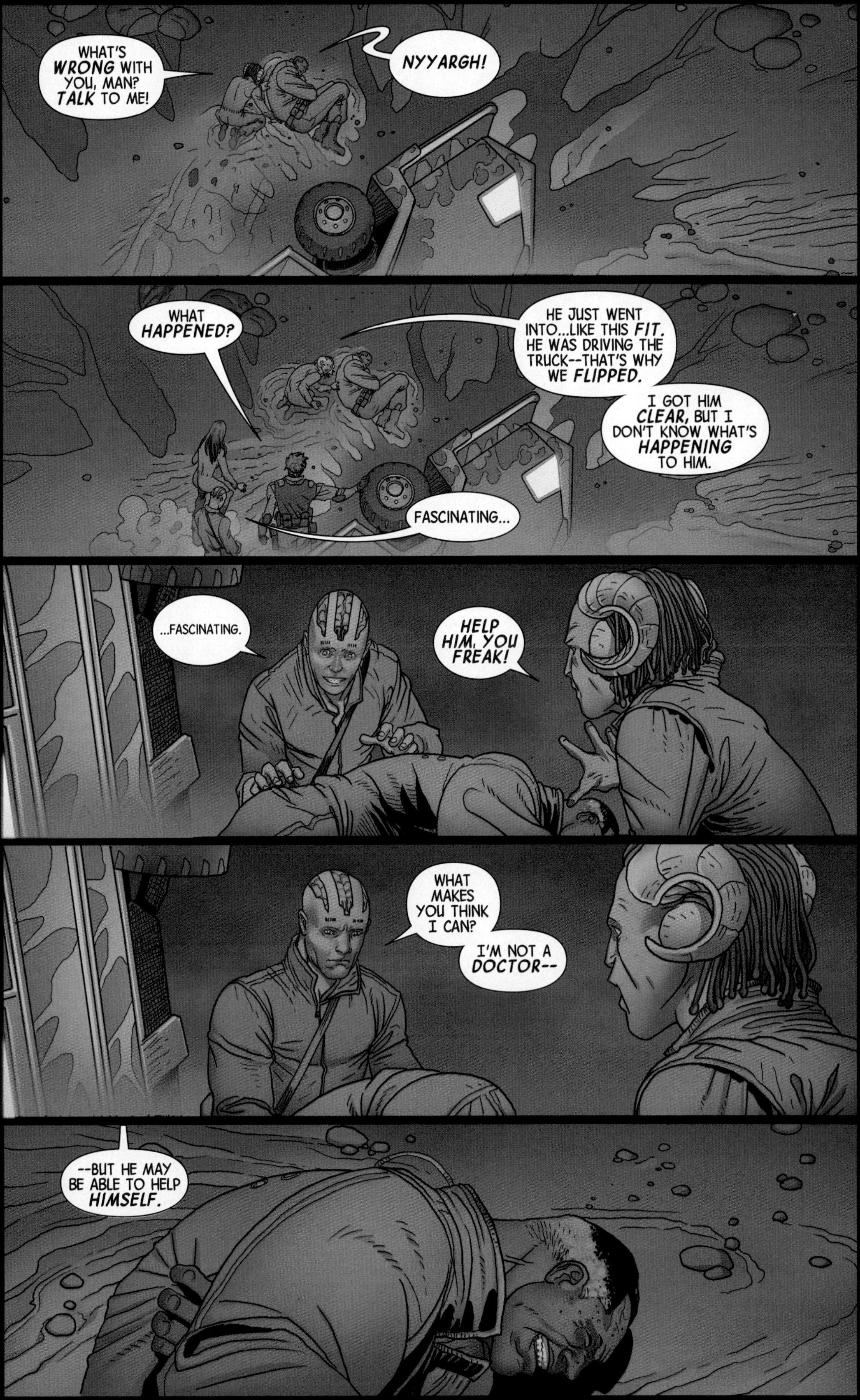
WHAT'S WRONG WITH YOU, MAN? TALK TO ME!
NYYARGH!
WHAT HAPPENED?
HE JUST WENT INTO...LIKE THIS FIT. HE WAS DRIVING THE TRUCK--THAT'S WHY WE FLIPPED.
I GOT HIM CLEAR, BUT I DON'T KNOW WHAT'S HAPPENING TO HIM.
FASCINATING...
...FASCINATING.
HELP HIM, YOU FREAK!
WHAT MAKES YOU THINK I CAN?
I'M NOT A DOCTOR--
--BUT HE MAY BE ABLE TO HELP HIMSELF.

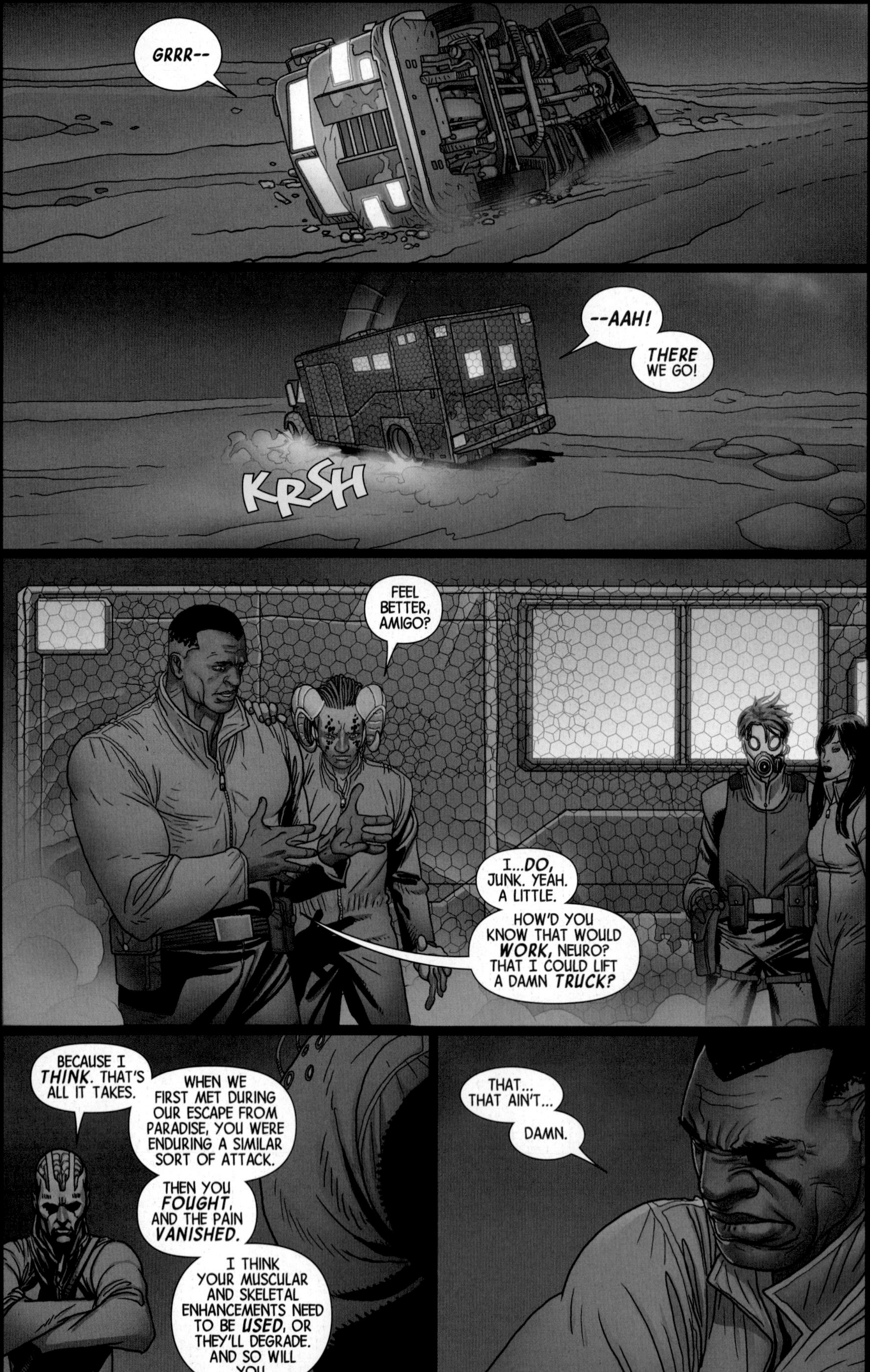
GRRR--
--AAH!
THERE WE GO!
KRSH
FEEL BETTER, AMIGO?
I...DO, JUNK. YEAH. A LITTLE.
HOW'D YOU KNOW THAT WOULD WORK, NEURO? THAT I COULD LIFT A DAMN TRUCK?
BECAUSE I THINK. THAT'S ALL IT TAKES.
WHEN WE FIRST MET DURING OUR ESCAPE FROM PARADISE, YOU WERE ENDURING A SIMILAR SORT OF ATTACK.
THEN YOU FOUGHT, AND THE PAIN VANISHED.
I THINK YOUR MUSCULAR AND SKELETAL ENHANCEMENTS NEED TO BE USED, OR THEY'LL DEGRADE. AND SO WILL YOU.
THAT... THAT AIN'T...
DAMN.

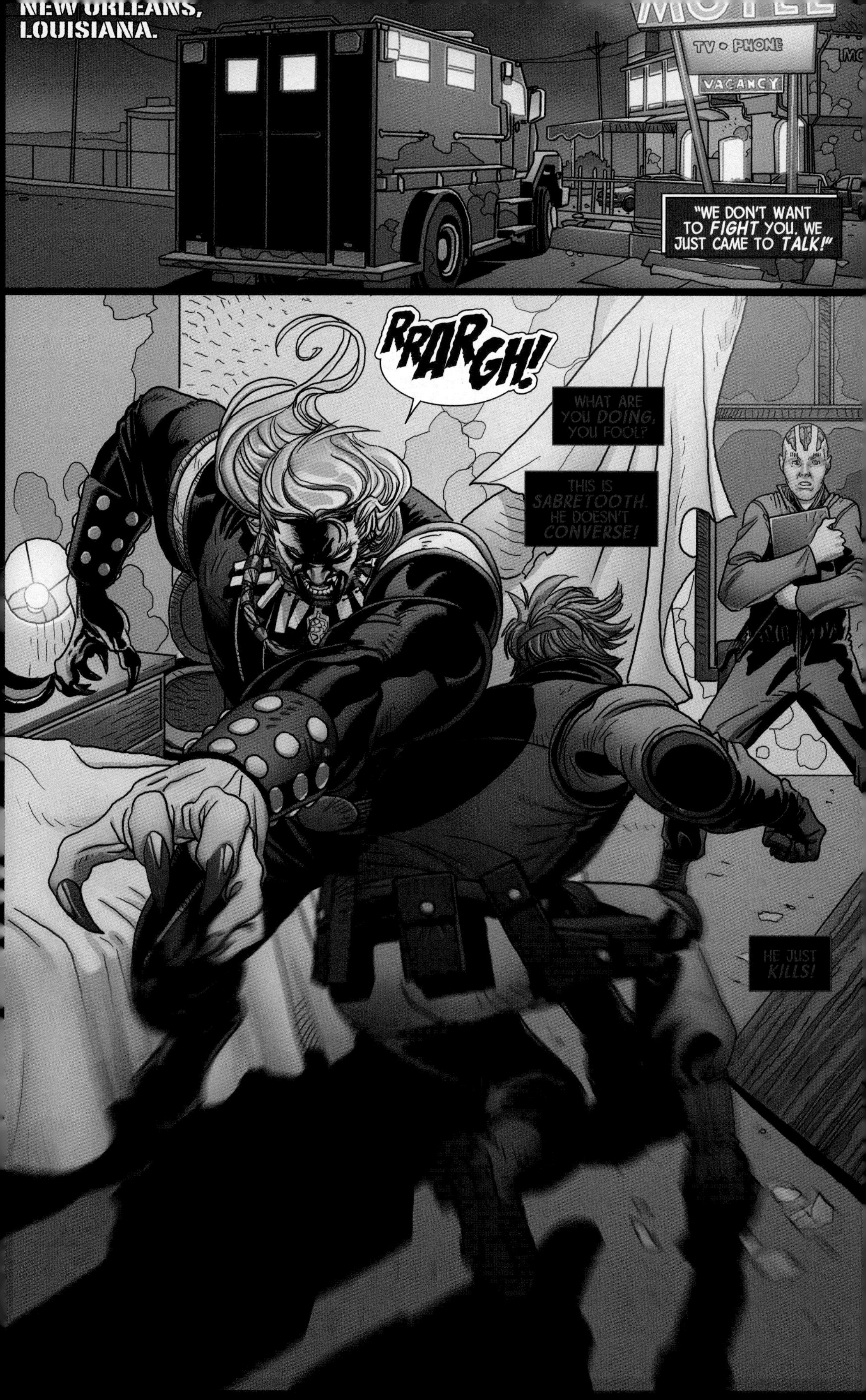
NEW ORLEANS, LOUISIANA.
MOTEL
TV • PHONE
VACANCY
"WE DON'T WANT TO FIGHT YOU. WE JUST CAME TO TALK!"
RRRARGH!
WHAT ARE YOU DOING, YOU FOOL?
THIS IS SABRETOOTH. HE DOESN'T CONVERSE!
HE JUST KILLS!

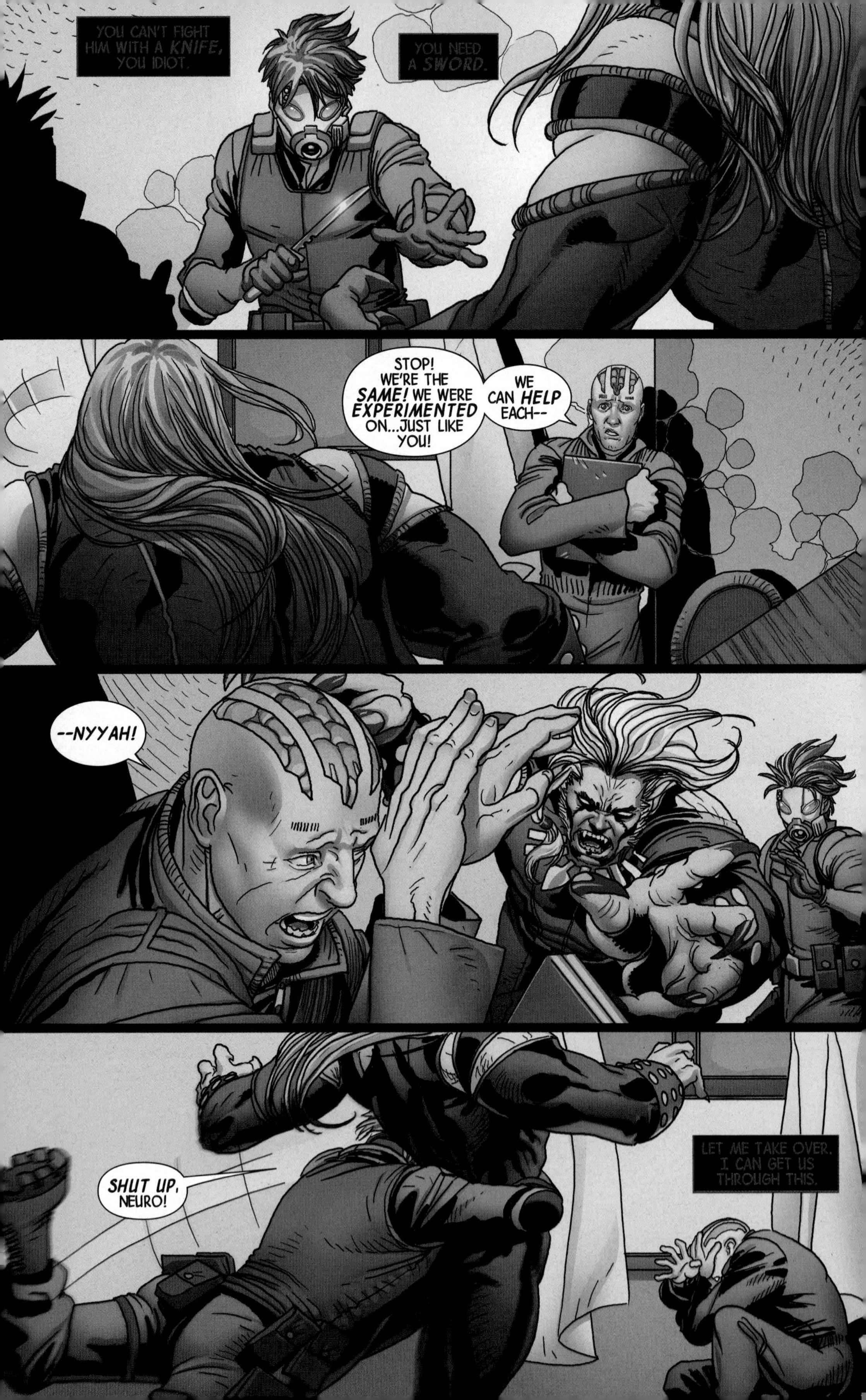

YOU CAN'T FIGHT HIM WITH A KNIFE, YOU IDIOT.
YOU NEED A SWORD.
STOP! WE'RE THE SAME! WE WERE EXPERIMENTED ON...JUST LIKE YOU!
WE CAN HELP EACH--
--NYYAH!
SHUT UP, NEURO!
LET ME TAKE OVER. I CAN GET US THROUGH THIS.

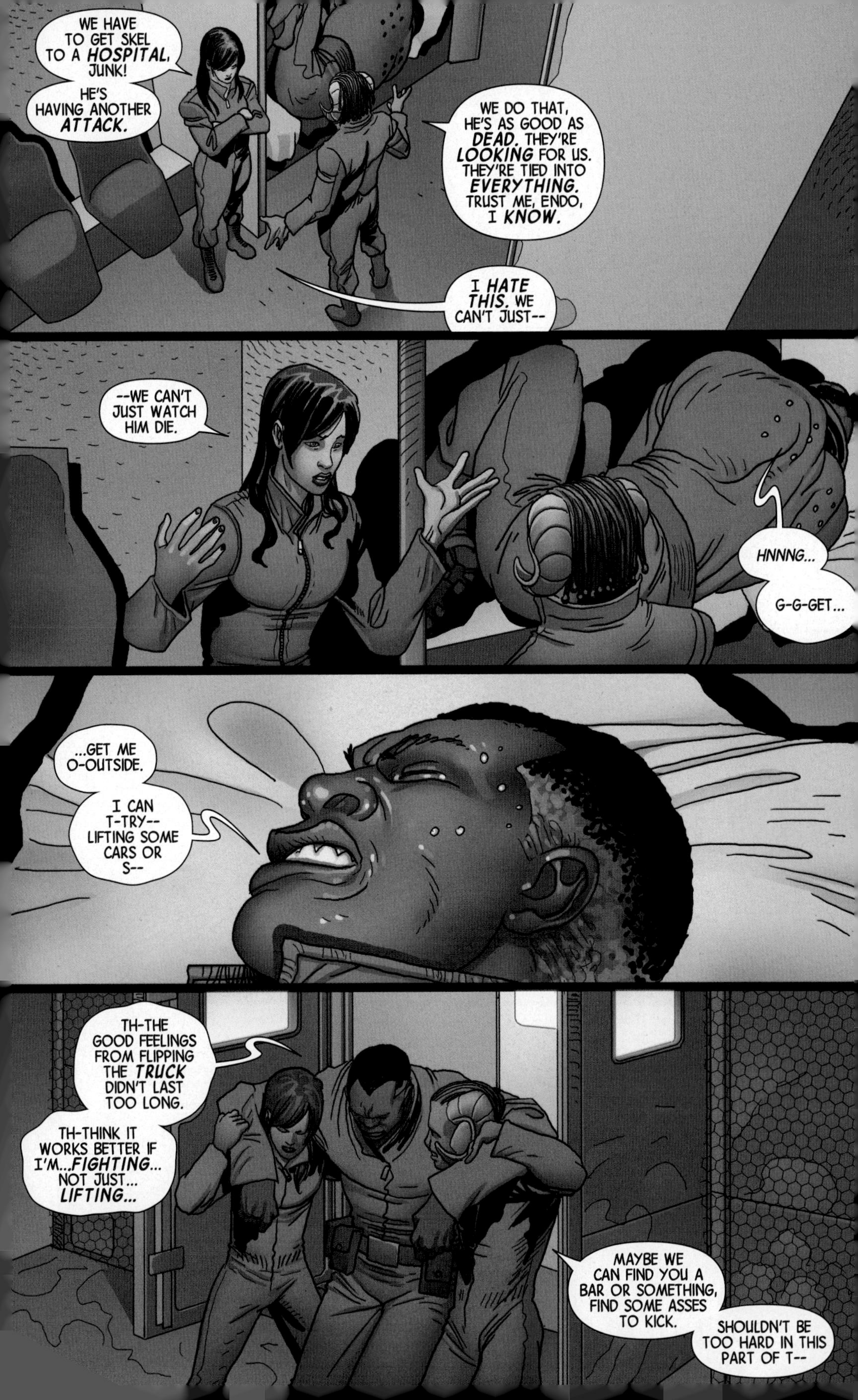
WE HAVE TO GET SKEL TO A HOSPITAL, JUNK!
HE'S HAVING ANOTHER ATTACK.
WE DO THAT, HE'S AS GOOD AS DEAD. THEY'RE LOOKING FOR US. THEY'RE TIED INTO EVERYTHING. TRUST ME, ENDO, I KNOW.
I HATE THIS. WE CAN'T JUST--
--WE CAN'T JUST WATCH HIM DIE.
HNNNG...
G-G-GET...
...GET ME O-OUTSIDE.
I CAN T-TRY-- LIFTING SOME CARS OR S--
TH-THE GOOD FEELINGS FROM FLIPPING THE TRUCK DIDN'T LAST TOO LONG.
TH-THINK IT WORKS BETTER IF I'M...FIGHTING... NOT JUST... LIFTING...
MAYBE WE CAN FIND YOU A BAR OR SOMETHING, FIND SOME ASSES TO KICK.
SHOULDN'T BE TOO HARD IN THIS PART OF T--

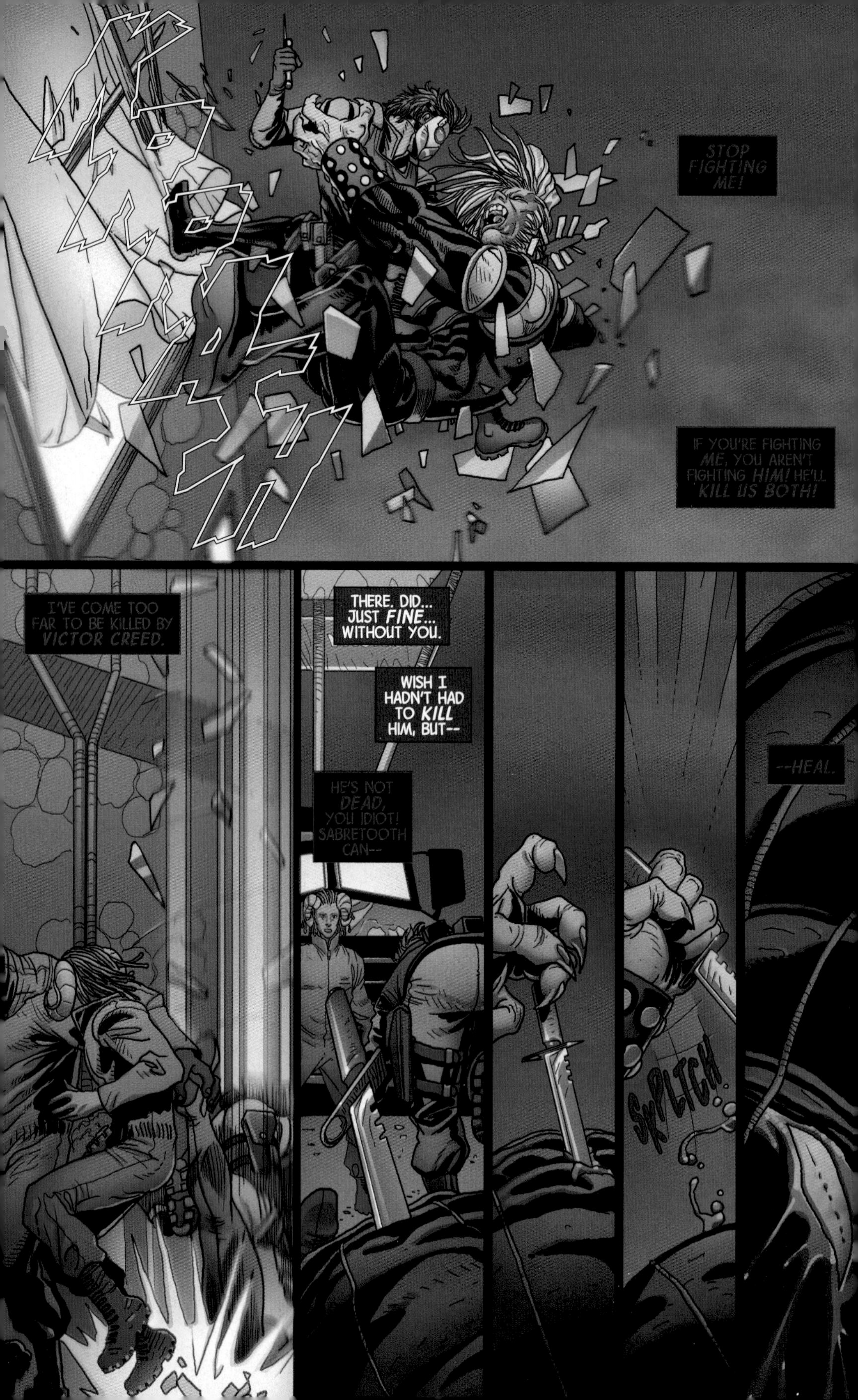
STOP FIGHTING ME!
IF YOU'RE FIGHTING ME, YOU AREN'T FIGHTING HIM! HE'LL KILL US BOTH!
I'VE COME TOO FAR TO BE KILLED BY VICTOR CREED.
THERE. DID... JUST FINE... WITHOUT YOU.
WISH I HADN'T HAD TO KILL HIM, BUT--
HE'S NOT DEAD, YOU IDIOT! SABRETOOTH CAN--
SKPLTCH
--HEAL.

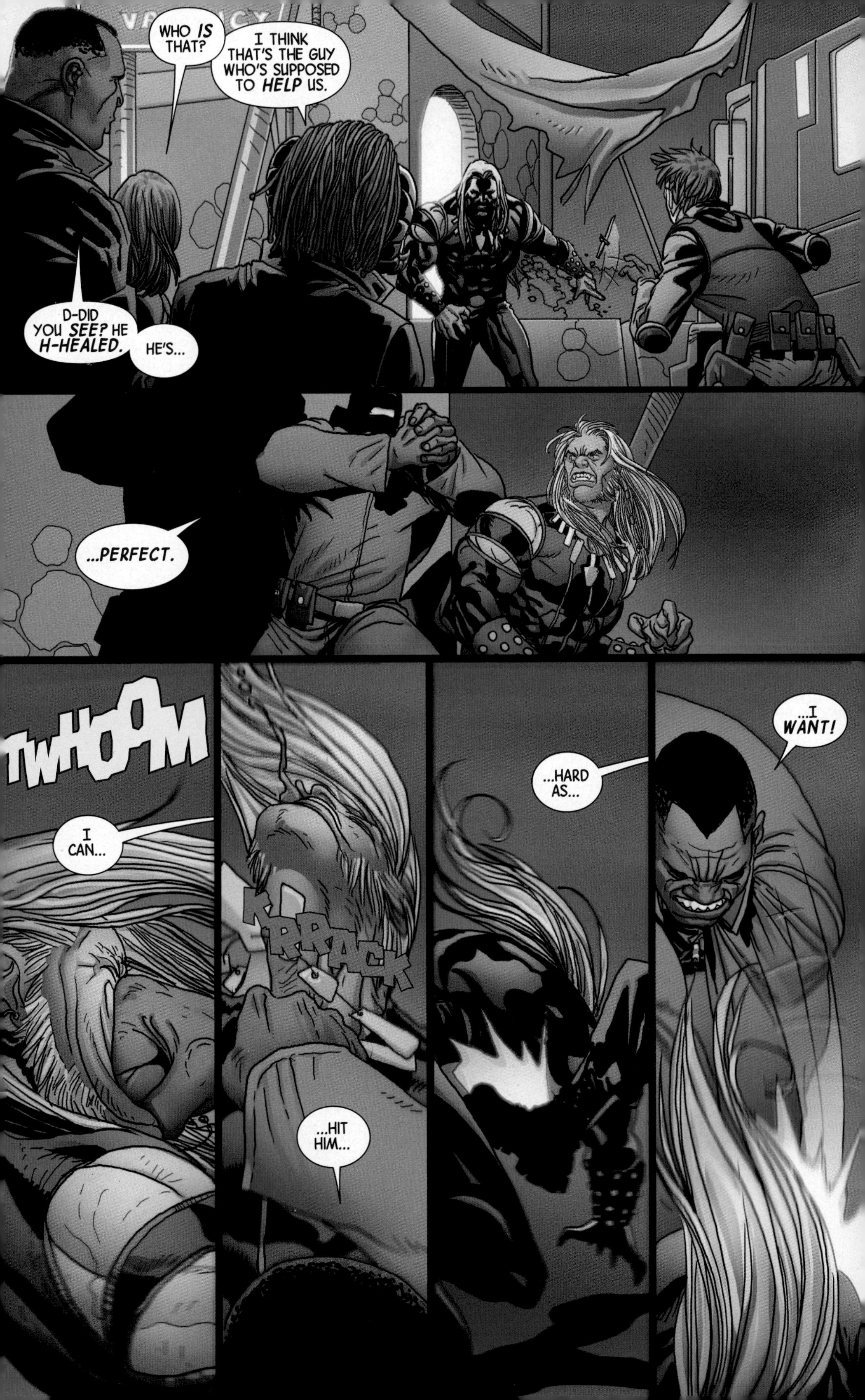
WHO IS THAT?
I THINK THAT'S THE GUY WHO'S SUPPOSED TO HELP US.
D-DID YOU SEE? HE H-HEALED.
HE'S...
...PERFECT.
TWHOOM
I CAN...
KRRACK
...HIT HIM...
...HARD AS...
...I WANT!

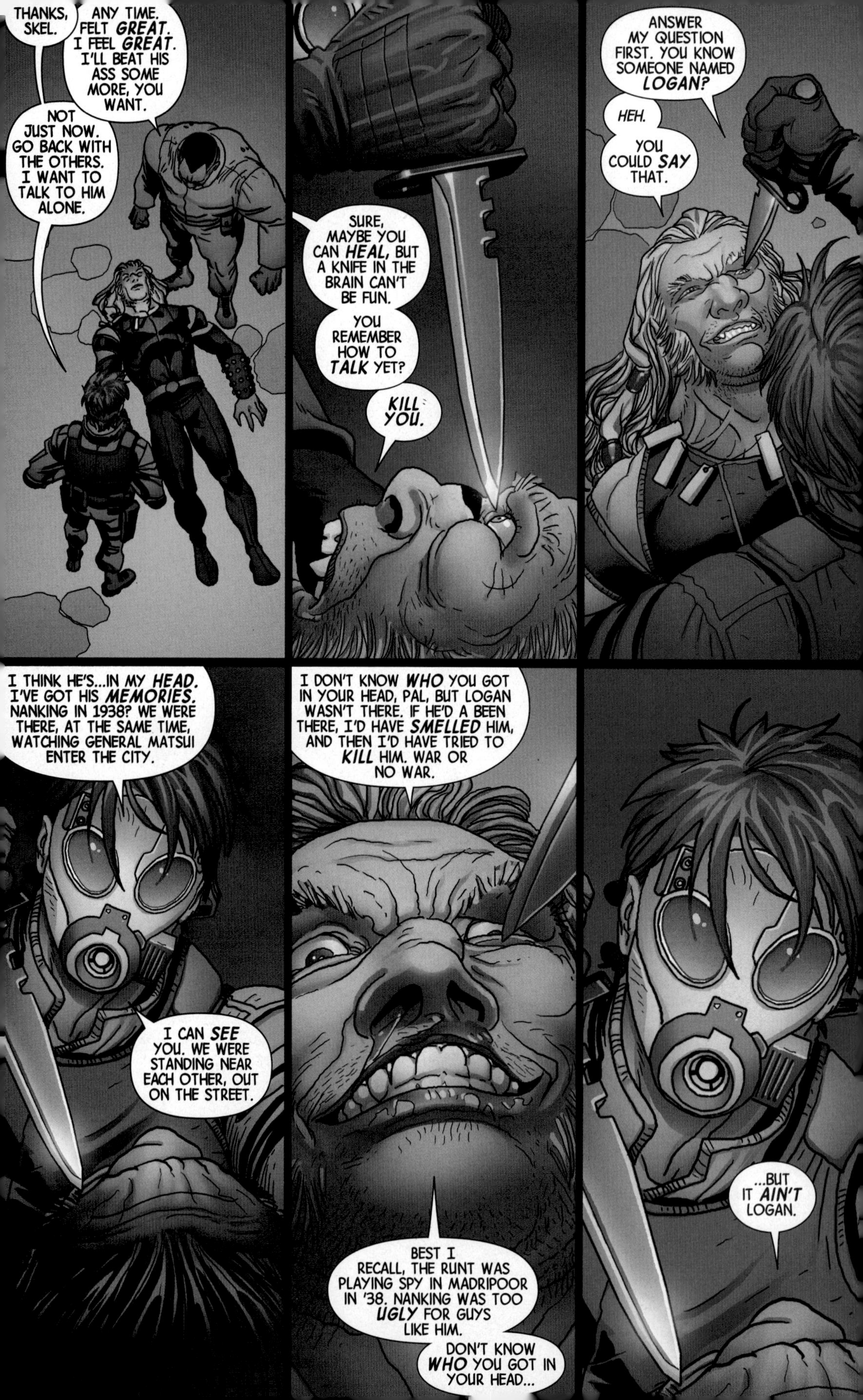
THANKS, SKEL.
ANY TIME. FELT GREAT. I FEEL GREAT. I'LL BEAT HIS ASS SOME MORE, YOU WANT.
NOT JUST NOW. GO BACK WITH THE OTHERS. I WANT TO TALK TO HIM ALONE.
SURE, MAYBE YOU CAN HEAL, BUT A KNIFE IN THE BRAIN CAN'T BE FUN.
YOU REMEMBER HOW TO TALK YET?
KILL YOU.
ANSWER MY QUESTION FIRST. YOU KNOW SOMEONE NAMED LOGAN?
HEH.
YOU COULD SAY THAT.
I THINK HE'S...IN MY HEAD. I'VE GOT HIS MEMORIES. NANKING IN 1938? WE WERE THERE, AT THE SAME TIME, WATCHING GENERAL MATSUI ENTER THE CITY.
I CAN SEE YOU. WE WERE STANDING NEAR EACH OTHER, OUT ON THE STREET.
I DON'T KNOW WHO YOU GOT IN YOUR HEAD, PAL, BUT LOGAN WASN'T THERE. IF HE'D A BEEN THERE, I'D HAVE SMELLED HIM, AND THEN I'D HAVE TRIED TO KILL HIM. WAR OR NO WAR.
BEST I RECALL, THE RUNT WAS PLAYING SPY IN MADRIPOOR IN '38. NANKING WAS TOO UGLY FOR GUYS LIKE HIM.
DON'T KNOW WHO YOU GOT IN YOUR HEAD...
...BUT IT AIN'T LOGAN.

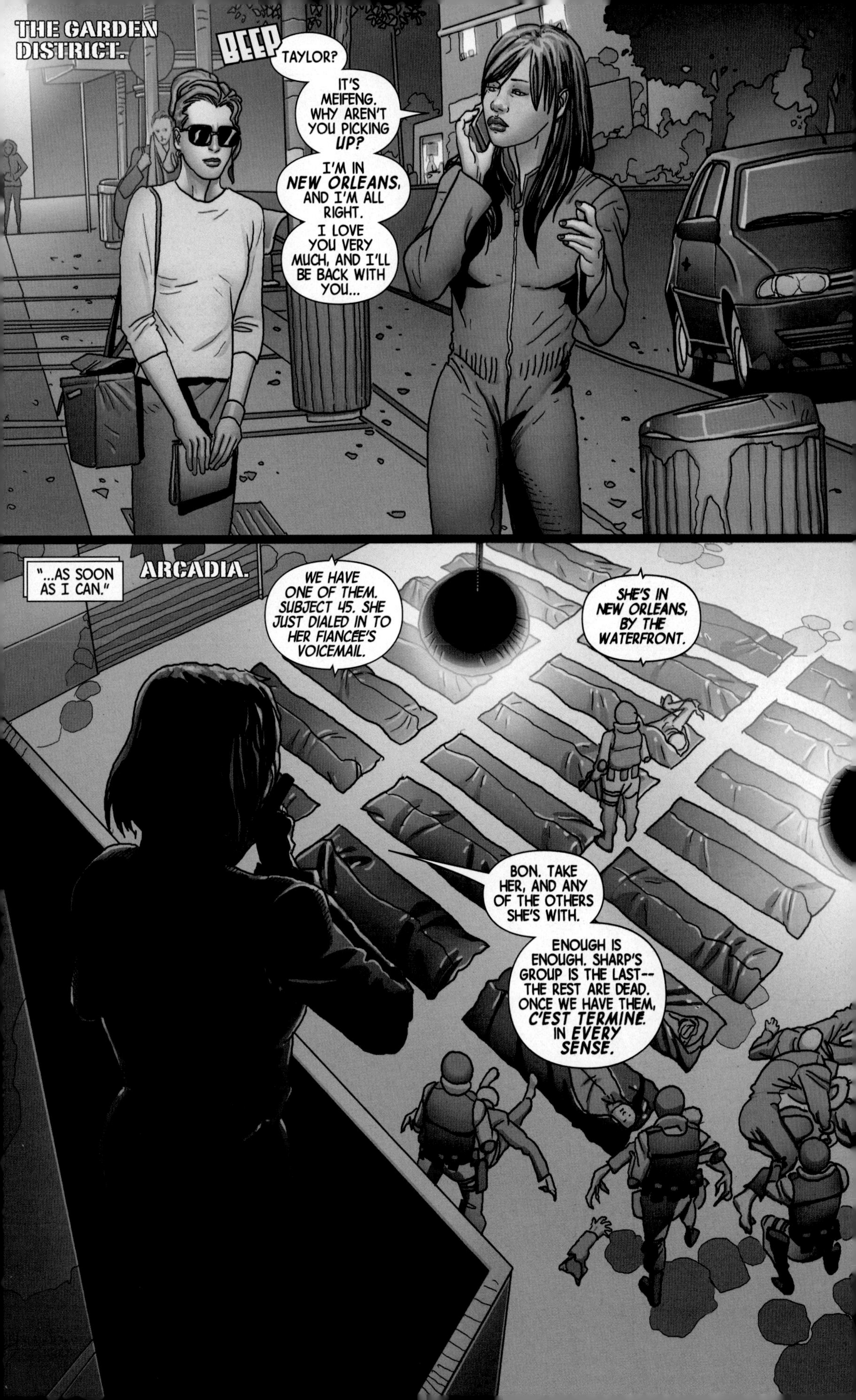
THE GARDEN DISTRICT.
BEEP
TAYLOR?
IT'S MEIFENG. WHY AREN'T YOU PICKING UP?
I'M IN NEW ORLEANS, AND I'M ALL RIGHT.
I LOVE YOU VERY MUCH, AND I'LL BE BACK WITH YOU...
"...AS SOON AS I CAN."
ARCADIA.
WE HAVE ONE OF THEM. SUBJECT 45. SHE JUST DIALED IN TO HER FIANCÉE'S VOICEMAIL.
SHE'S IN NEW ORLEANS, BY THE WATERFRONT.
BON. TAKE HER, AND ANY OF THE OTHERS SHE'S WITH.
ENOUGH IS ENOUGH. SHARP'S GROUP IS THE LAST-- THE REST ARE DEAD. ONCE WE HAVE THEM, C'EST TERMINE. IN EVERY SENSE.

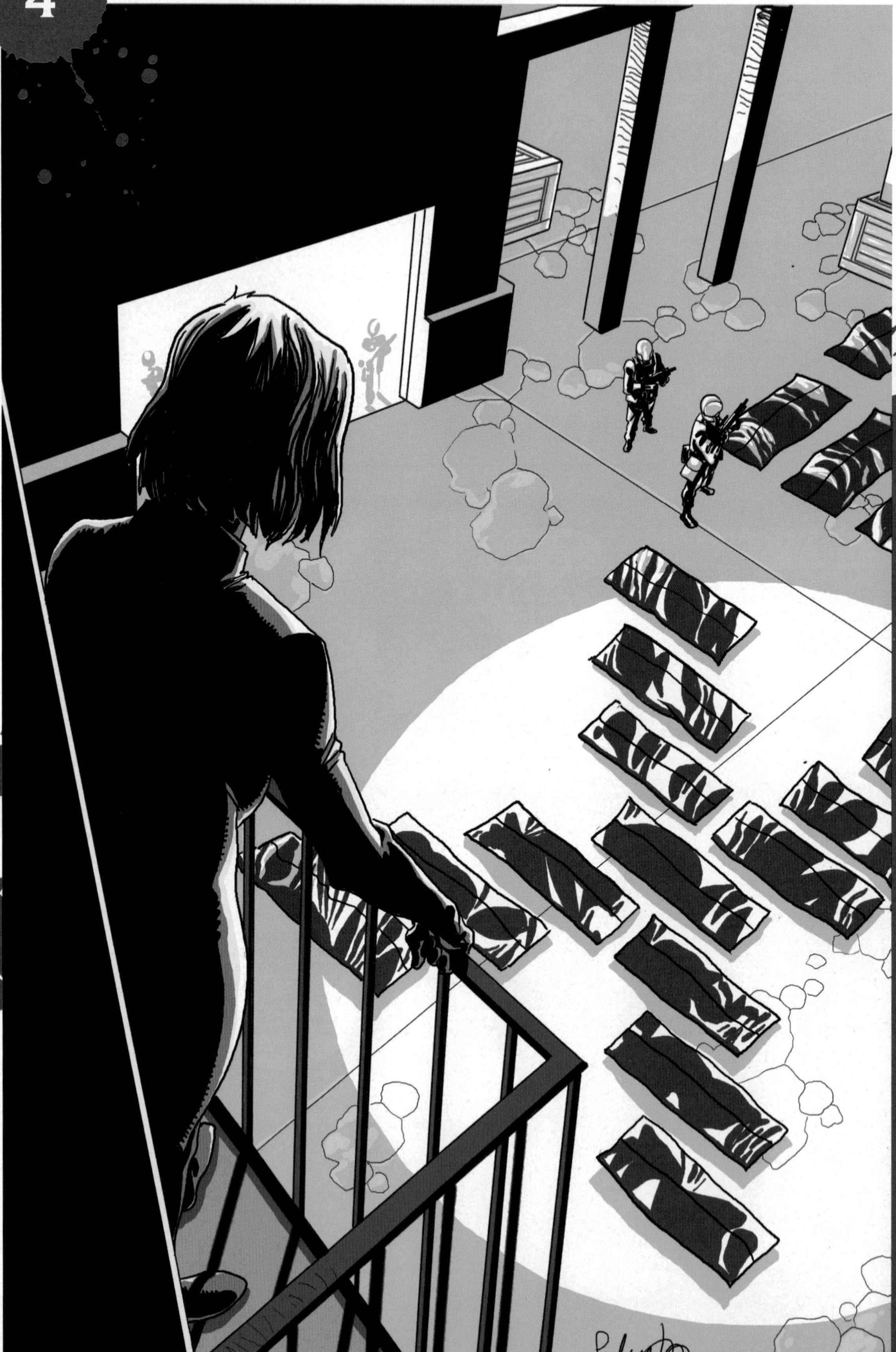

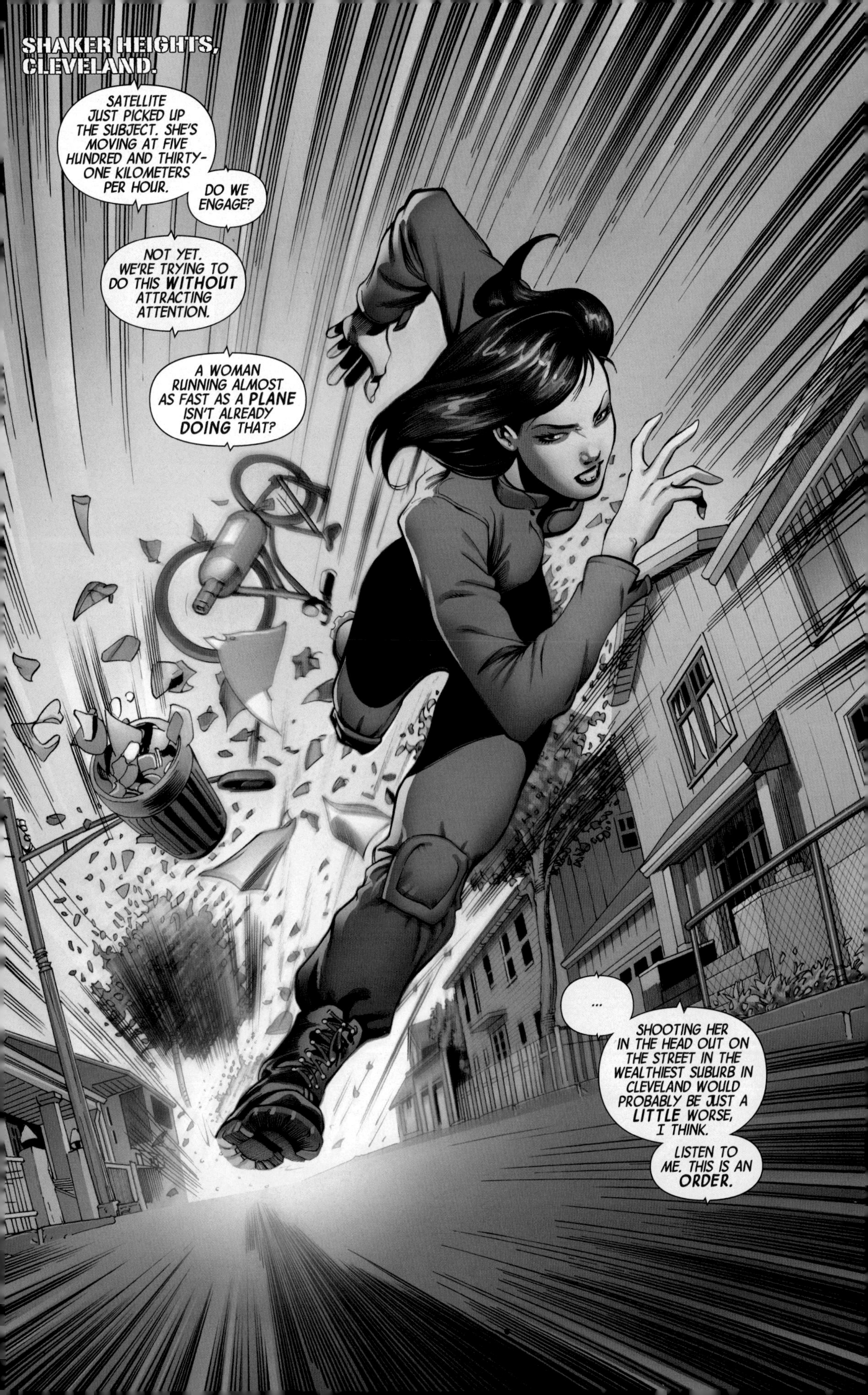
SHAKER HEIGHTS, CLEVELAND.
SATELLITE JUST PICKED UP THE SUBJECT. SHE'S MOVING AT FIVE HUNDRED AND THIRTY-ONE KILOMETERS PER HOUR.
DO WE ENGAGE?
NOT YET. WE'RE TRYING TO DO THIS WITHOUT ATTRACTING ATTENTION.
A WOMAN RUNNING ALMOST AS FAST AS A PLANE ISN'T ALREADY DOING THAT?
...
SHOOTING HER IN THE HEAD OUT ON THE STREET IN THE WEALTHIEST SUBURB IN CLEVELAND WOULD PROBABLY BE JUST A LITTLE WORSE, I THINK.
LISTEN TO ME. THIS IS AN ORDER.

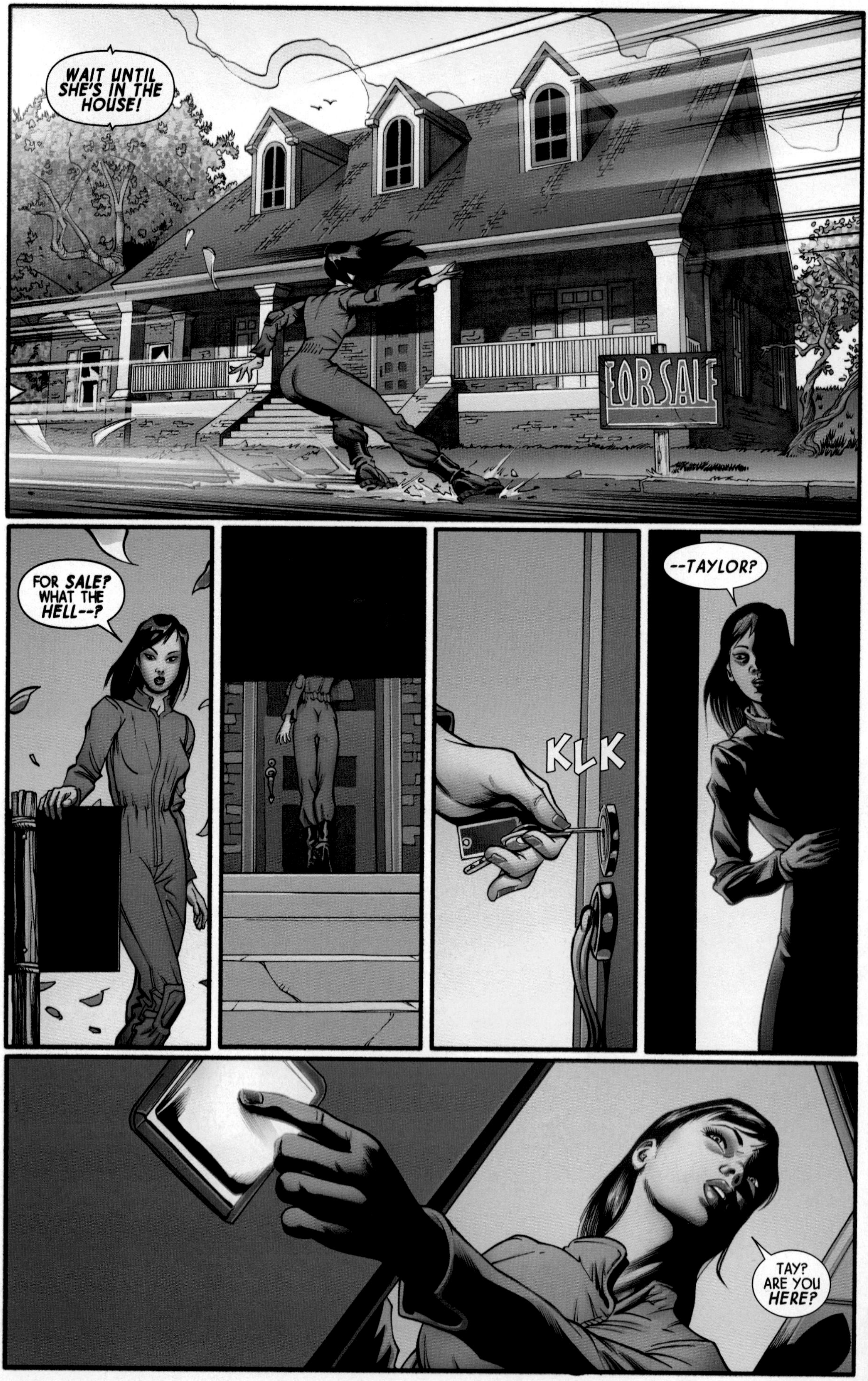
WAIT UNTIL SHE'S IN THE HOUSE!
FOR SALE
FOR SALE? WHAT THE HELL--?
KLK
--TAYLOR?
TAY? ARE YOU HERE?

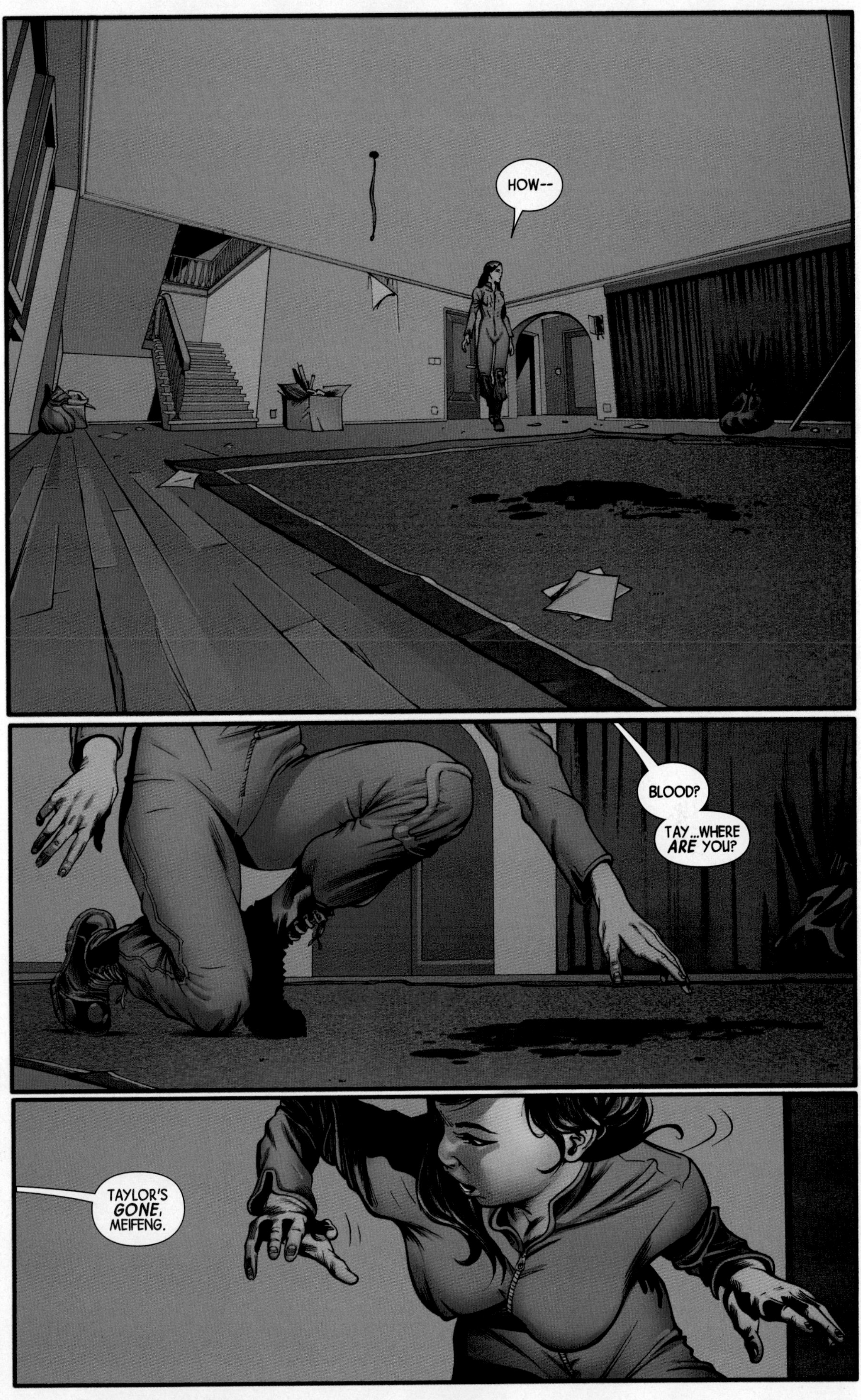
HOW--
BLOOD?
TAY...WHERE ARE YOU?
TAYLOR'S GONE, MEIFENG.

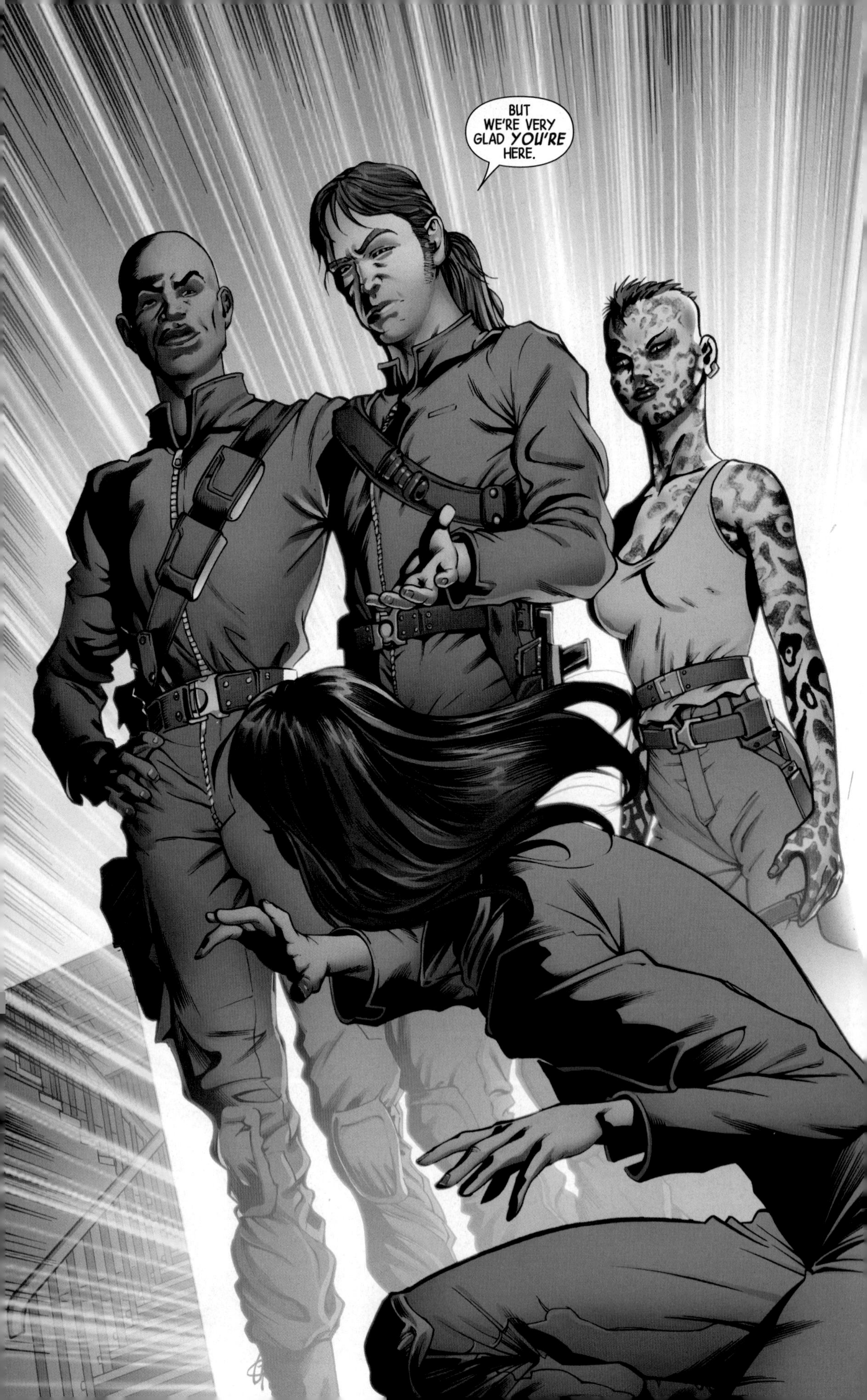
BUT WE'RE VERY GLAD YOU'RE HERE.

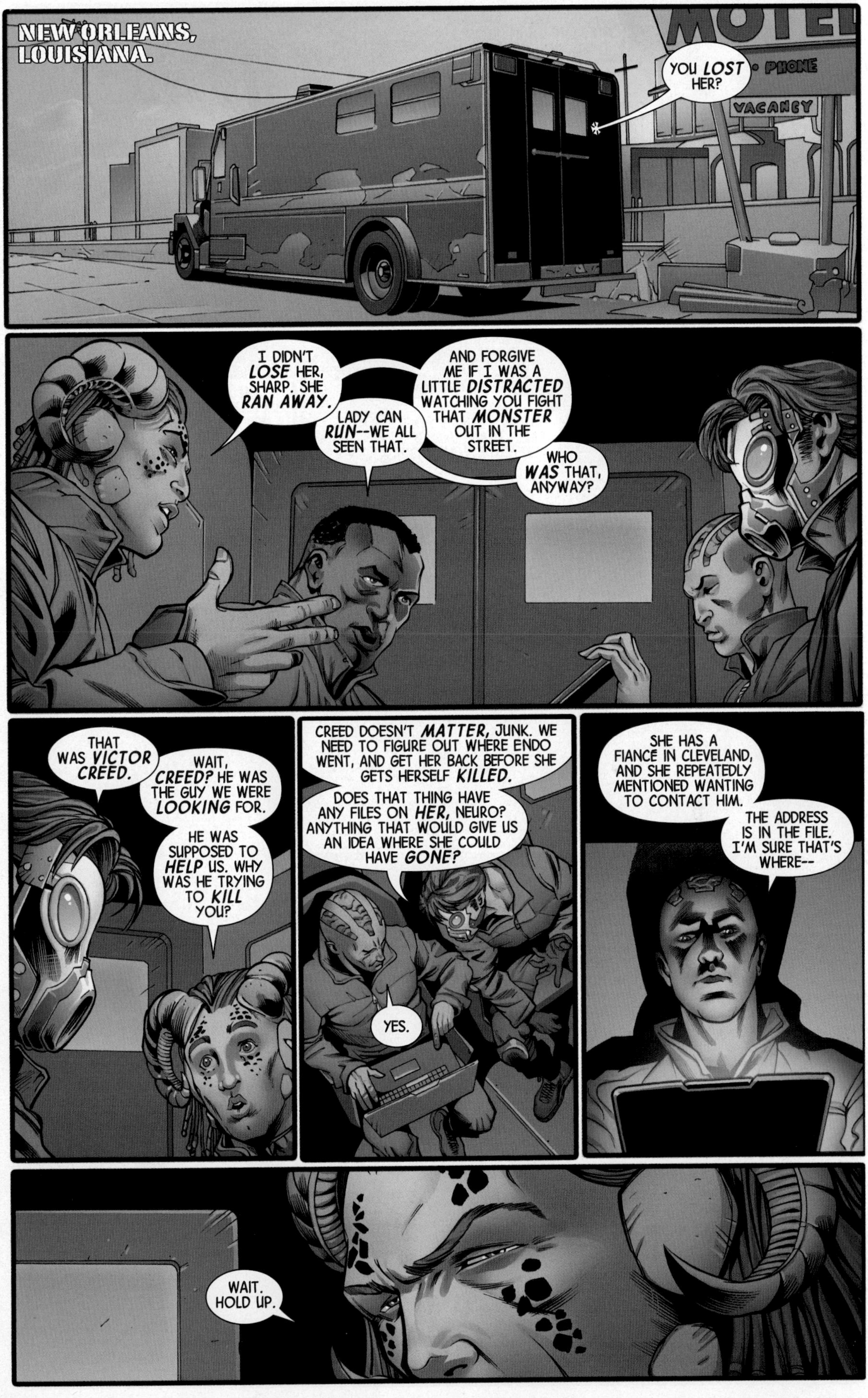
NEW ORLEANS, LOUISIANA.
YOU LOST HER?
MOTEL
PHONE
VACANCY
I DIDN'T LOSE HER, SHARP. SHE RAN AWAY.
AND FORGIVE ME IF I WAS A LITTLE DISTRACTED WATCHING YOU FIGHT THAT MONSTER OUT IN THE STREET.
LADY CAN RUN--WE ALL SEEN THAT.
WHO WAS THAT, ANYWAY?
THAT WAS VICTOR CREED.
WAIT, CREED? HE WAS THE GUY WE WERE LOOKING FOR.
HE WAS SUPPOSED TO HELP US. WHY WAS HE TRYING TO KILL YOU?
CREED DOESN'T MATTER, JUNK. WE NEED TO FIGURE OUT WHERE ENDO WENT, AND GET HER BACK BEFORE SHE GETS HERSELF KILLED.
DOES THAT THING HAVE ANY FILES ON HER, NEURO? ANYTHING THAT WOULD GIVE US AN IDEA WHERE SHE COULD HAVE GONE?
YES.
SHE HAS A FIANCÉ IN CLEVELAND, AND SHE REPEATEDLY MENTIONED WANTING TO CONTACT HIM.
THE ADDRESS IS IN THE FILE. I'M SURE THAT'S WHERE--
WAIT. HOLD UP.

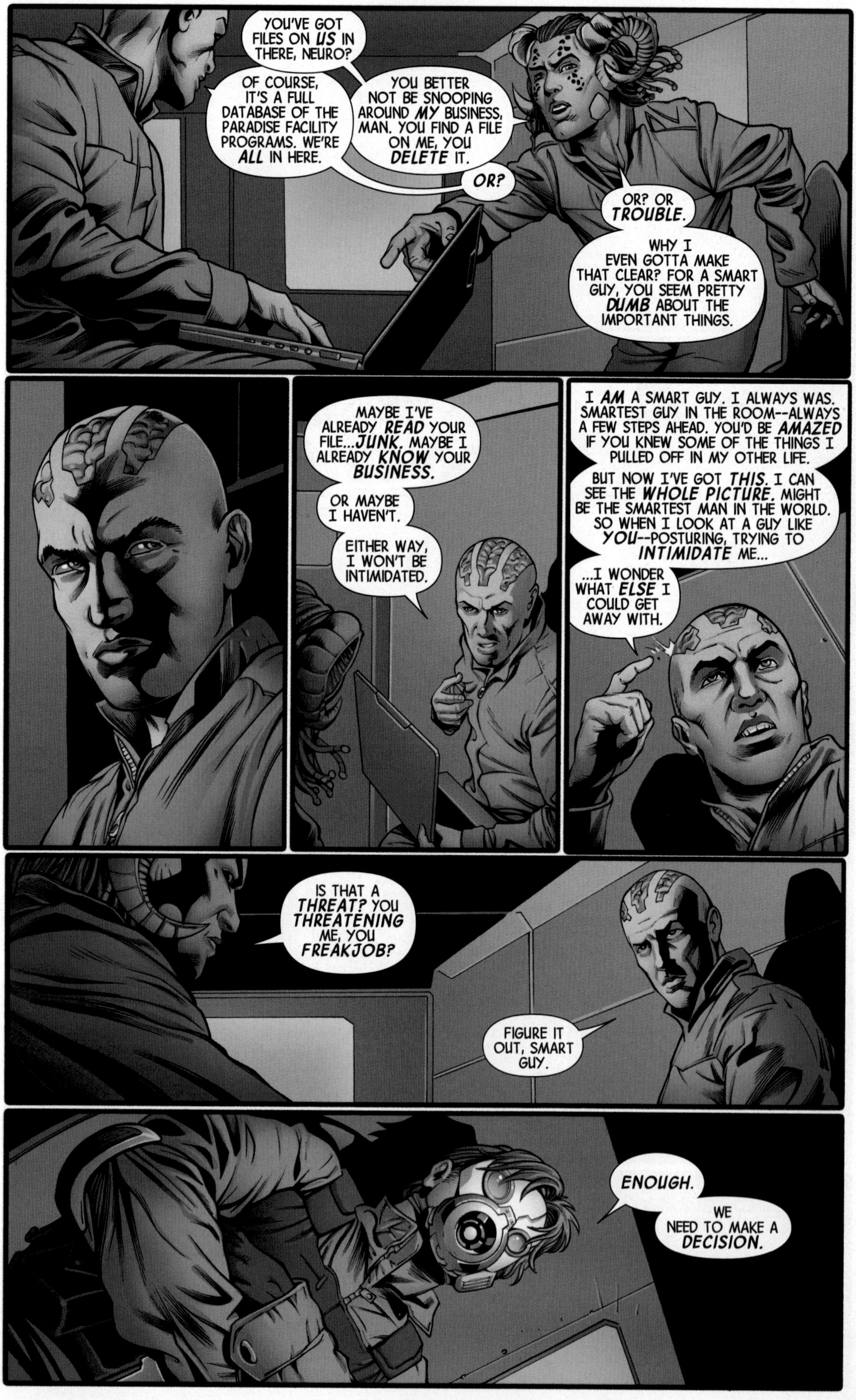
YOU'VE GOT FILES ON US IN THERE, NEURO?
OF COURSE, IT'S A FULL DATABASE OF THE PARADISE FACILITY PROGRAMS. WE'RE ALL IN HERE.
YOU BETTER NOT BE SNOOPING AROUND MY BUSINESS, MAN. YOU FIND A FILE ON ME, YOU DELETE IT.
OR?
OR? OR TROUBLE.
WHY I EVEN GOTTA MAKE THAT CLEAR? FOR A SMART GUY, YOU SEEM PRETTY DUMB ABOUT THE IMPORTANT THINGS.
MAYBE I'VE ALREADY READ YOUR FILE...JUNK. MAYBE I ALREADY KNOW YOUR BUSINESS.
OR MAYBE I HAVEN'T.
EITHER WAY, I WON'T BE INTIMIDATED.
I AM A SMART GUY. I ALWAYS WAS. SMARTEST GUY IN THE ROOM--ALWAYS A FEW STEPS AHEAD. YOU'D BE AMAZED IF YOU KNEW SOME OF THE THINGS I PULLED OFF IN MY OTHER LIFE.
BUT NOW I'VE GOT THIS. I CAN SEE THE WHOLE PICTURE. MIGHT BE THE SMARTEST MAN IN THE WORLD. SO WHEN I LOOK AT A GUY LIKE YOU--POSTURING, TRYING TO INTIMIDATE ME...
...I WONDER WHAT ELSE I COULD GET AWAY WITH.
IS THAT A THREAT? YOU THREATENING ME, YOU FREAKJOB?
FIGURE IT OUT, SMART GUY.
ENOUGH.
WE NEED TO MAKE A DECISION.

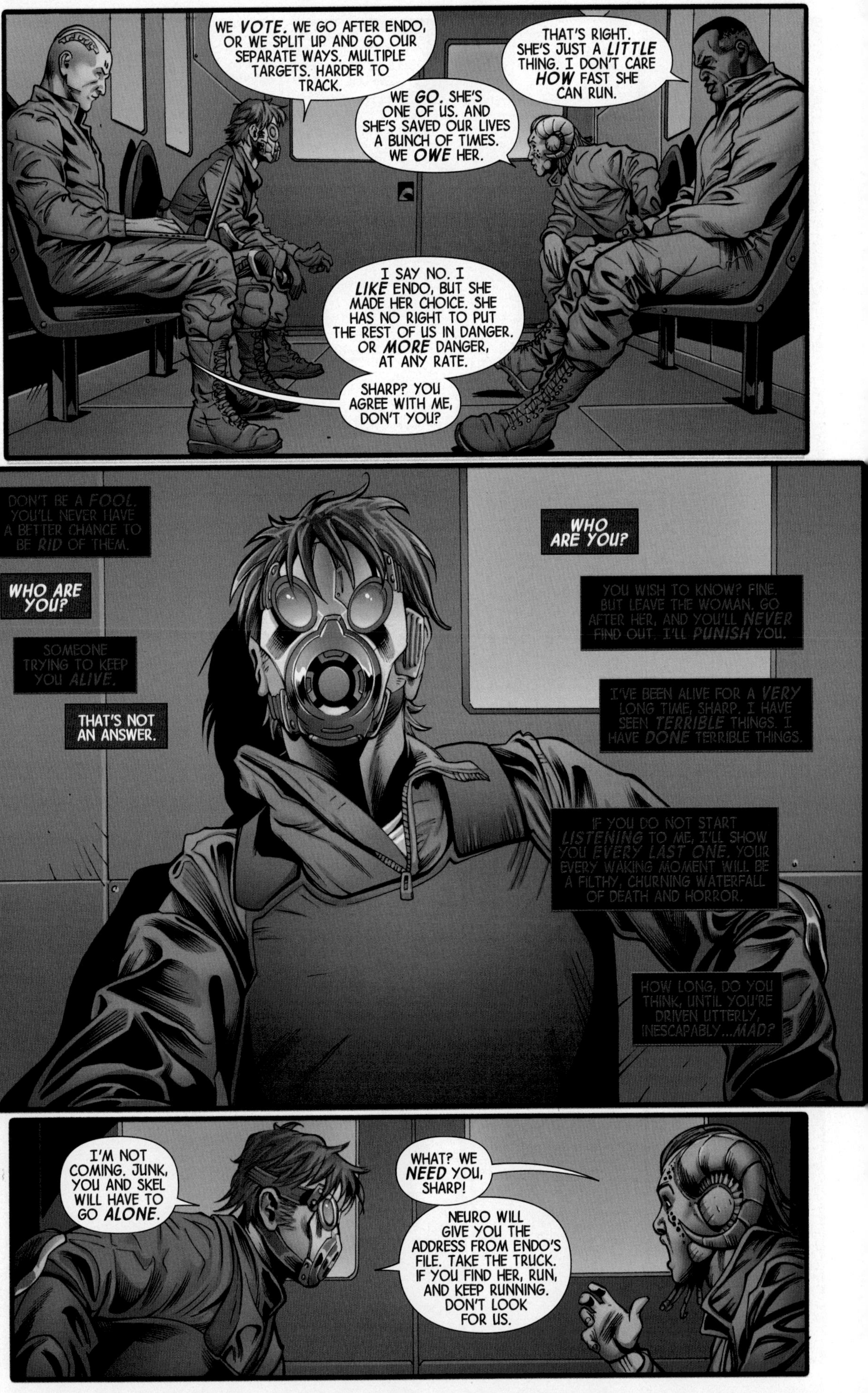
WE VOTE. WE GO AFTER ENDO, OR WE SPLIT UP AND GO OUR SEPARATE WAYS. MULTIPLE TARGETS. HARDER TO TRACK.
WE GO. SHE'S ONE OF US. AND SHE'S SAVED OUR LIVES A BUNCH OF TIMES. WE OWE HER.
THAT'S RIGHT. SHE'S JUST A LITTLE THING. I DON'T CARE HOW FAST SHE CAN RUN.
I SAY NO. I LIKE ENDO, BUT SHE MADE HER CHOICE. SHE HAS NO RIGHT TO PUT THE REST OF US IN DANGER. OR MORE DANGER, AT ANY RATE.
SHARP? YOU AGREE WITH ME, DON'T YOU?
DON'T BE A FOOL. YOU'LL NEVER HAVE A BETTER CHANCE TO BE RID OF THEM.
WHO ARE YOU?
SOMEONE TRYING TO KEEP YOU ALIVE.
THAT'S NOT AN ANSWER.
WHO ARE YOU?
YOU WISH TO KNOW? FINE. BUT LEAVE THE WOMAN. GO AFTER HER, AND YOU'LL NEVER FIND OUT. I'LL PUNISH YOU.
I'VE BEEN ALIVE FOR A VERY LONG TIME, SHARP. I HAVE SEEN TERRIBLE THINGS. I HAVE DONE TERRIBLE THINGS.
IF YOU DO NOT START LISTENING TO ME, I'LL SHOW YOU EVERY LAST ONE. YOUR EVERY WAKING MOMENT WILL BE A FILTHY, CHURNING WATERFALL OF DEATH AND HORROR.
HOW LONG, DO YOU THINK, UNTIL YOU'RE DRIVEN UTTERLY, INESCAPABLY...MAD?
I'M NOT COMING. JUNK, YOU AND SKEL WILL HAVE TO GO ALONE.
WHAT? WE NEED YOU, SHARP!
NEURO WILL GIVE YOU THE ADDRESS FROM ENDO'S FILE. TAKE THE TRUCK. IF YOU FIND HER, RUN, AND KEEP RUNNING. DON'T LOOK FOR US.

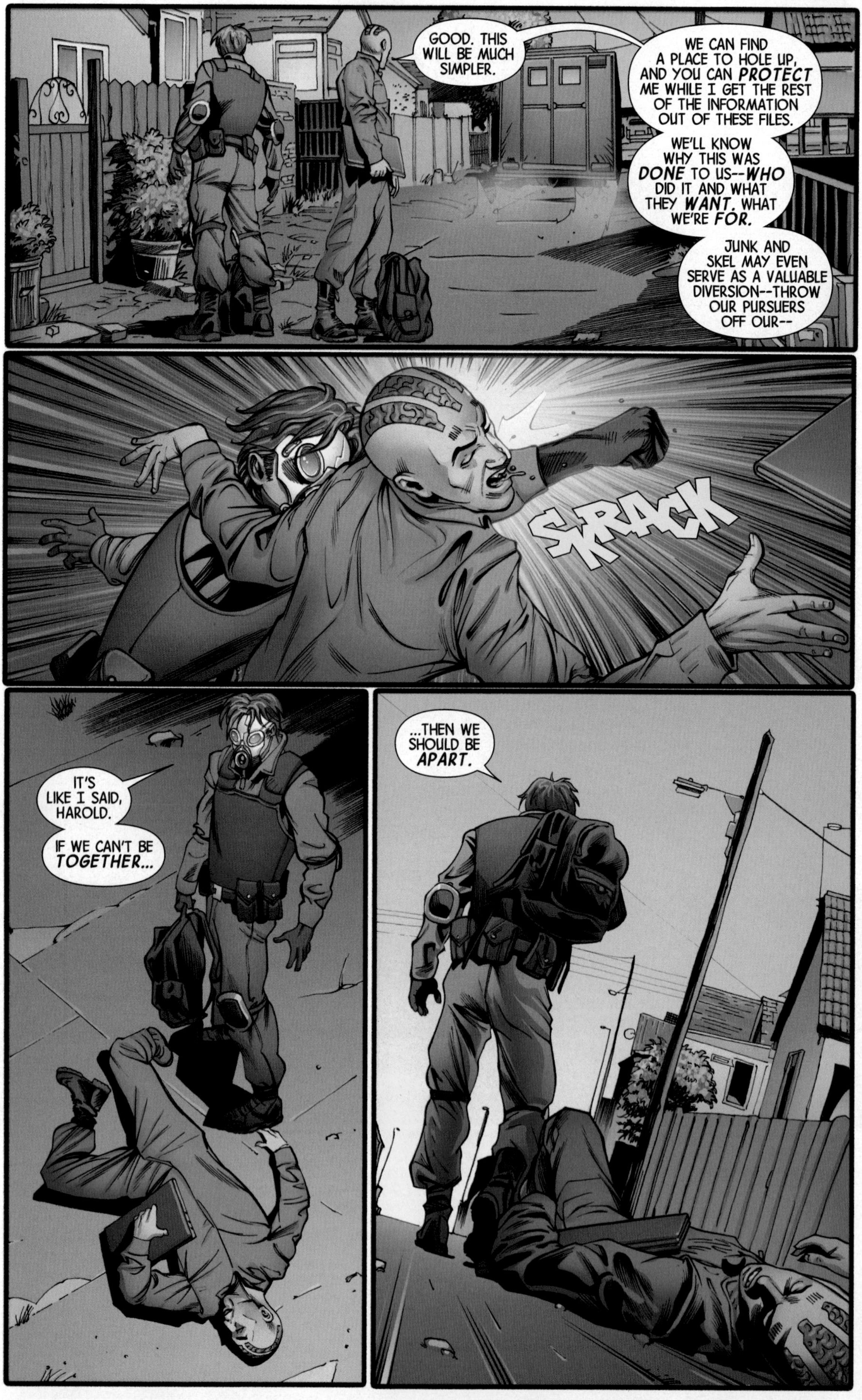
GOOD. THIS WILL BE MUCH SIMPLER.
WE CAN FIND A PLACE TO HOLE UP, AND YOU CAN PROTECT ME WHILE I GET THE REST OF THE INFORMATION OUT OF THESE FILES.
WE'LL KNOW WHY THIS WAS DONE TO US--WHO DID IT AND WHAT THEY WANT. WHAT WE'RE FOR.
JUNK AND SKEL MAY EVEN SERVE AS A VALUABLE DIVERSION--THROW OUR PURSUERS OFF OUR--
SKRACK
IT'S LIKE I SAID, HAROLD.
IF WE CAN'T BE TOGETHER...
...THEN WE SHOULD BE APART.

WHO *ARE* YOU? WHAT DID YOU DO TO MY *HOUSE*?

WHERE IS *TAYLOR*?

WHAT DID YOU DO TO MY *FIANCEE*?

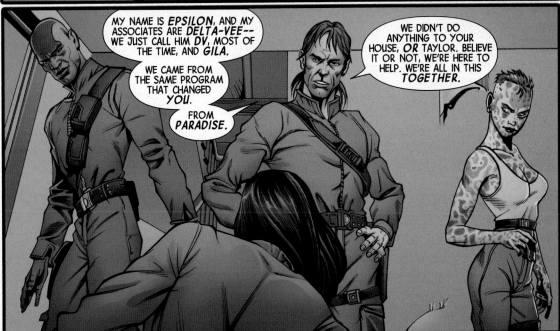

MY NAME IS *EPSILON*, AND MY ASSOCIATES ARE *DELTA-VEE*-- WE JUST CALL HIM *DV*, MOST OF THE TIME, AND *GILA*.

WE CAME FROM THE SAME PROGRAM THAT CHANGED *YOU*.

FROM *PARADISE*.

WE DIDN'T DO ANYTHING TO YOUR HOUSE, *OR* TAYLOR. BELIEVE IT OR NOT, WE'RE HERE TO HELP. WE'RE ALL IN THIS *TOGETHER*.

YOU'RE *LYING*. THAT'S A *BLOOD STAIN* ON THE CARPET, ISN'T IT?

SHHHZZZAPP

IN FACT, YES, IT IS. VERY PERCEPTIVE.

LITTLE HELP, DV?

SSSPP

YES, SIR. ON IT.

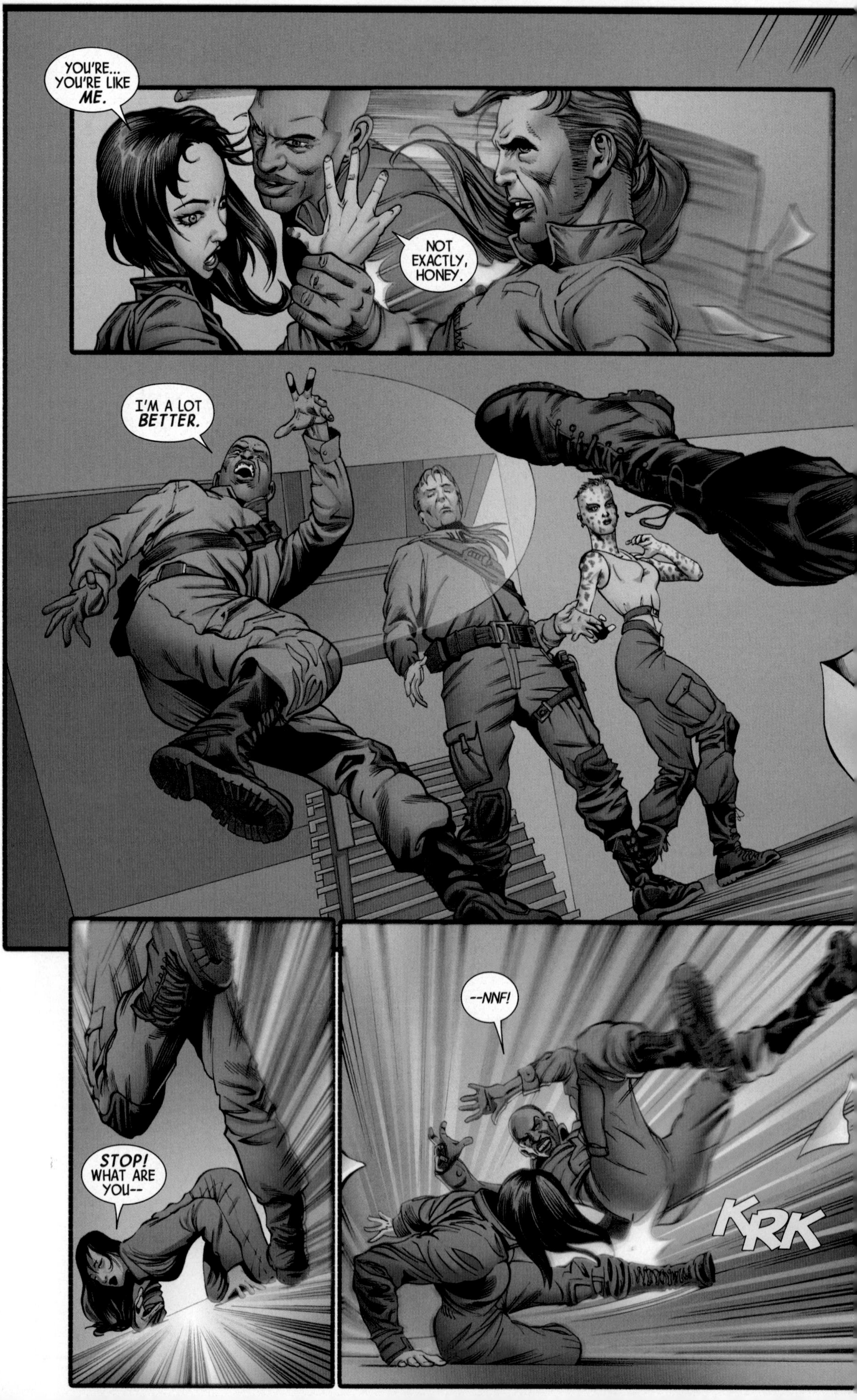
YOU'RE... YOU'RE LIKE ME.
NOT EXACTLY, HONEY.
I'M A LOT BETTER.
STOP! WHAT ARE YOU--
--NNF!
KRK

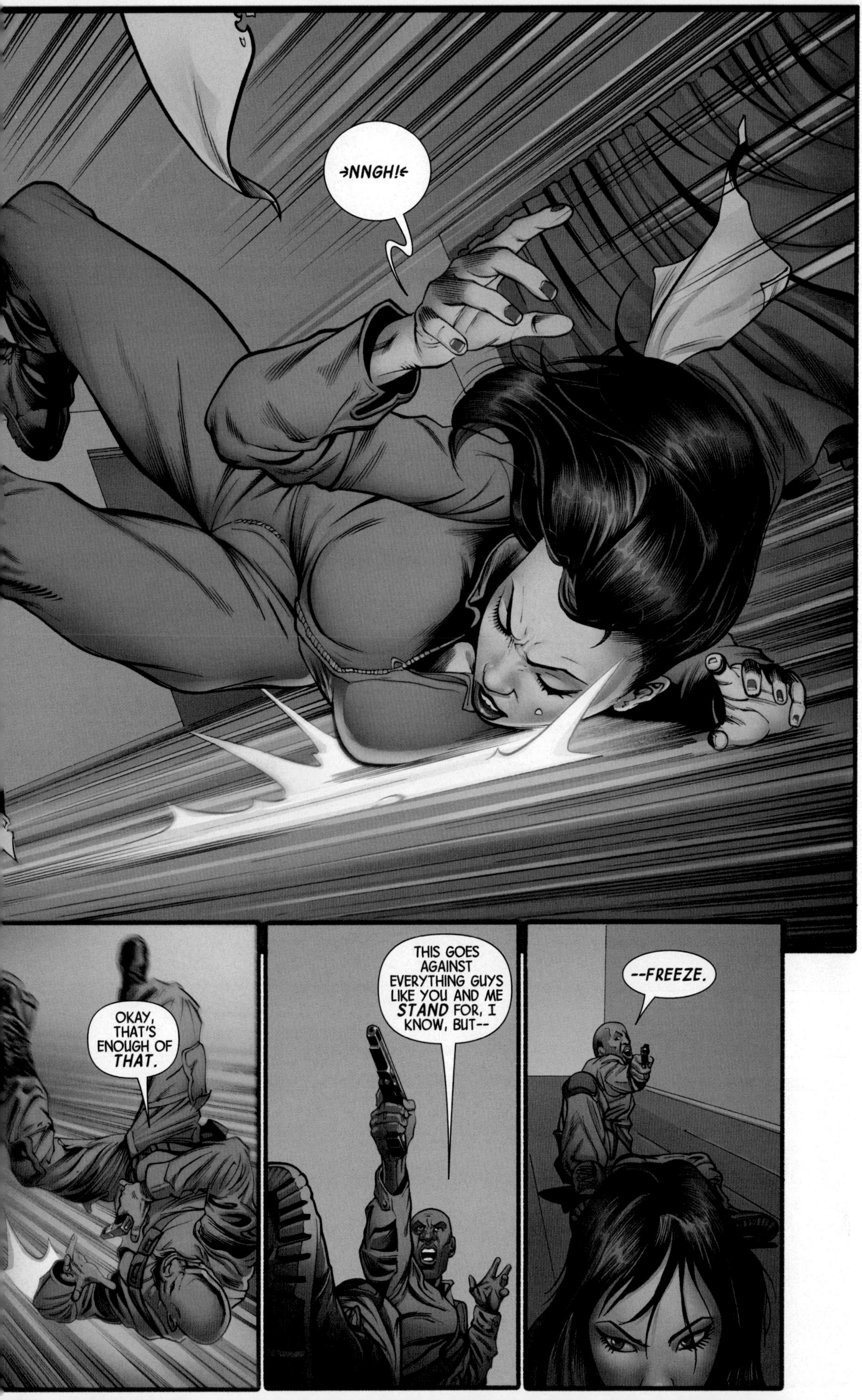

NNGH!
OKAY, THAT'S ENOUGH OF THAT.
THIS GOES AGAINST EVERYTHING GUYS LIKE YOU AND ME STAND FOR, I KNOW, BUT--
--FREEZE.

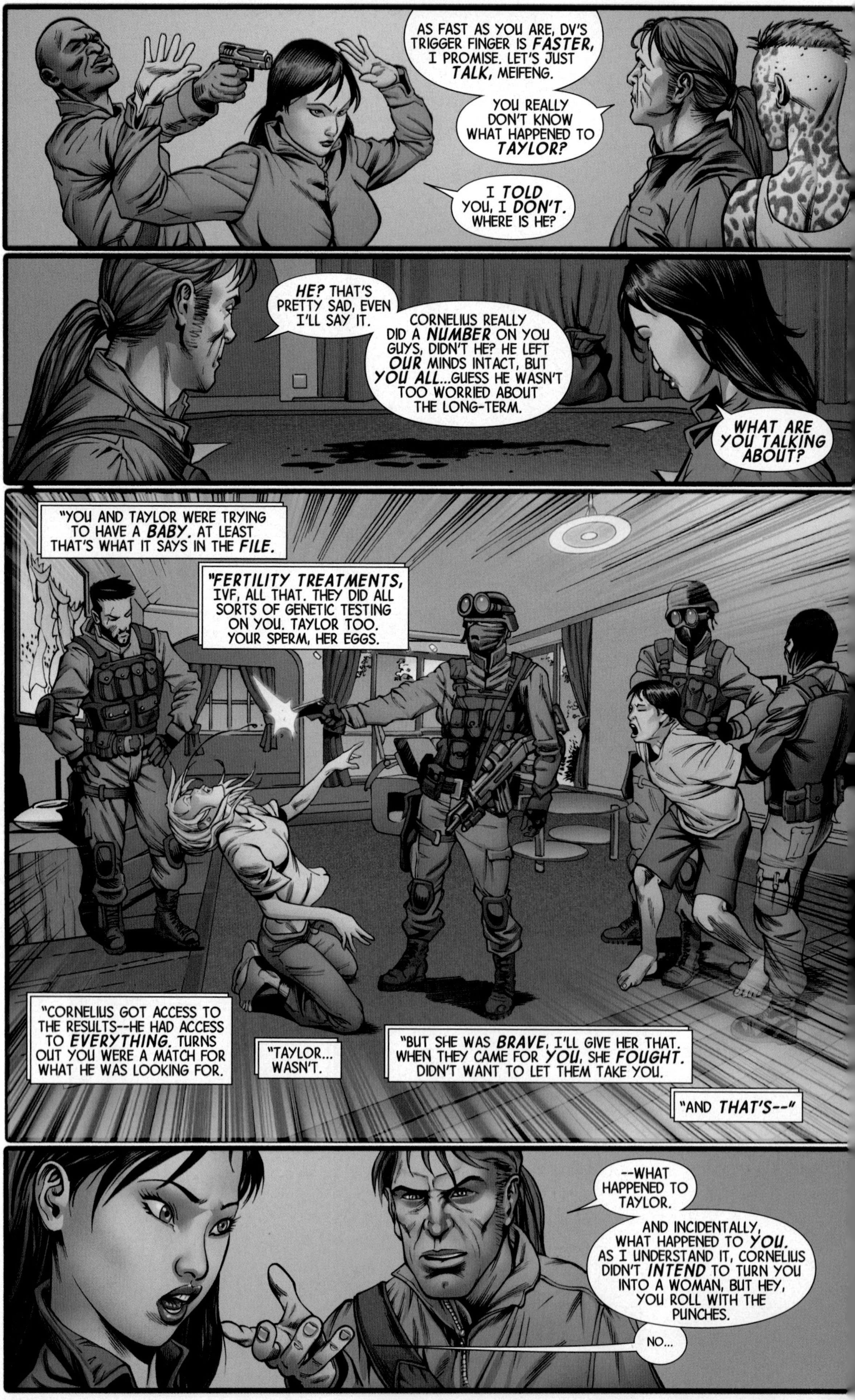
AS FAST AS YOU ARE, DV'S TRIGGER FINGER IS FASTER, I PROMISE. LET'S JUST TALK, MEIFENG.
YOU REALLY DON'T KNOW WHAT HAPPENED TO TAYLOR?
I TOLD YOU, I DON'T. WHERE IS HE?
HE? THAT'S PRETTY SAD, EVEN I'LL SAY IT.
CORNELIUS REALLY DID A NUMBER ON YOU GUYS, DIDN'T HE? HE LEFT OUR MINDS INTACT, BUT YOU ALL...GUESS HE WASN'T TOO WORRIED ABOUT THE LONG-TERM.
WHAT ARE YOU TALKING ABOUT?
"YOU AND TAYLOR WERE TRYING TO HAVE A BABY. AT LEAST THAT'S WHAT IT SAYS IN THE FILE.
"FERTILITY TREATMENTS, IVF, ALL THAT. THEY DID ALL SORTS OF GENETIC TESTING ON YOU. TAYLOR TOO. YOUR SPERM, HER EGGS.
"CORNELIUS GOT ACCESS TO THE RESULTS--HE HAD ACCESS TO EVERYTHING. TURNS OUT YOU WERE A MATCH FOR WHAT HE WAS LOOKING FOR.
"TAYLOR... WASN'T.
"BUT SHE WAS BRAVE, I'LL GIVE HER THAT. WHEN THEY CAME FOR YOU, SHE FOUGHT. DIDN'T WANT TO LET THEM TAKE YOU.
"AND THAT'S--"
--WHAT HAPPENED TO TAYLOR.
AND INCIDENTALLY, WHAT HAPPENED TO YOU. AS I UNDERSTAND IT, CORNELIUS DIDN'T INTEND TO TURN YOU INTO A WOMAN, BUT HEY, YOU ROLL WITH THE PUNCHES.
NO...

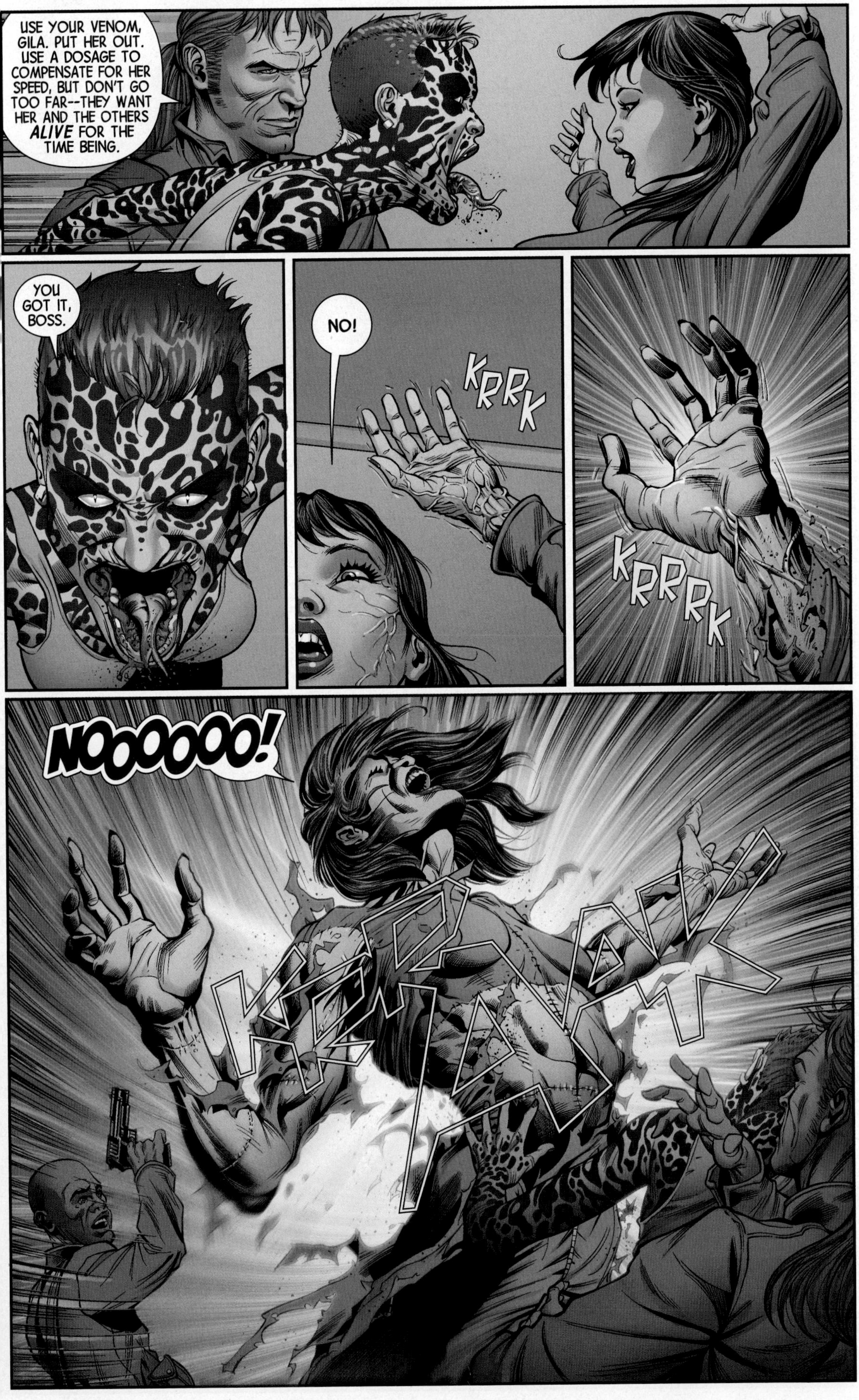
USE YOUR VENOM, GILA. PUT HER OUT. USE A DOSAGE TO COMPENSATE FOR HER SPEED, BUT DON'T GO TOO FAR--THEY WANT HER AND THE OTHERS *ALIVE* FOR THE TIME BEING.
YOU GOT IT, BOSS.
NO!
KRRK
KRRRK
NOOOOOO!

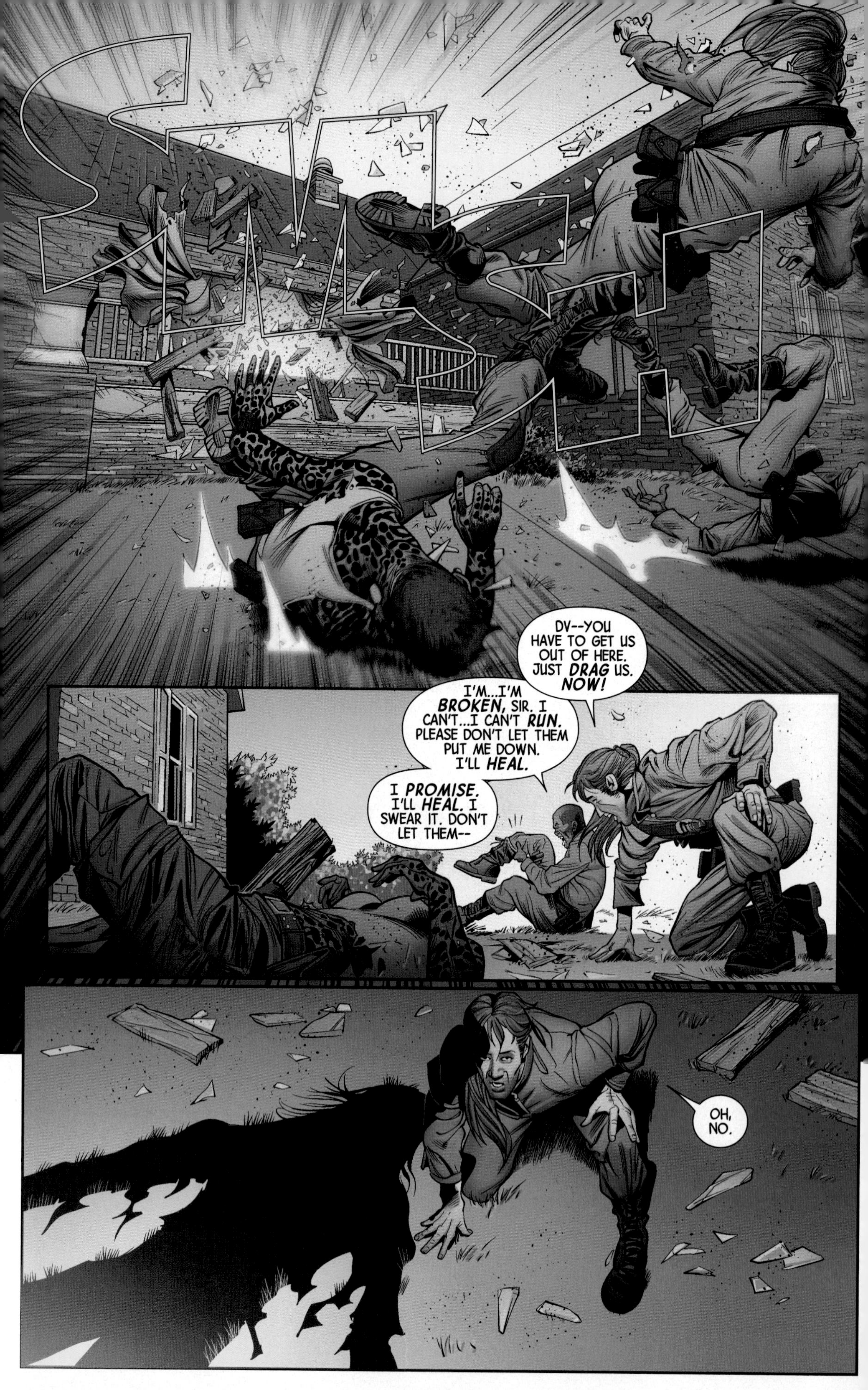
SMASH
DV--YOU HAVE TO GET US OUT OF HERE. JUST DRAG US. NOW!
I'M...I'M BROKEN, SIR. I CAN'T...I CAN'T RUN. PLEASE DON'T LET THEM PUT ME DOWN. I'LL HEAL.
I PROMISE. I'LL HEAL. I SWEAR IT. DON'T LET THEM--
OH, NO.

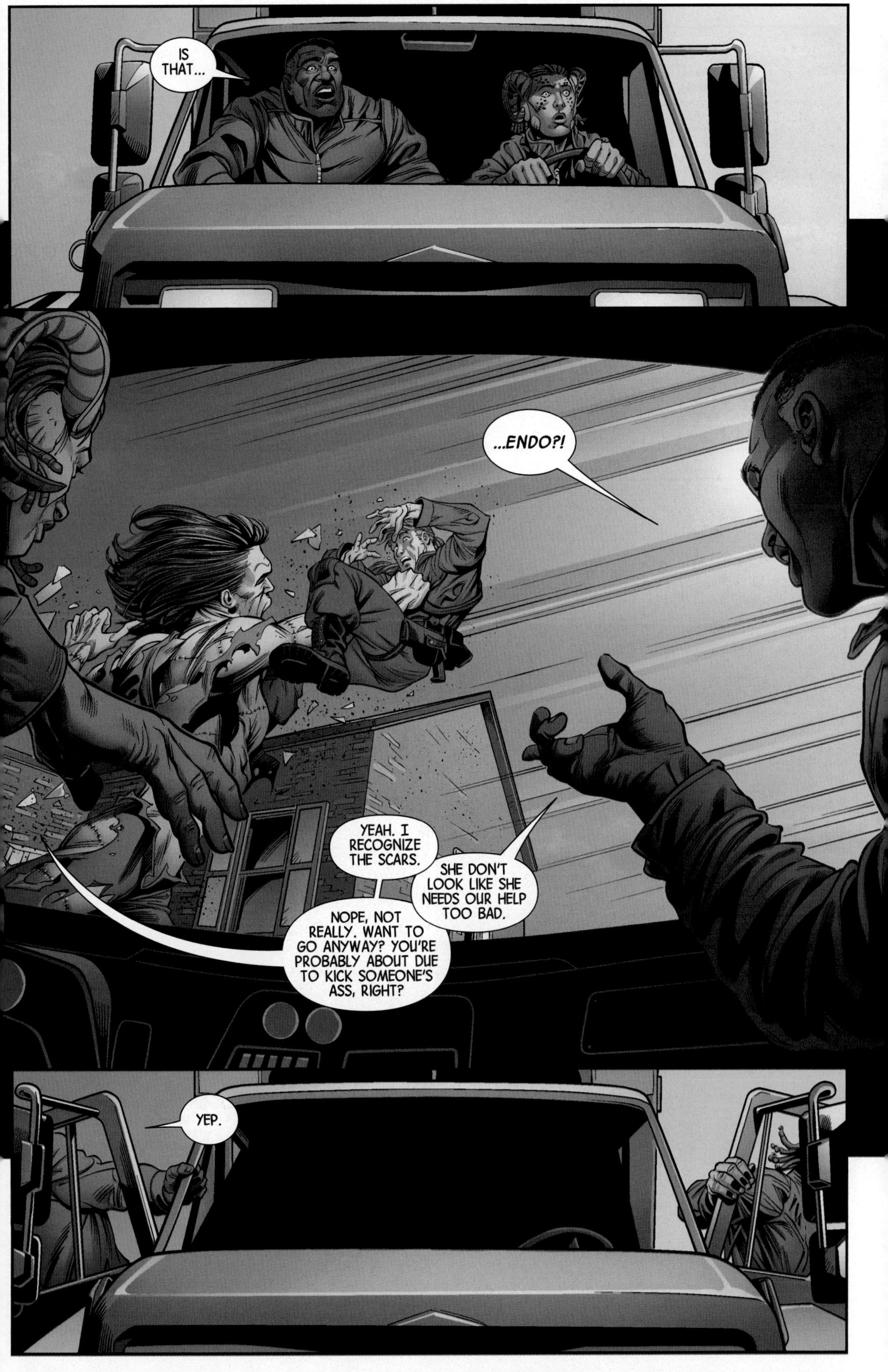
IS THAT...
...ENDO?!
YEAH. I RECOGNIZE THE SCARS.
SHE DON'T LOOK LIKE SHE NEEDS OUR HELP TOO BAD.
NOPE, NOT REALLY. WANT TO GO ANYWAY? YOU'RE PROBABLY ABOUT DUE TO KICK SOMEONE'S ASS, RIGHT?
YEP.

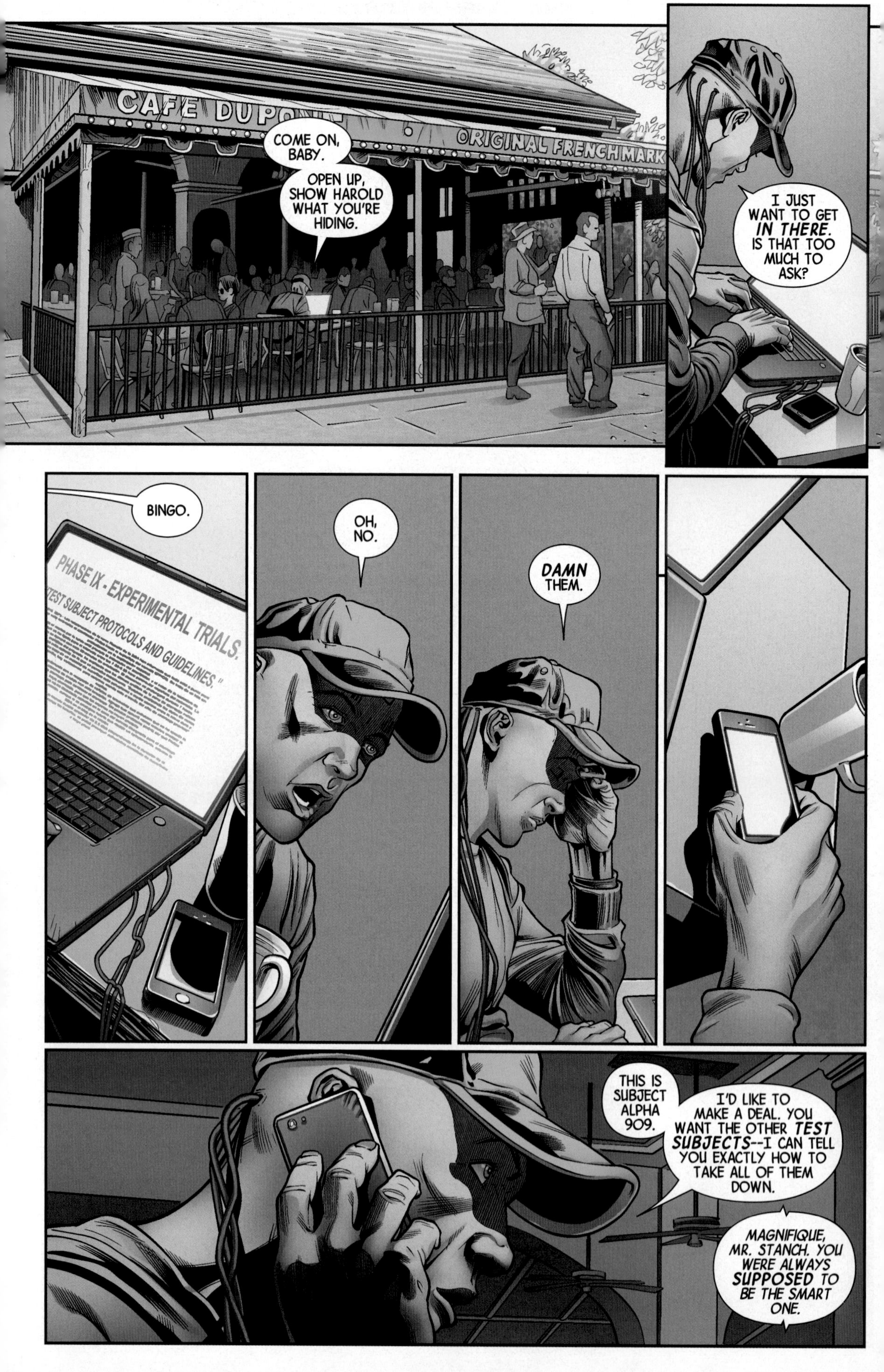
COME ON, BABY.
OPEN UP, SHOW HAROLD WHAT YOU'RE HIDING.
I JUST WANT TO GET *IN THERE*. IS THAT TOO MUCH TO ASK?
BINGO.
PHASE IX - EXPERIMENTAL TRIALS.
TEST SUBJECT PROTOCOLS AND GUIDELINES.
OH, NO.
DAMN THEM.
THIS IS SUBJECT ALPHA 909.
I'D LIKE TO MAKE A DEAL. YOU WANT THE OTHER *TEST SUBJECTS*--I CAN TELL YOU EXACTLY HOW TO TAKE ALL OF THEM DOWN.
MAGNIFIQUE, MR. STANCH. YOU WERE ALWAYS **SUPPOSED** *TO BE THE SMART ONE.*

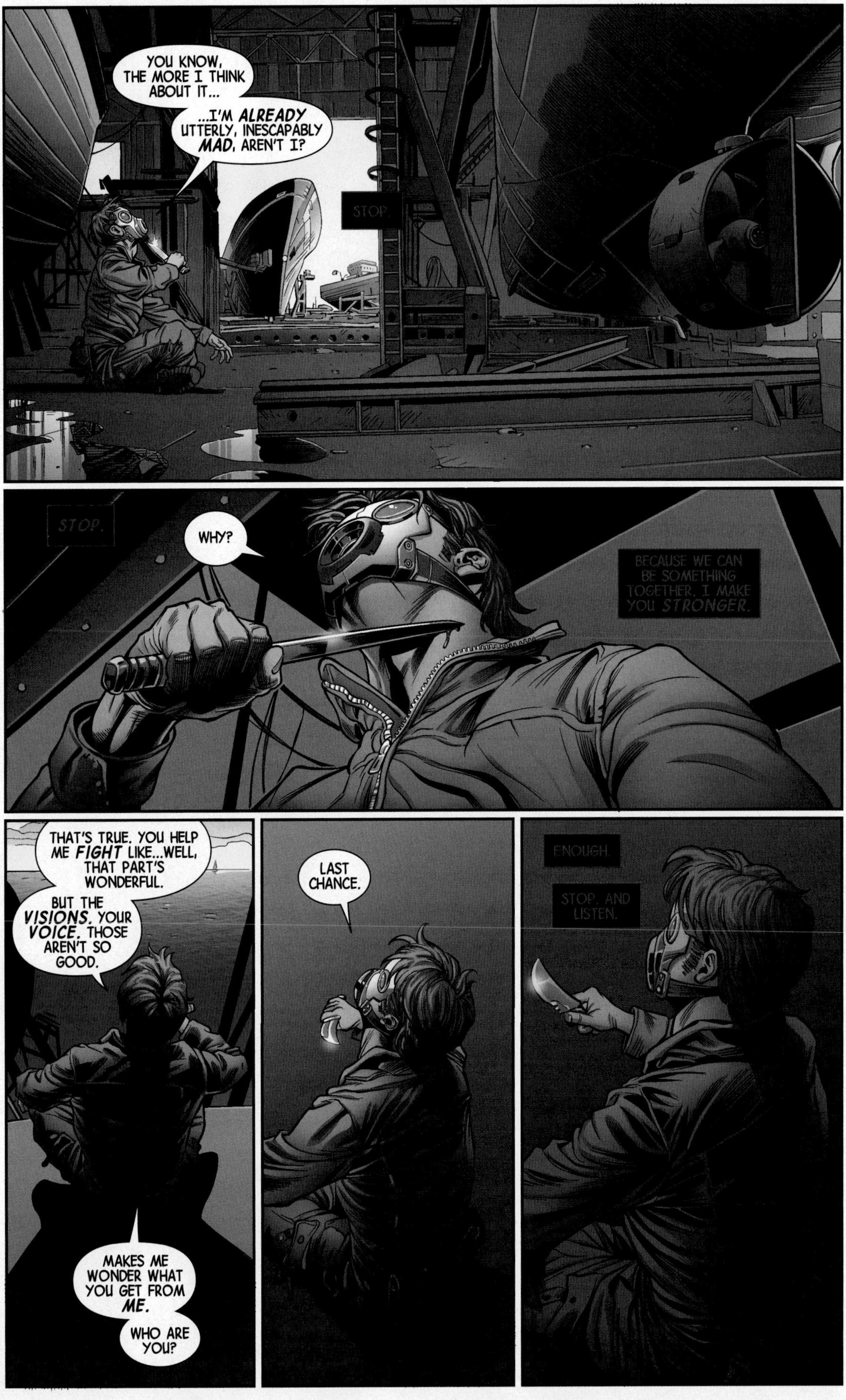
YOU KNOW, THE MORE I THINK ABOUT IT...
...I'M ALREADY UTTERLY, INESCAPABLY MAD, AREN'T I?
STOP.
STOP.
WHY?
BECAUSE WE CAN BE SOMETHING TOGETHER. I MAKE YOU STRONGER.
THAT'S TRUE. YOU HELP ME FIGHT LIKE...WELL, THAT PART'S WONDERFUL.
BUT THE VISIONS. YOUR VOICE. THOSE AREN'T SO GOOD.
MAKES ME WONDER WHAT YOU GET FROM ME.
WHO ARE YOU?
LAST CHANCE.
ENOUGH.
STOP. AND LISTEN.

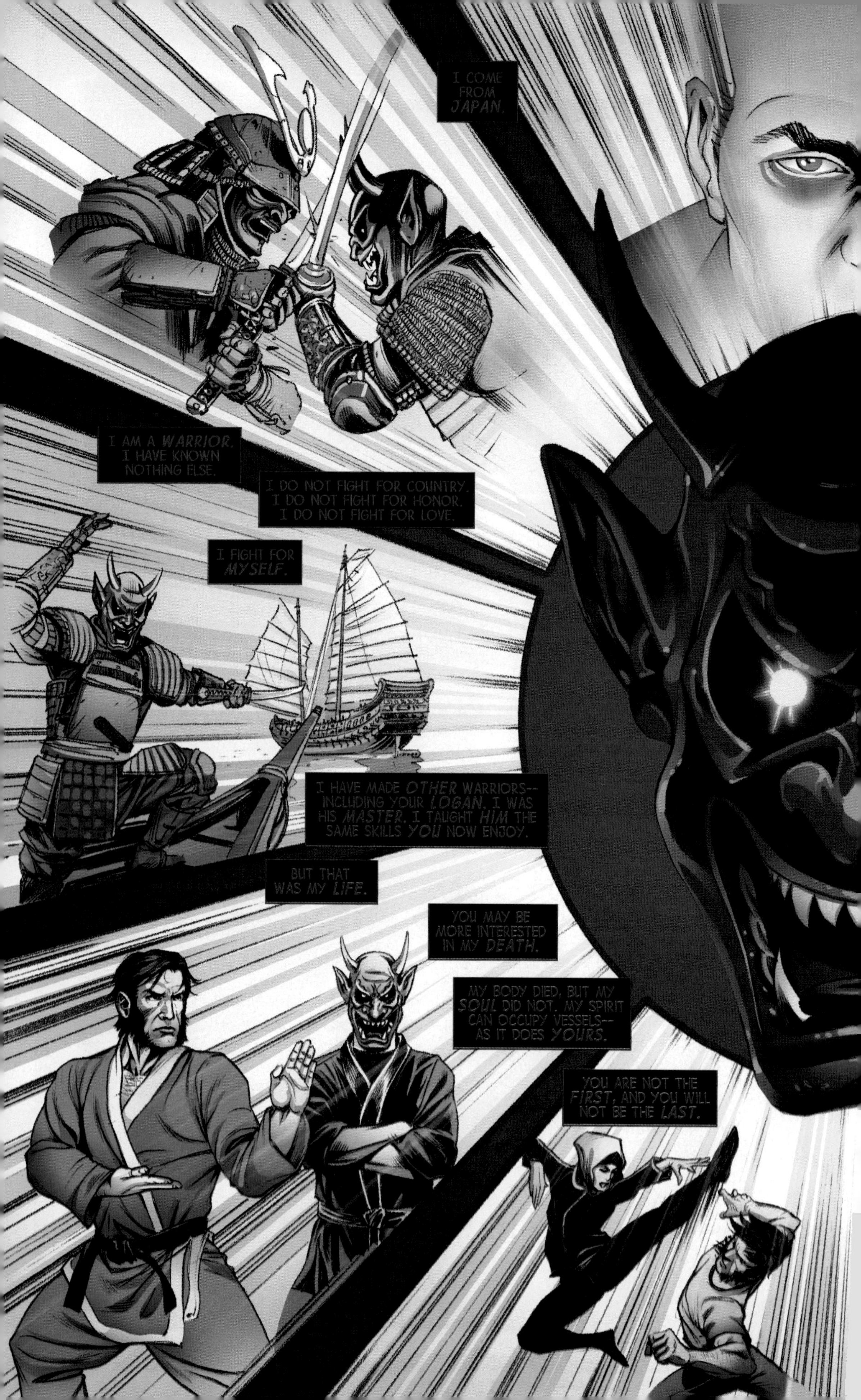
I COME FROM *JAPAN*.
I AM A *WARRIOR*. I HAVE KNOWN NOTHING ELSE.
I DO NOT FIGHT FOR COUNTRY. I DO NOT FIGHT FOR HONOR. I DO NOT FIGHT FOR LOVE.
I FIGHT FOR *MYSELF*.
I HAVE MADE *OTHER* WARRIORS-- INCLUDING YOUR *LOGAN*. I WAS HIS *MASTER*. I TAUGHT *HIM* THE SAME SKILLS *YOU* NOW ENJOY.
BUT THAT WAS MY *LIFE*.
YOU MAY BE MORE INTERESTED IN MY *DEATH*.
MY BODY DIED, BUT MY *SOUL* DID NOT. MY SPIRIT CAN OCCUPY VESSELS-- AS IT DOES *YOURS*.
YOU ARE NOT THE *FIRST*, AND YOU WILL NOT BE THE *LAST*.

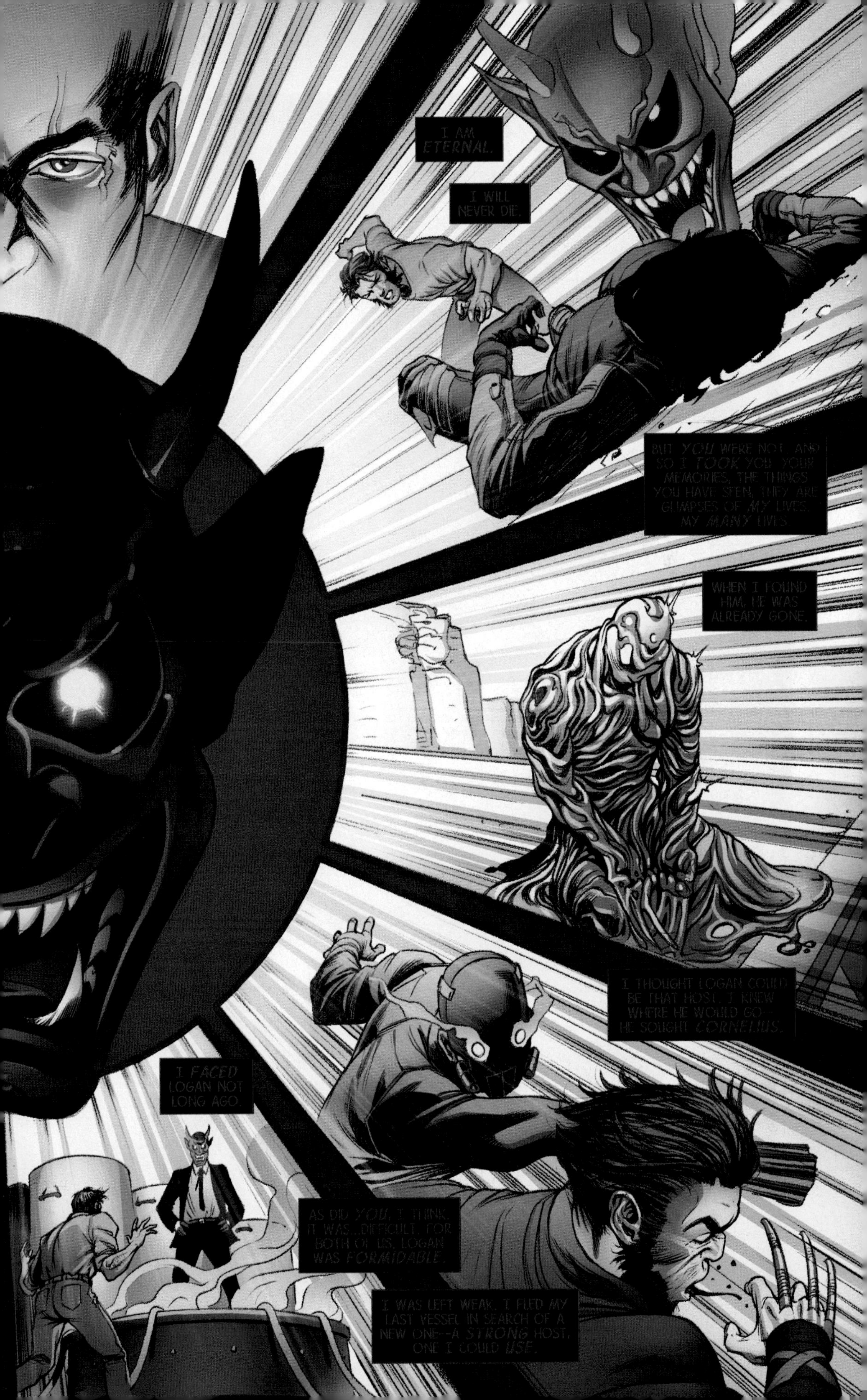
I AM ETERNAL.
I WILL NEVER DIE.
BUT YOU WERE NOT, AND SO I TOOK YOU YOUR MEMORIES. THE THINGS YOU HAVE SEEN, THEY ARE GLIMPSES OF MY LIVES. MY MANY LIVES.
WHEN I FOUND HIM, HE WAS ALREADY GONE.
I THOUGHT LOGAN COULD BE THAT HOST. I KNEW WHERE HE WOULD GO-- HE SOUGHT CORNELIUS.
I FACED LOGAN NOT LONG AGO.
AS DID YOU, I THINK. IT WAS...DIFFICULT. FOR BOTH OF US. LOGAN WAS FORMIDABLE.
I WAS LEFT WEAK. I FLED MY LAST VESSEL IN SEARCH OF A NEW ONE--A STRONG HOST. ONE I COULD USE.

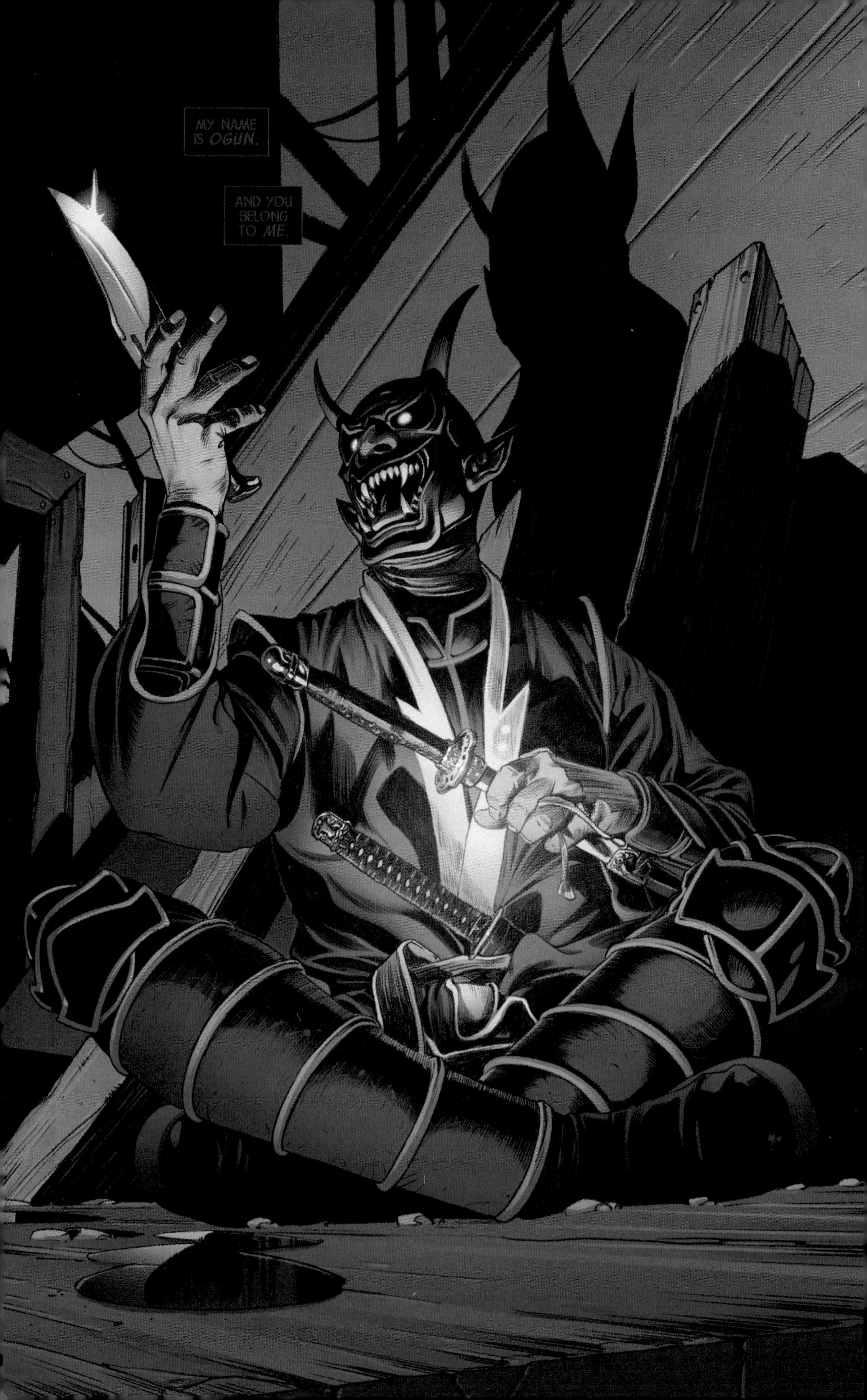
MY NAME IS OGUN.
AND YOU BELONG TO ME.

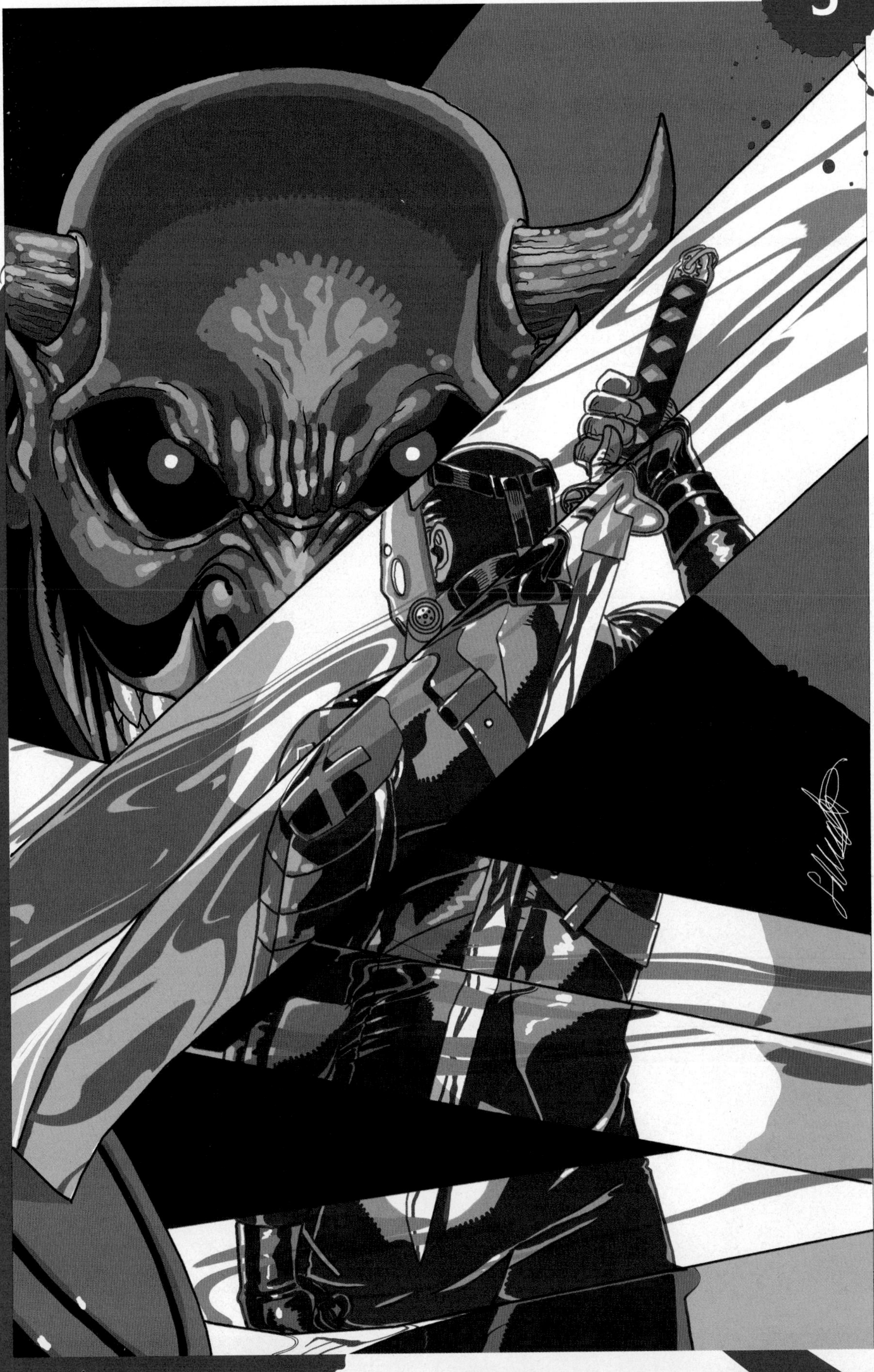

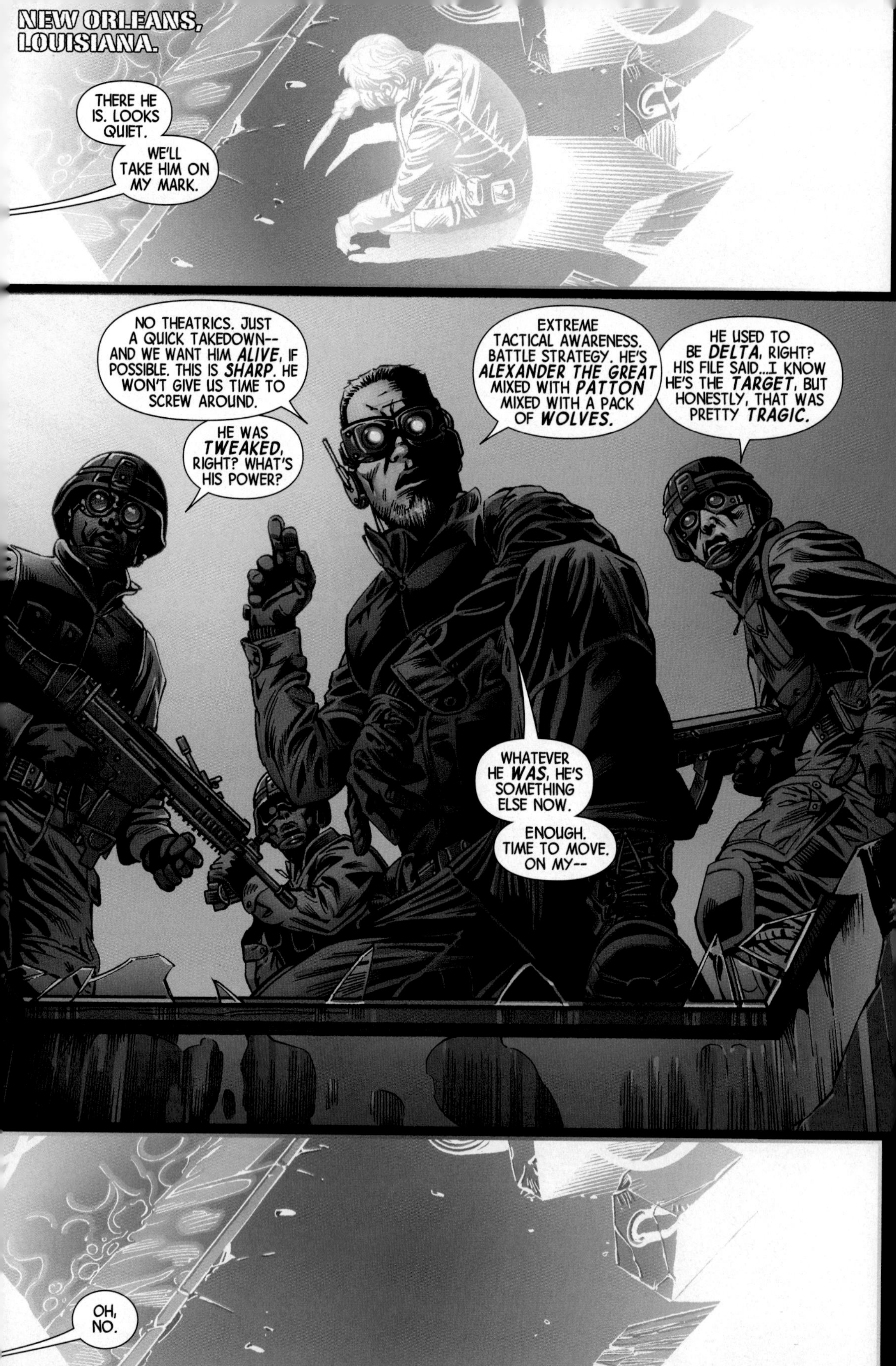
NEW ORLEANS, LOUISIANA.
THERE HE IS. LOOKS QUIET.
WE'LL TAKE HIM ON MY MARK.
NO THEATRICS. JUST A QUICK TAKEDOWN-- AND WE WANT HIM ALIVE, IF POSSIBLE. THIS IS SHARP. HE WON'T GIVE US TIME TO SCREW AROUND.
HE WAS TWEAKED, RIGHT? WHAT'S HIS POWER?
EXTREME TACTICAL AWARENESS. BATTLE STRATEGY. HE'S ALEXANDER THE GREAT MIXED WITH PATTON MIXED WITH A PACK OF WOLVES.
HE USED TO BE DELTA, RIGHT? HIS FILE SAID...I KNOW HE'S THE TARGET, BUT HONESTLY, THAT WAS PRETTY TRAGIC.
WHATEVER HE WAS, HE'S SOMETHING ELSE NOW.
ENOUGH. TIME TO MOVE. ON MY--
OH, NO.

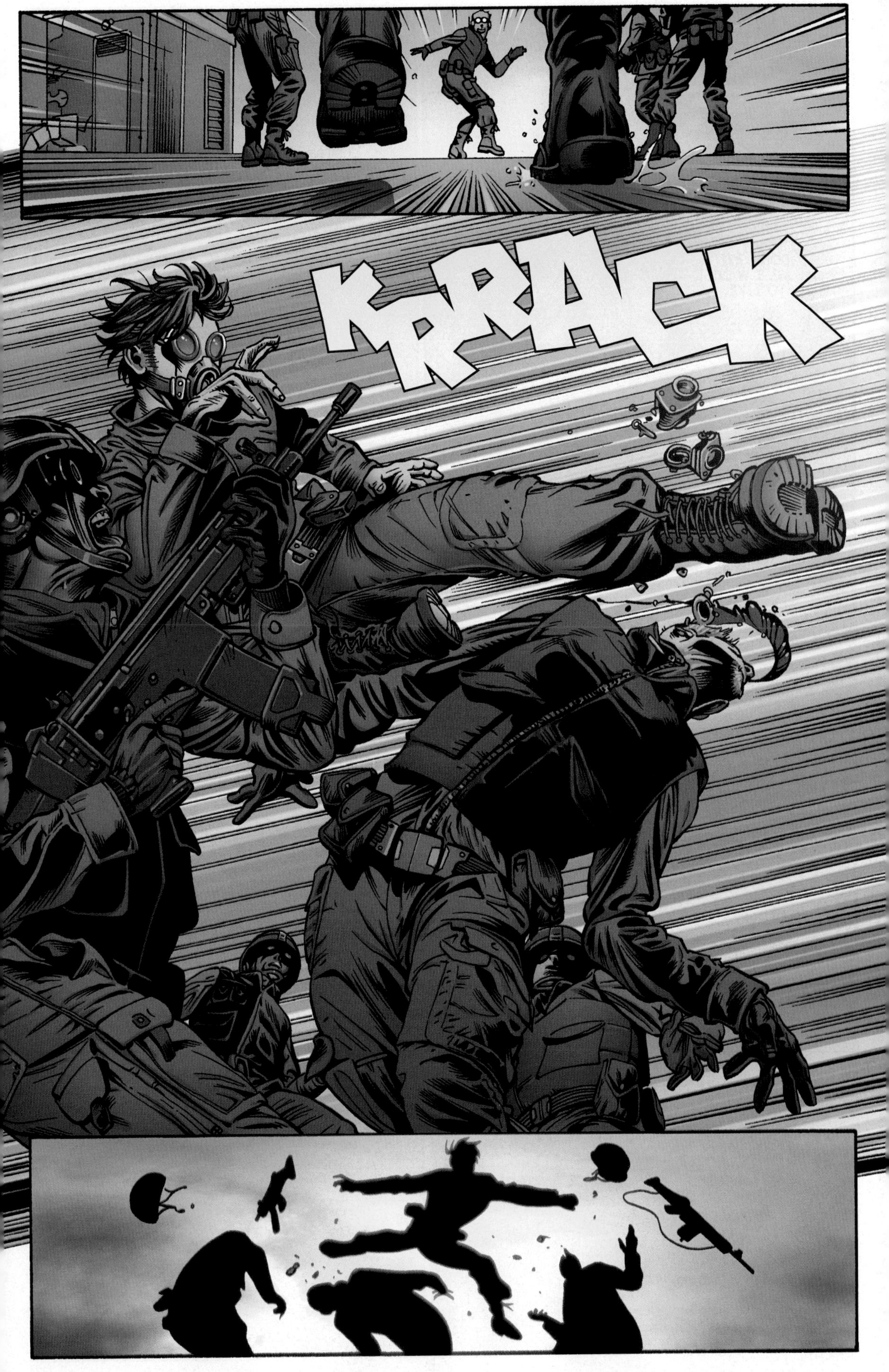
KRRACK

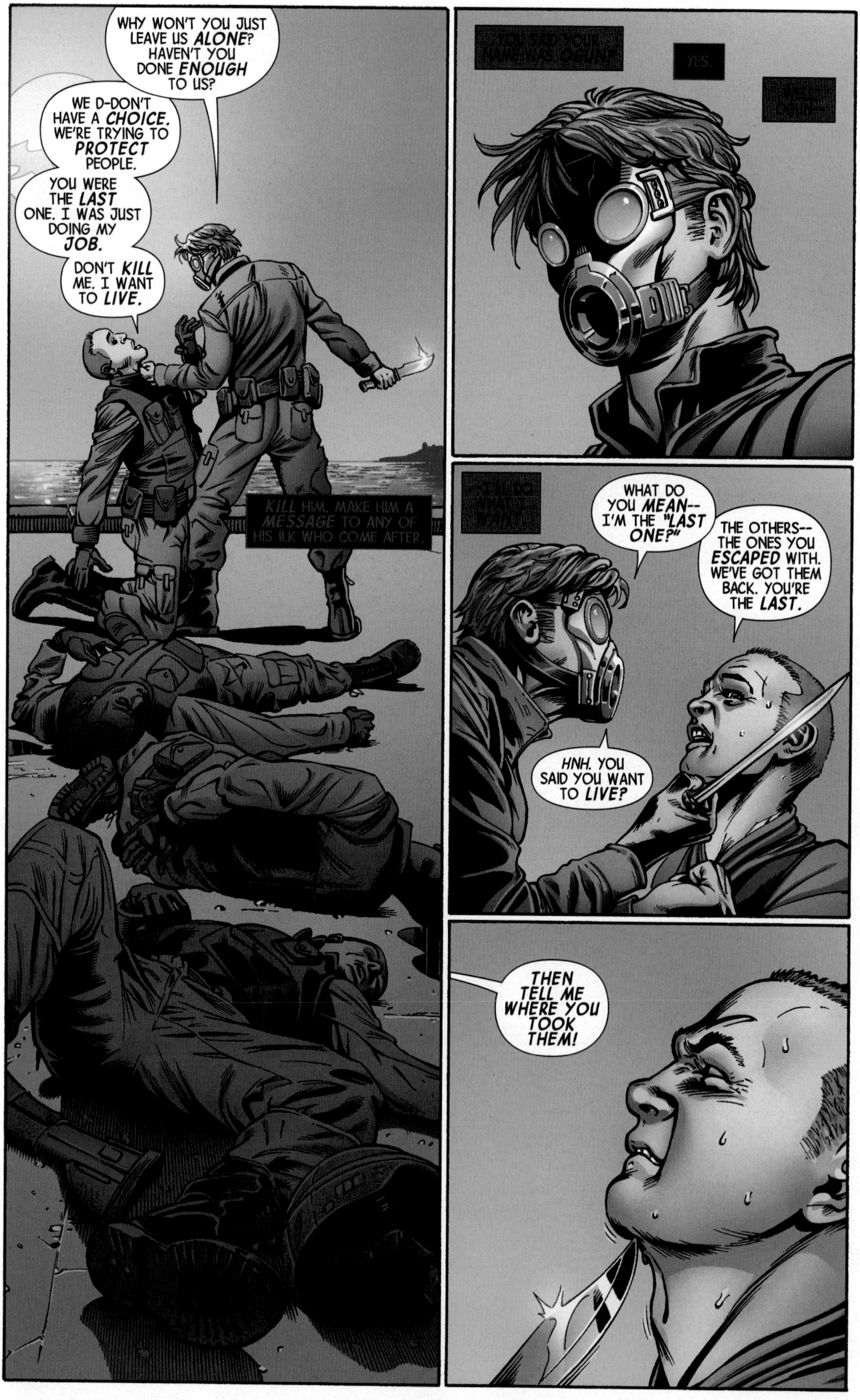
WHY WON'T YOU JUST LEAVE US ALONE? HAVEN'T YOU DONE ENOUGH TO US?
WE D-DON'T HAVE A CHOICE. WE'RE TRYING TO PROTECT PEOPLE.
YOU WERE THE LAST ONE. I WAS JUST DOING MY JOB.
DON'T KILL ME. I WANT TO LIVE.
KILL HIM. MAKE HIM A MESSAGE TO ANY OF HIS ILK WHO COME AFTER.
YOU SAID YOUR NAME WAS OGUN?
YES.
WHAT DO YOU MEAN-- I'M THE "LAST ONE?"
THE OTHERS-- THE ONES YOU ESCAPED WITH. WE'VE GOT THEM BACK. YOU'RE THE LAST.
HNH. YOU SAID YOU WANT TO LIVE?
THEN TELL ME WHERE YOU TOOK THEM!

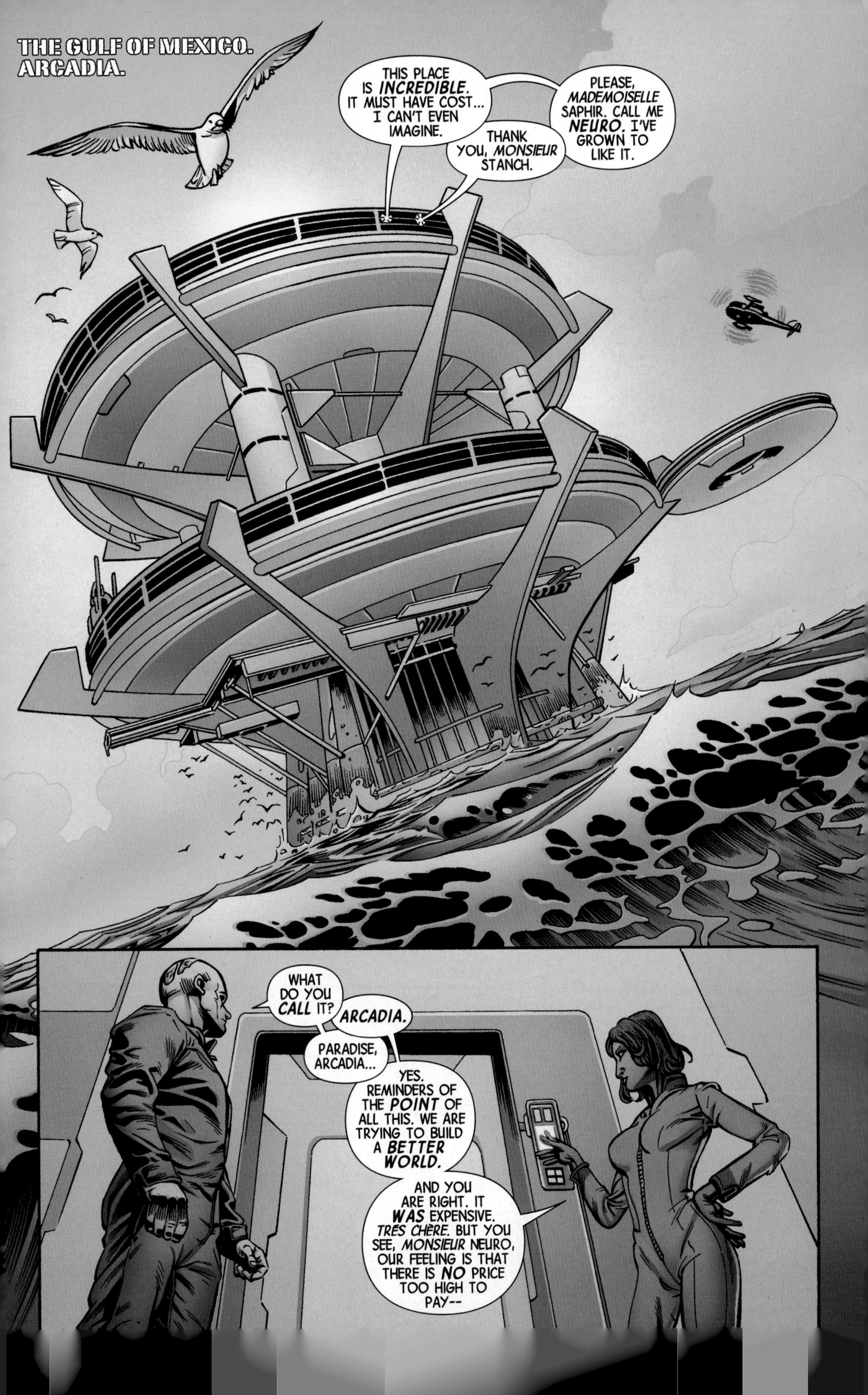
THE GULF OF MEXICO. ARCADIA.
THIS PLACE IS INCREDIBLE. IT MUST HAVE COST... I CAN'T EVEN IMAGINE.
THANK YOU, MONSIEUR STANCH.
PLEASE, MADEMOISELLE SAPHIR. CALL ME NEURO. I'VE GROWN TO LIKE IT.
WHAT DO YOU CALL IT?
ARCADIA.
PARADISE, ARCADIA...
YES. REMINDERS OF THE POINT OF ALL THIS. WE ARE TRYING TO BUILD A BETTER WORLD.
AND YOU ARE RIGHT. IT WAS EXPENSIVE. TRÈS CHÈRE. BUT YOU SEE, MONSIEUR NEURO, OUR FEELING IS THAT THERE IS NO PRICE TOO HIGH TO PAY--

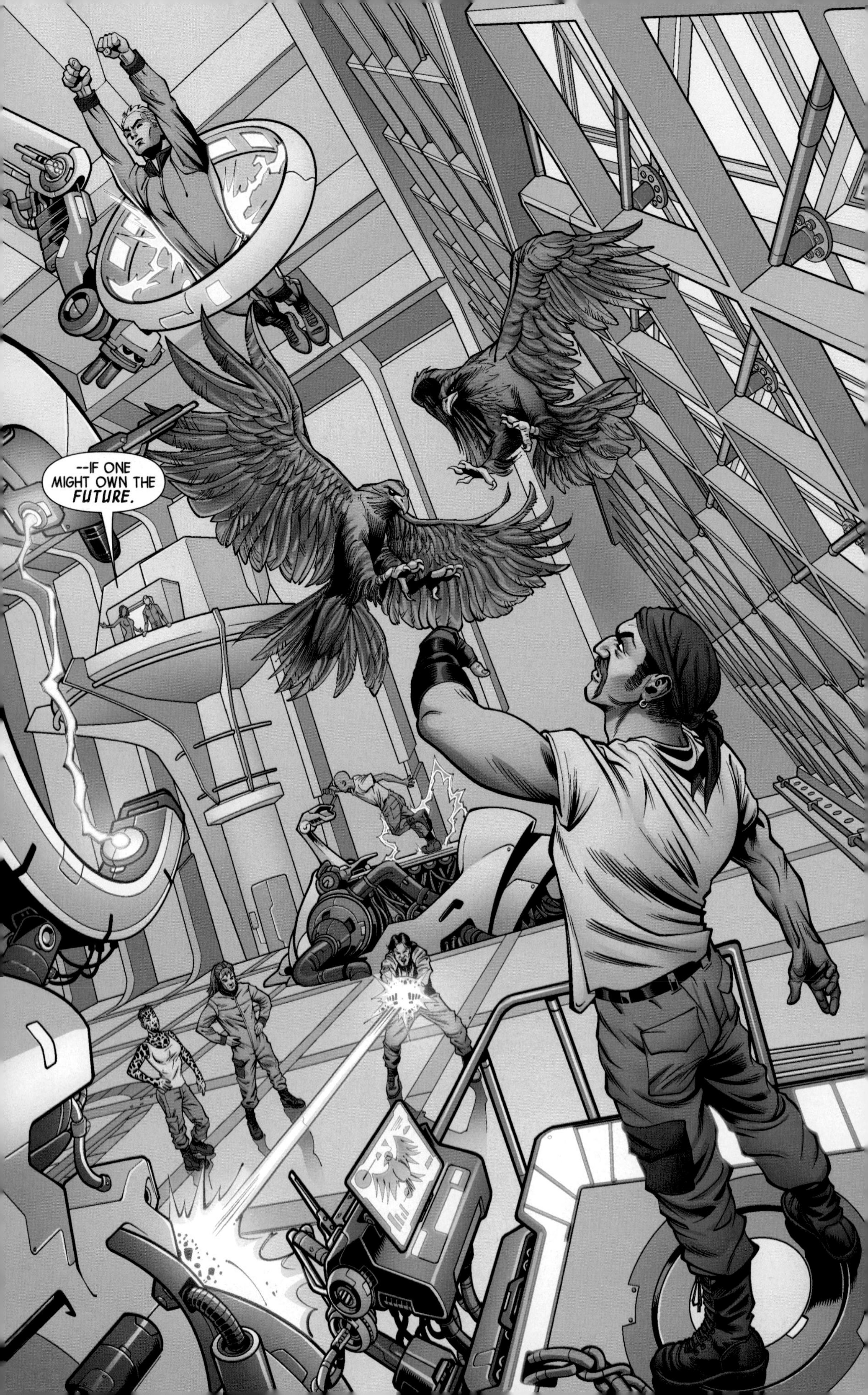
--IF ONE MIGHT OWN THE *FUTURE.*

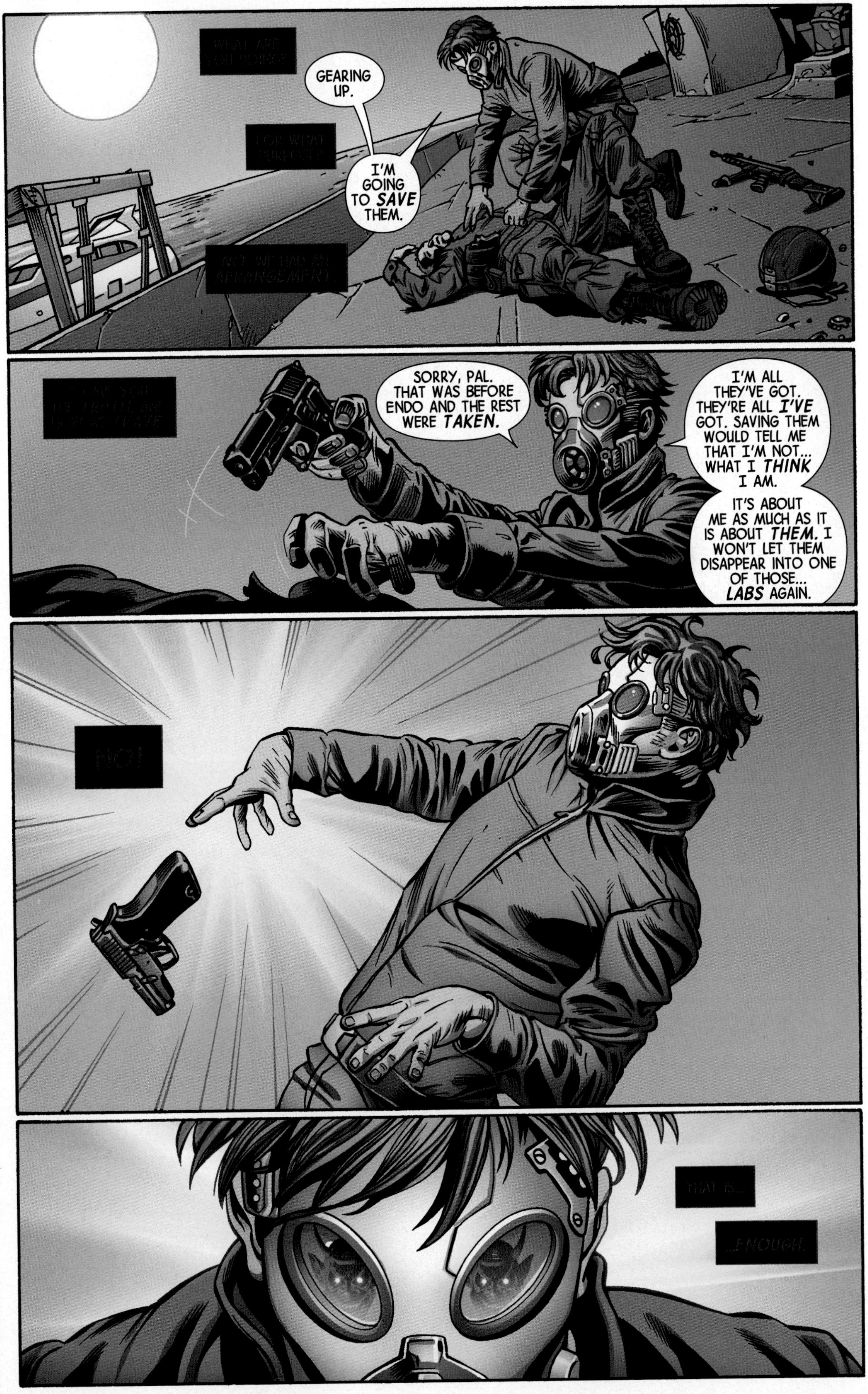
WHAT ARE YOU DOING?
GEARING UP.
FOR WHAT PURPOSE?
I'M GOING TO SAVE THEM.
NO. WE HAD AN ARRANGEMENT.
SORRY, PAL. THAT WAS BEFORE ENDO AND THE REST WERE TAKEN.
I'M ALL THEY'VE GOT. THEY'RE ALL I'VE GOT. SAVING THEM WOULD TELL ME THAT I'M NOT... WHAT I THINK I AM.
IT'S ABOUT ME AS MUCH AS IT IS ABOUT THEM. I WON'T LET THEM DISAPPEAR INTO ONE OF THOSE... LABS AGAIN.
NO!
THAT IS...
...ENOUGH.

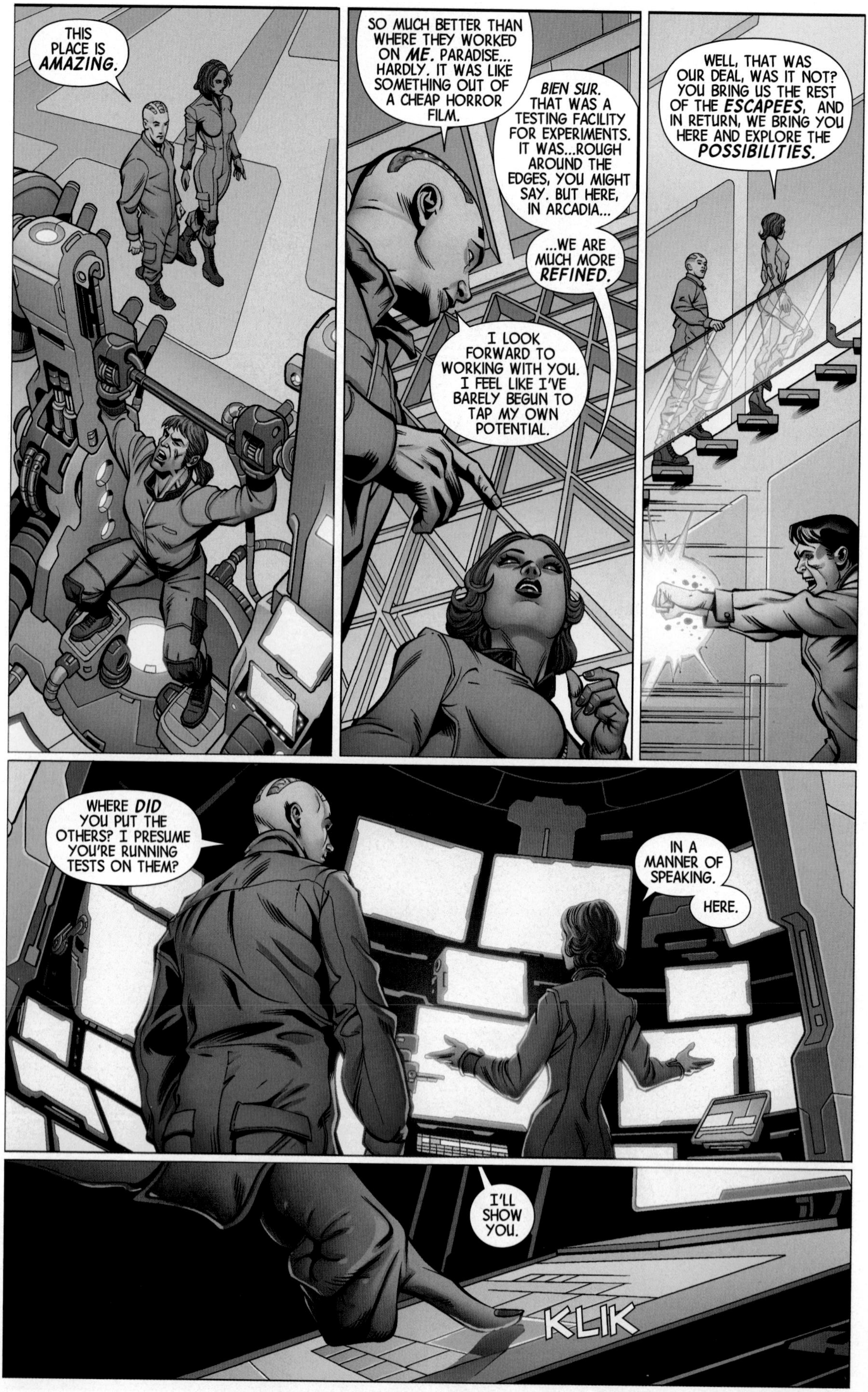
THIS PLACE IS AMAZING.
SO MUCH BETTER THAN WHERE THEY WORKED ON ME. PARADISE... HARDLY. IT WAS LIKE SOMETHING OUT OF A CHEAP HORROR FILM.
BIEN SUR. THAT WAS A TESTING FACILITY FOR EXPERIMENTS. IT WAS...ROUGH AROUND THE EDGES, YOU MIGHT SAY. BUT HERE, IN ARCADIA...
...WE ARE MUCH MORE REFINED.
I LOOK FORWARD TO WORKING WITH YOU. I FEEL LIKE I'VE BARELY BEGUN TO TAP MY OWN POTENTIAL.
WELL, THAT WAS OUR DEAL, WAS IT NOT? YOU BRING US THE REST OF THE ESCAPEES, AND IN RETURN, WE BRING YOU HERE AND EXPLORE THE POSSIBILITIES.
WHERE DID YOU PUT THE OTHERS? I PRESUME YOU'RE RUNNING TESTS ON THEM?
IN A MANNER OF SPEAKING.
HERE.
I'LL SHOW YOU.
KLIK

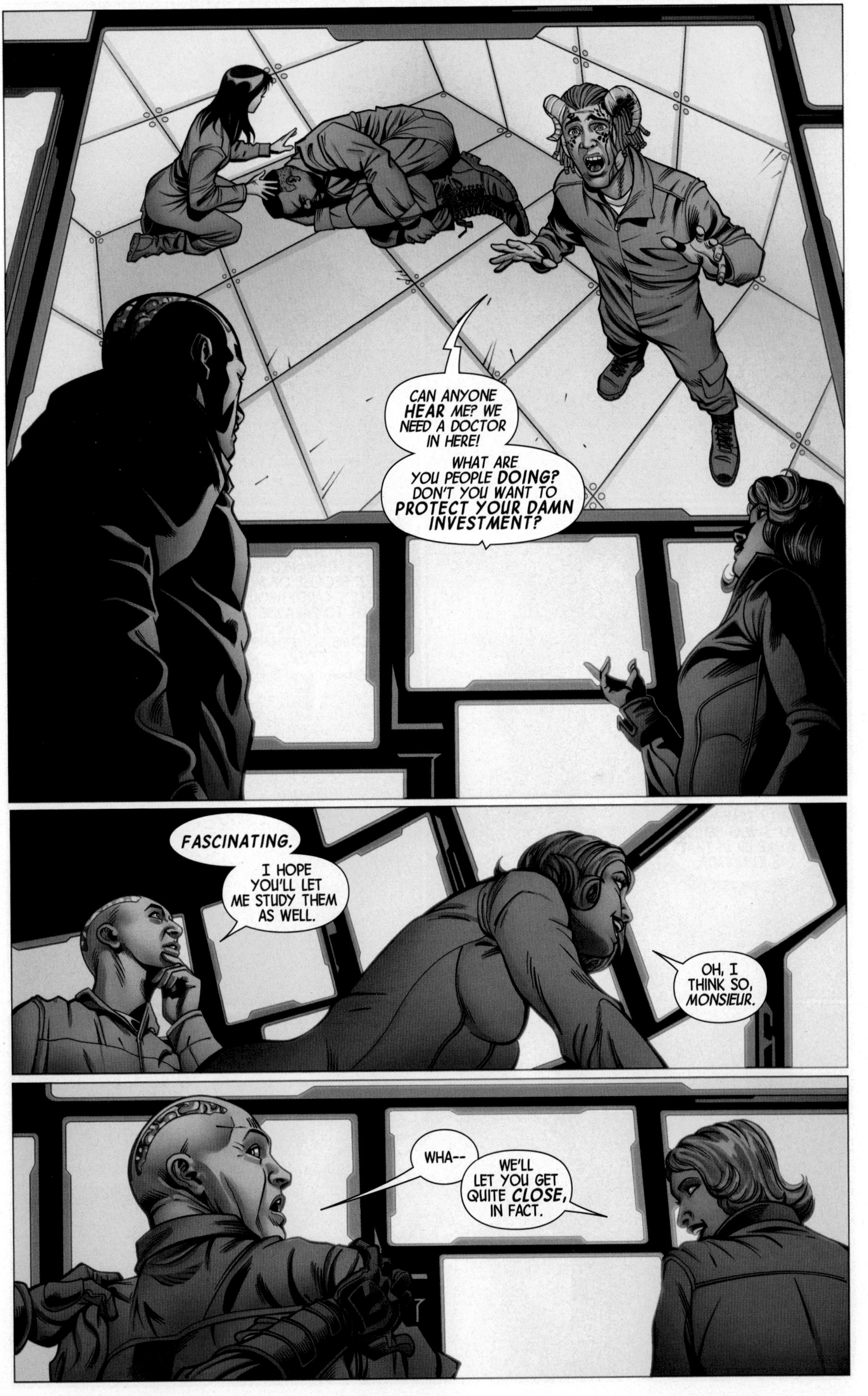
CAN ANYONE HEAR ME? WE NEED A DOCTOR IN HERE!
WHAT ARE YOU PEOPLE DOING? DON'T YOU WANT TO PROTECT YOUR DAMN INVESTMENT?
FASCINATING.
I HOPE YOU'LL LET ME STUDY THEM AS WELL.
OH, I THINK SO, MONSIEUR.
WHA--
WE'LL LET YOU GET QUITE CLOSE, IN FACT.

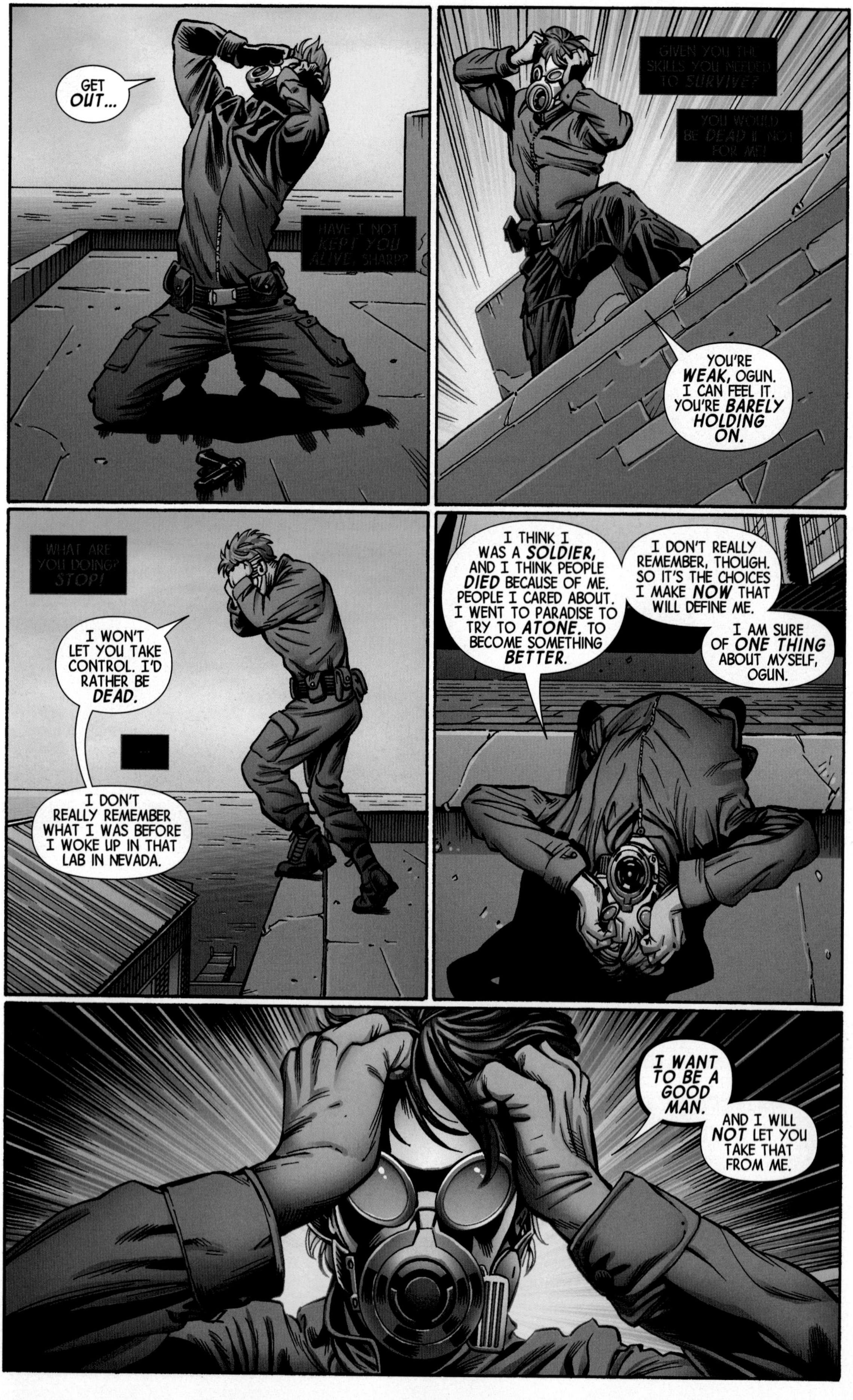

GET OUT...
HAVE I NOT KEPT YOU ALIVE, SHARP?
GIVEN YOU THE SKILLS YOU NEEDED TO SURVIVE?
YOU WOULD BE DEAD IF NOT FOR ME!
YOU'RE WEAK, OGUN. I CAN FEEL IT. YOU'RE BARELY HOLDING ON.
WHAT ARE YOU DOING? STOP!
I WON'T LET YOU TAKE CONTROL. I'D RATHER BE DEAD.
...
I DON'T REALLY REMEMBER WHAT I WAS BEFORE I WOKE UP IN THAT LAB IN NEVADA.
I THINK I WAS A SOLDIER, AND I THINK PEOPLE DIED BECAUSE OF ME. PEOPLE I CARED ABOUT. I WENT TO PARADISE TO TRY TO ATONE, TO BECOME SOMETHING BETTER.
I DON'T REALLY REMEMBER, THOUGH. SO IT'S THE CHOICES I MAKE NOW THAT WILL DEFINE ME.
I AM SURE OF ONE THING ABOUT MYSELF, OGUN.
I WANT TO BE A GOOD MAN.
AND I WILL NOT LET YOU TAKE THAT FROM ME.

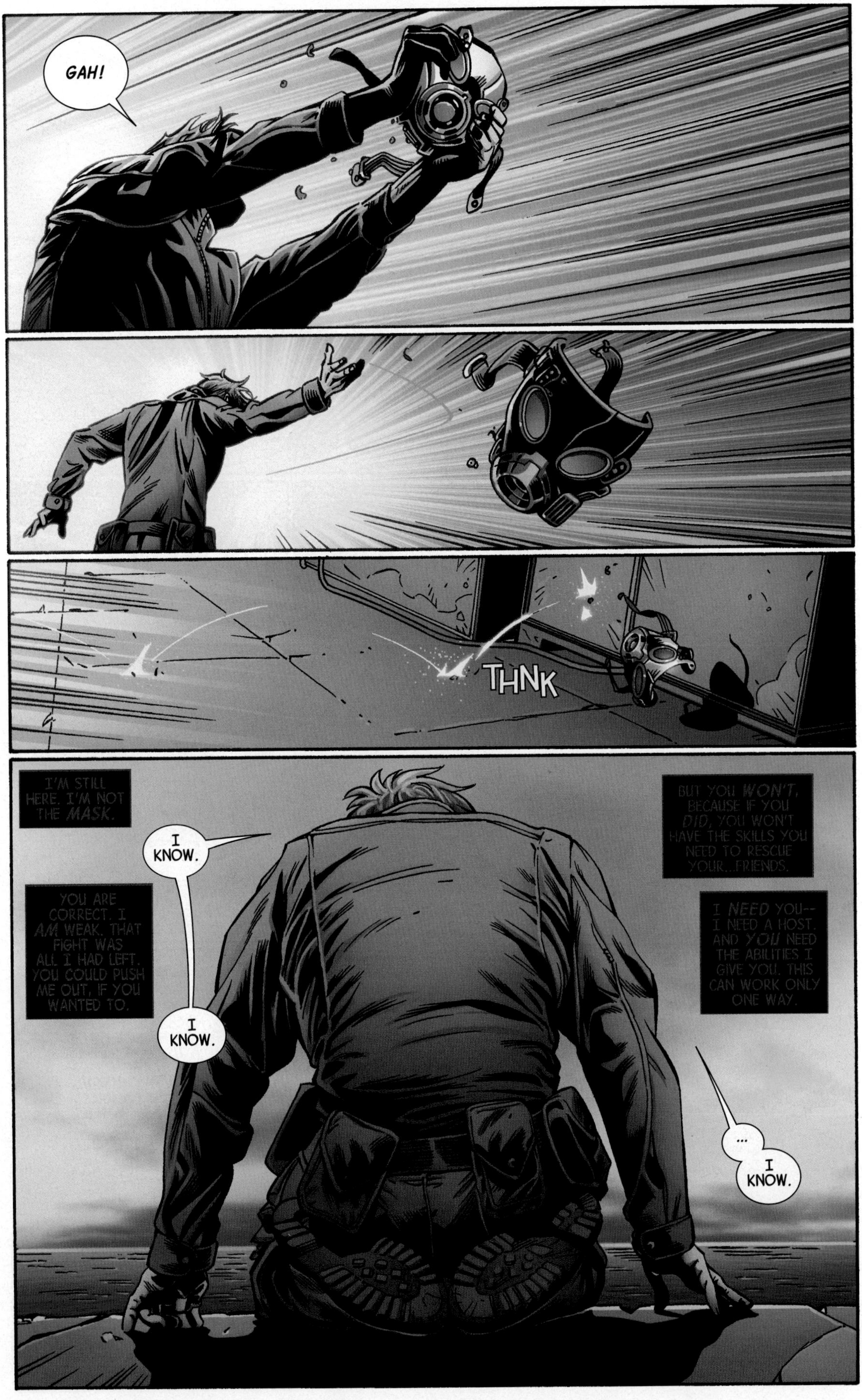
GAH!
THNK
I'M STILL HERE. I'M NOT THE MASK.
I KNOW.
YOU ARE CORRECT. I AM WEAK. THAT FIGHT WAS ALL I HAD LEFT. YOU COULD PUSH ME OUT, IF YOU WANTED TO.
I KNOW.
BUT YOU WON'T, BECAUSE IF YOU DID, YOU WON'T HAVE THE SKILLS YOU NEED TO RESCUE YOUR...FRIENDS.
I NEED YOU-- I NEED A HOST. AND YOU NEED THE ABILITIES I GIVE YOU. THIS CAN WORK ONLY ONE WAY.
...
I KNOW.

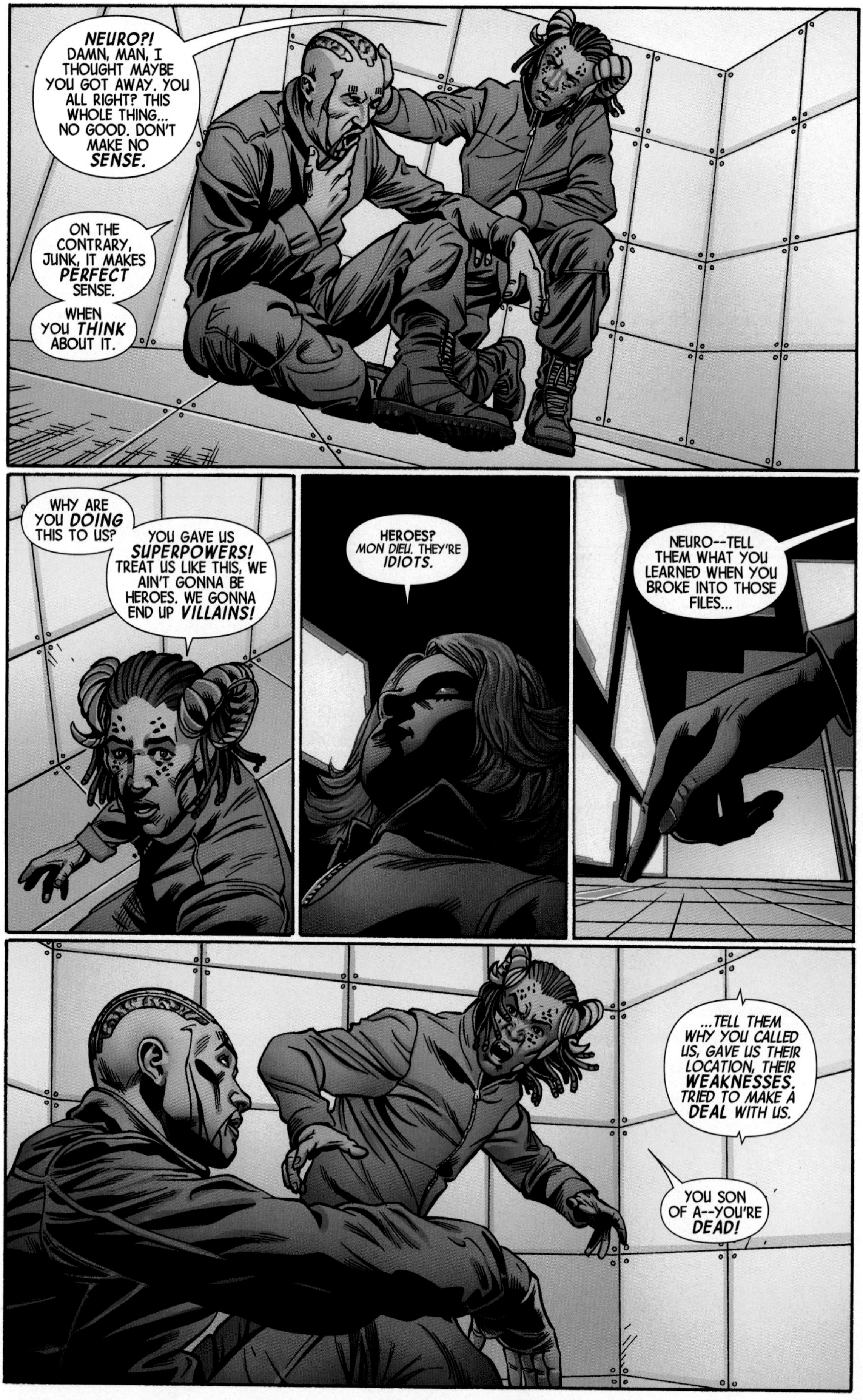
NEURO?! DAMN, MAN, I THOUGHT MAYBE YOU GOT AWAY. YOU ALL RIGHT? THIS WHOLE THING... NO GOOD. DON'T MAKE NO SENSE.
ON THE CONTRARY, JUNK, IT MAKES PERFECT SENSE.
WHEN YOU THINK ABOUT IT.
WHY ARE YOU DOING THIS TO US?
YOU GAVE US SUPERPOWERS! TREAT US LIKE THIS, WE AIN'T GONNA BE HEROES. WE GONNA END UP VILLAINS!
HEROES? MON DIEU. THEY'RE IDIOTS.
NEURO--TELL THEM WHAT YOU LEARNED WHEN YOU BROKE INTO THOSE FILES...
...TELL THEM WHY YOU CALLED US, GAVE US THEIR LOCATION, THEIR WEAKNESSES. TRIED TO MAKE A DEAL WITH US.
YOU SON OF A--YOU'RE DEAD!

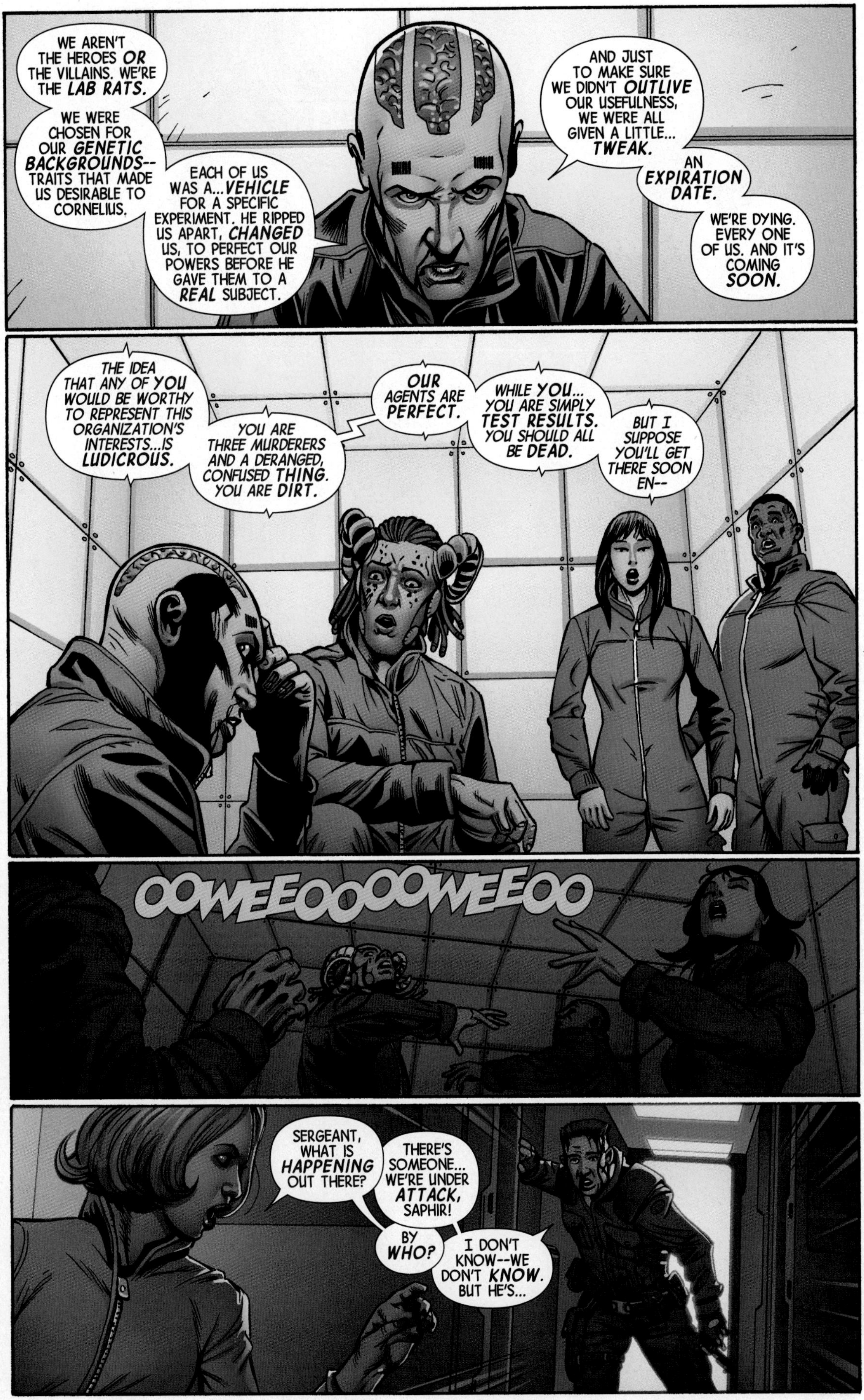
WE AREN'T THE HEROES OR THE VILLAINS. WE'RE THE LAB RATS.
WE WERE CHOSEN FOR OUR GENETIC BACKGROUNDS-- TRAITS THAT MADE US DESIRABLE TO CORNELIUS.
EACH OF US WAS A...VEHICLE FOR A SPECIFIC EXPERIMENT. HE RIPPED US APART, CHANGED US, TO PERFECT OUR POWERS BEFORE HE GAVE THEM TO A REAL SUBJECT.
AND JUST TO MAKE SURE WE DIDN'T OUTLIVE OUR USEFULNESS, WE WERE ALL GIVEN A LITTLE... TWEAK.
AN EXPIRATION DATE.
WE'RE DYING. EVERY ONE OF US. AND IT'S COMING SOON.
THE IDEA THAT ANY OF YOU WOULD BE WORTHY TO REPRESENT THIS ORGANIZATION'S INTERESTS...IS LUDICROUS.
YOU ARE THREE MURDERERS AND A DERANGED, CONFUSED THING. YOU ARE DIRT.
OUR AGENTS ARE PERFECT.
WHILE YOU... YOU ARE SIMPLY TEST RESULTS. YOU SHOULD ALL BE DEAD.
BUT I SUPPOSE YOU'LL GET THERE SOON EN--
OOWEEOOOOWEEOO
SERGEANT, WHAT IS HAPPENING OUT THERE?
THERE'S SOMEONE... WE'RE UNDER ATTACK, SAPHIR!
BY WHO?
I DON'T KNOW--WE DON'T KNOW. BUT HE'S...

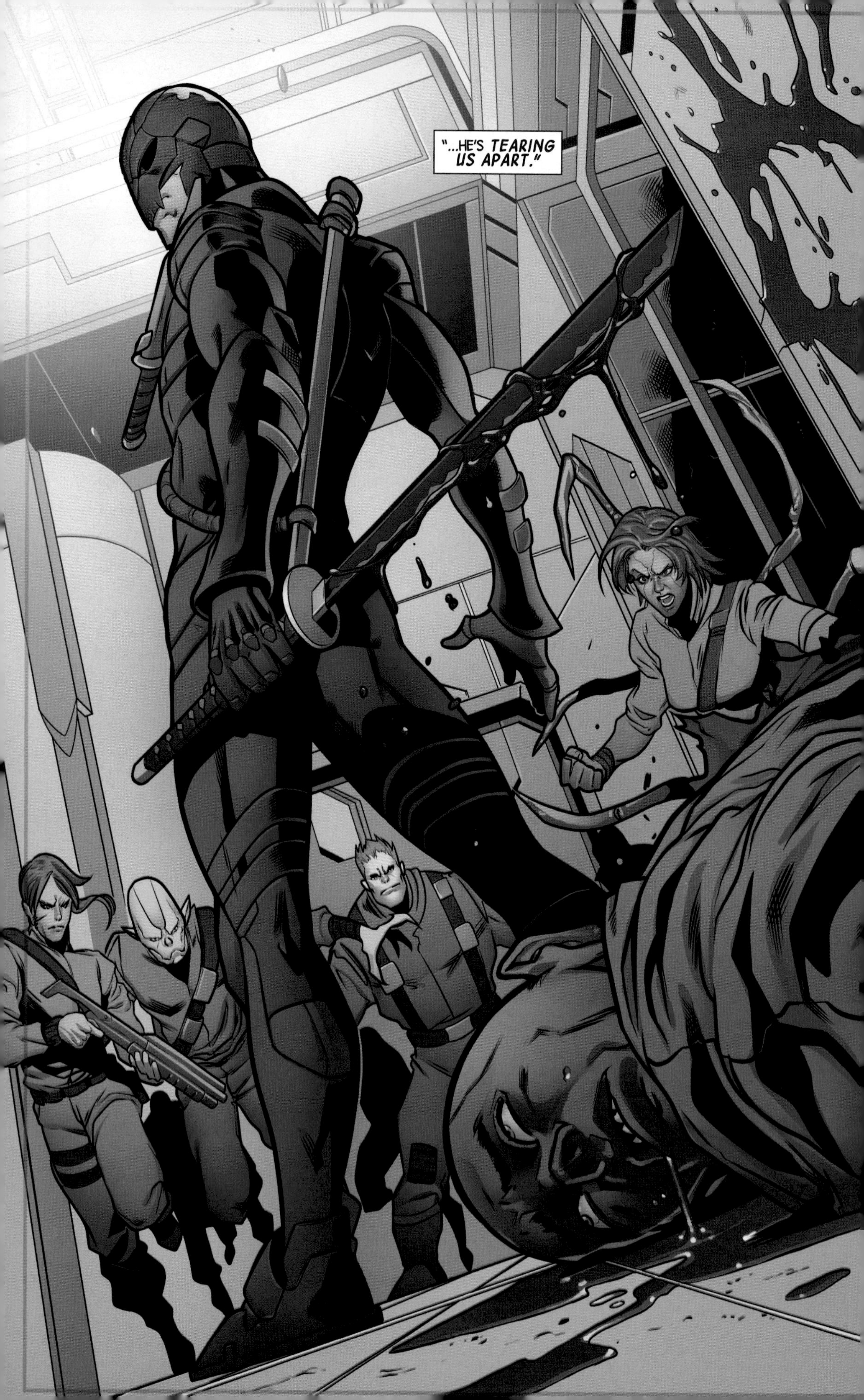
"...HE'S TEARING US APART."

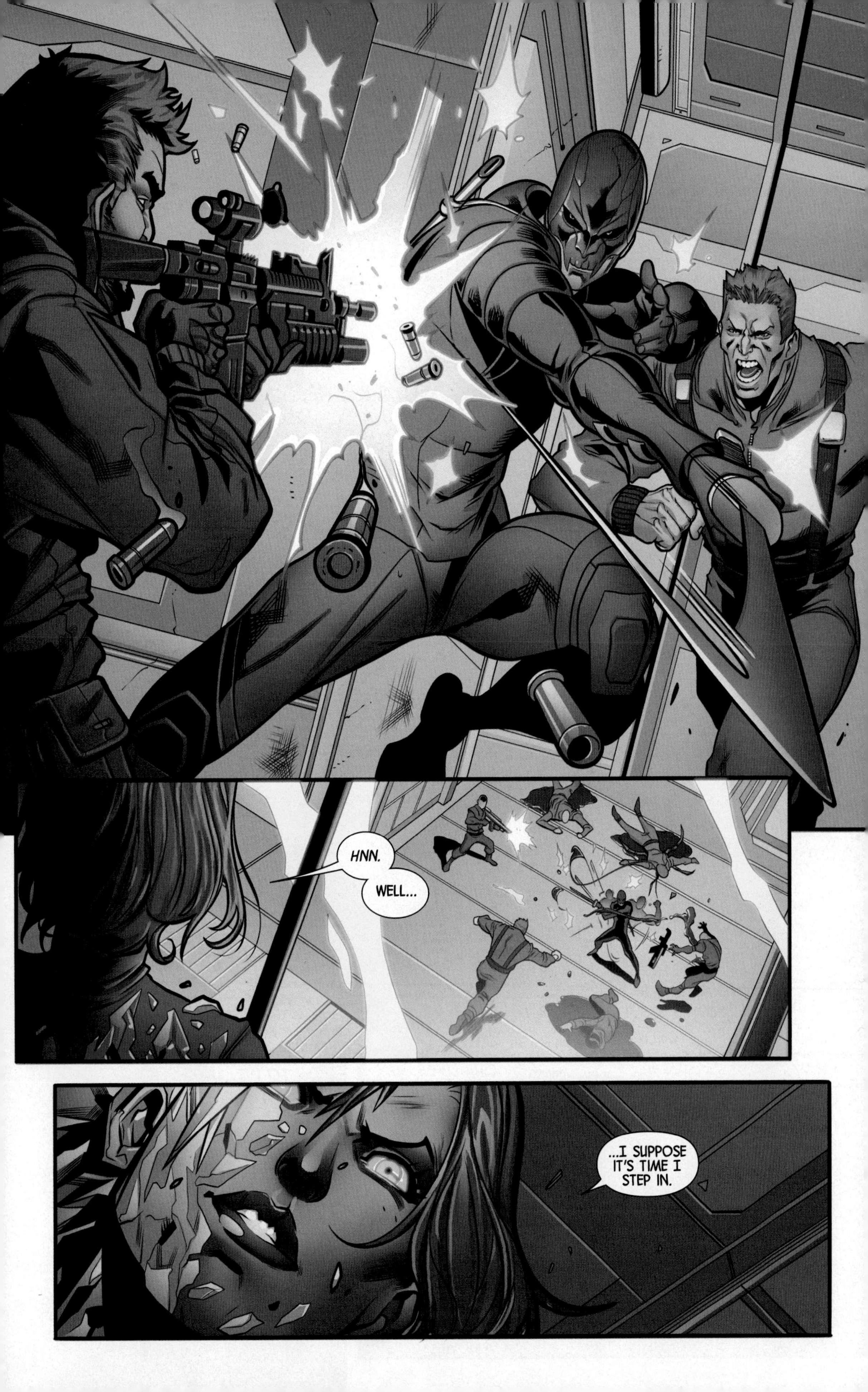
HNN.
WELL...
...I SUPPOSE IT'S TIME I STEP IN.

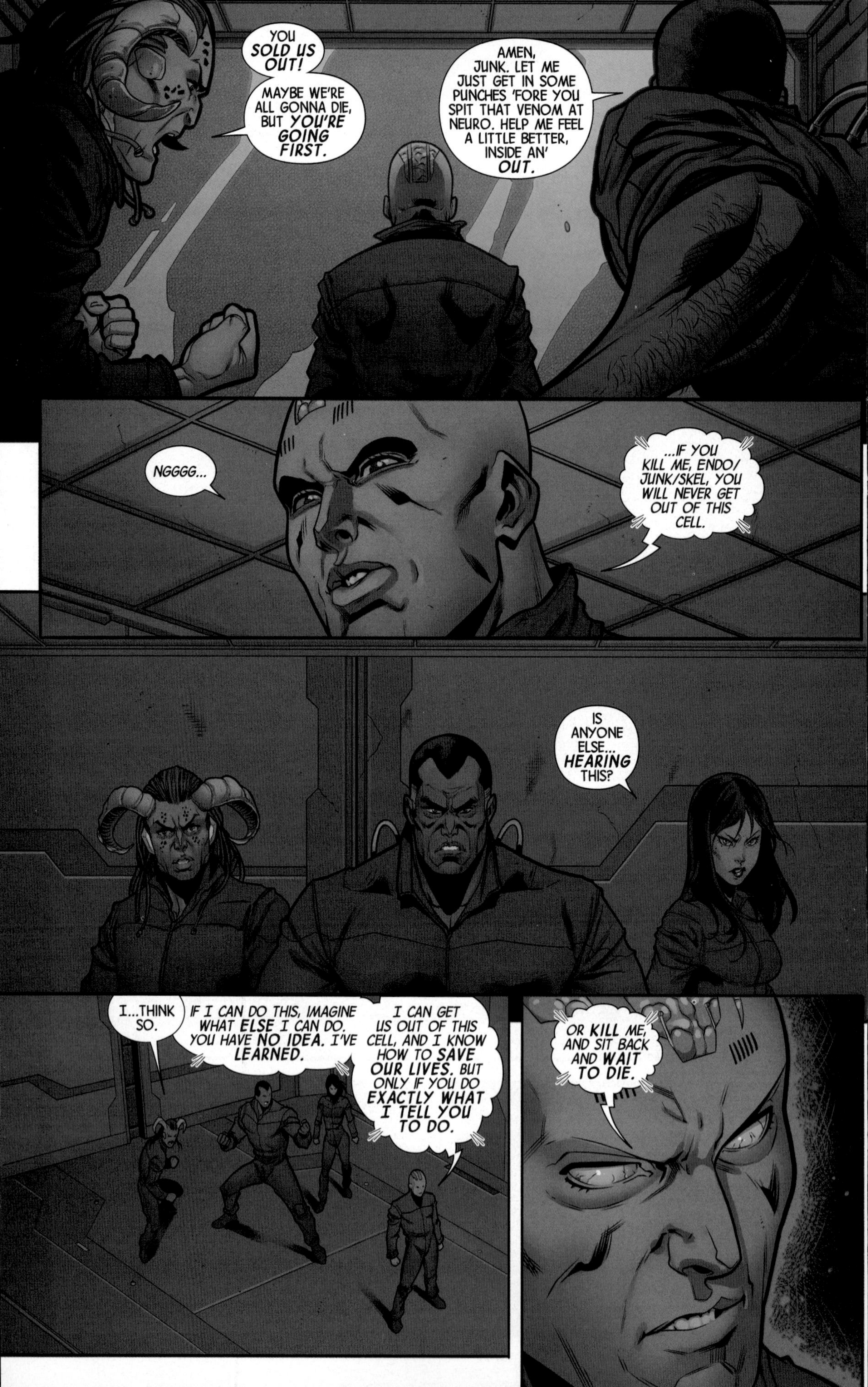
YOU SOLD US OUT!
MAYBE WE'RE ALL GONNA DIE, BUT YOU'RE GOING FIRST.
AMEN, JUNK. LET ME JUST GET IN SOME PUNCHES 'FORE YOU SPIT THAT VENOM AT NEURO. HELP ME FEEL A LITTLE BETTER, INSIDE AN' OUT.
NGGGG...
...IF YOU KILL ME, ENDO/JUNK/SKEL, YOU WILL NEVER GET OUT OF THIS CELL.
IS ANYONE ELSE... HEARING THIS?
I...THINK SO.
IF I CAN DO THIS, IMAGINE WHAT ELSE I CAN DO. YOU HAVE NO IDEA. I'VE LEARNED.
I CAN GET US OUT OF THIS CELL, AND I KNOW HOW TO SAVE OUR LIVES. BUT ONLY IF YOU DO EXACTLY WHAT I TELL YOU TO DO.
OR KILL ME, AND SIT BACK AND WAIT TO DIE.

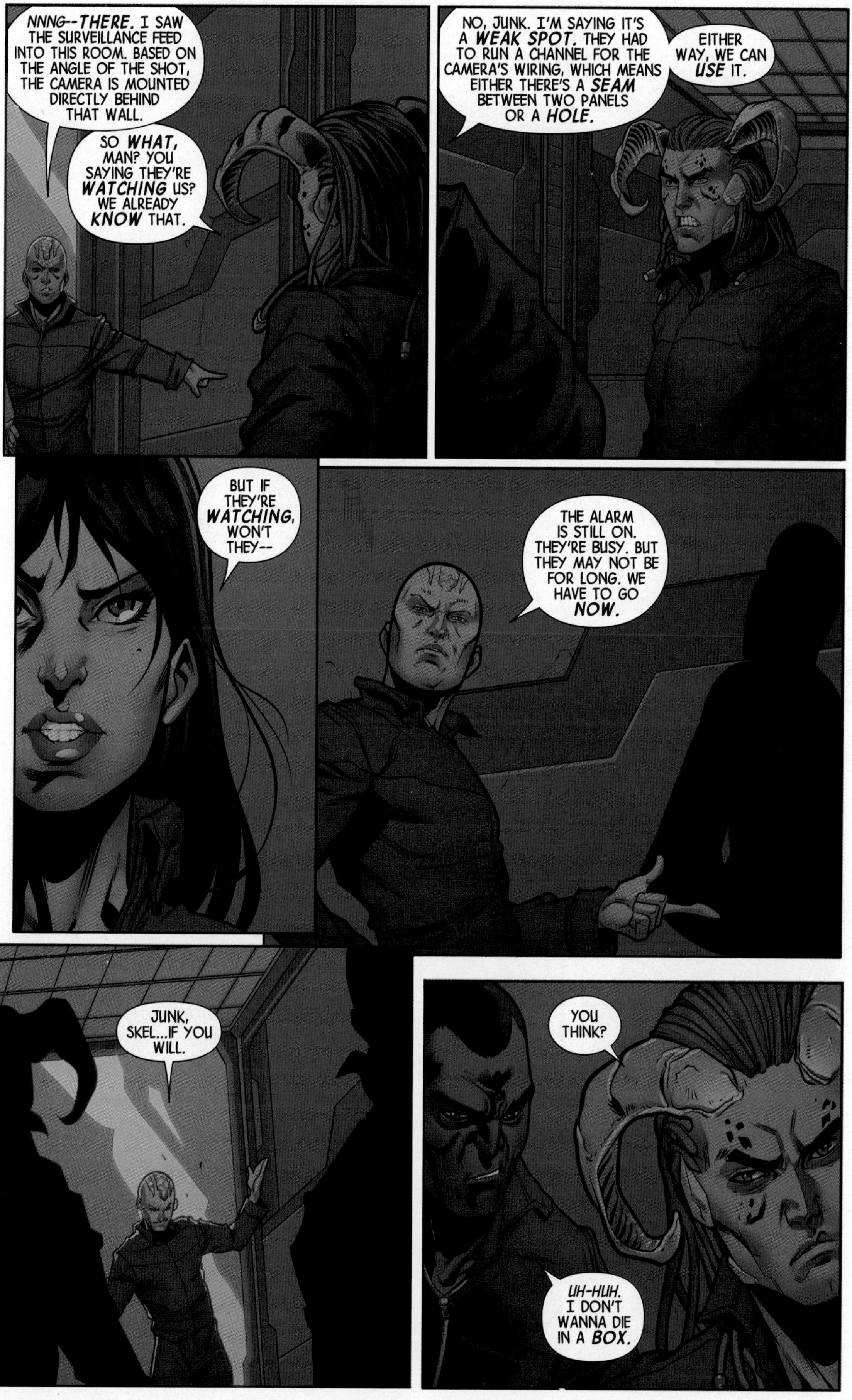
NNNG--THERE. I SAW THE SURVEILLANCE FEED INTO THIS ROOM. BASED ON THE ANGLE OF THE SHOT, THE CAMERA IS MOUNTED DIRECTLY BEHIND THAT WALL.
SO WHAT, MAN? YOU SAYING THEY'RE WATCHING US? WE ALREADY KNOW THAT.
NO, JUNK. I'M SAYING IT'S A WEAK SPOT. THEY HAD TO RUN A CHANNEL FOR THE CAMERA'S WIRING, WHICH MEANS EITHER THERE'S A SEAM BETWEEN TWO PANELS OR A HOLE.
EITHER WAY, WE CAN USE IT.
BUT IF THEY'RE WATCHING, WON'T THEY--
THE ALARM IS STILL ON. THEY'RE BUSY. BUT THEY MAY NOT BE FOR LONG. WE HAVE TO GO NOW.
JUNK, SKEL...IF YOU WILL.
YOU THINK?
UH-HUH. I DON'T WANNA DIE IN A BOX.

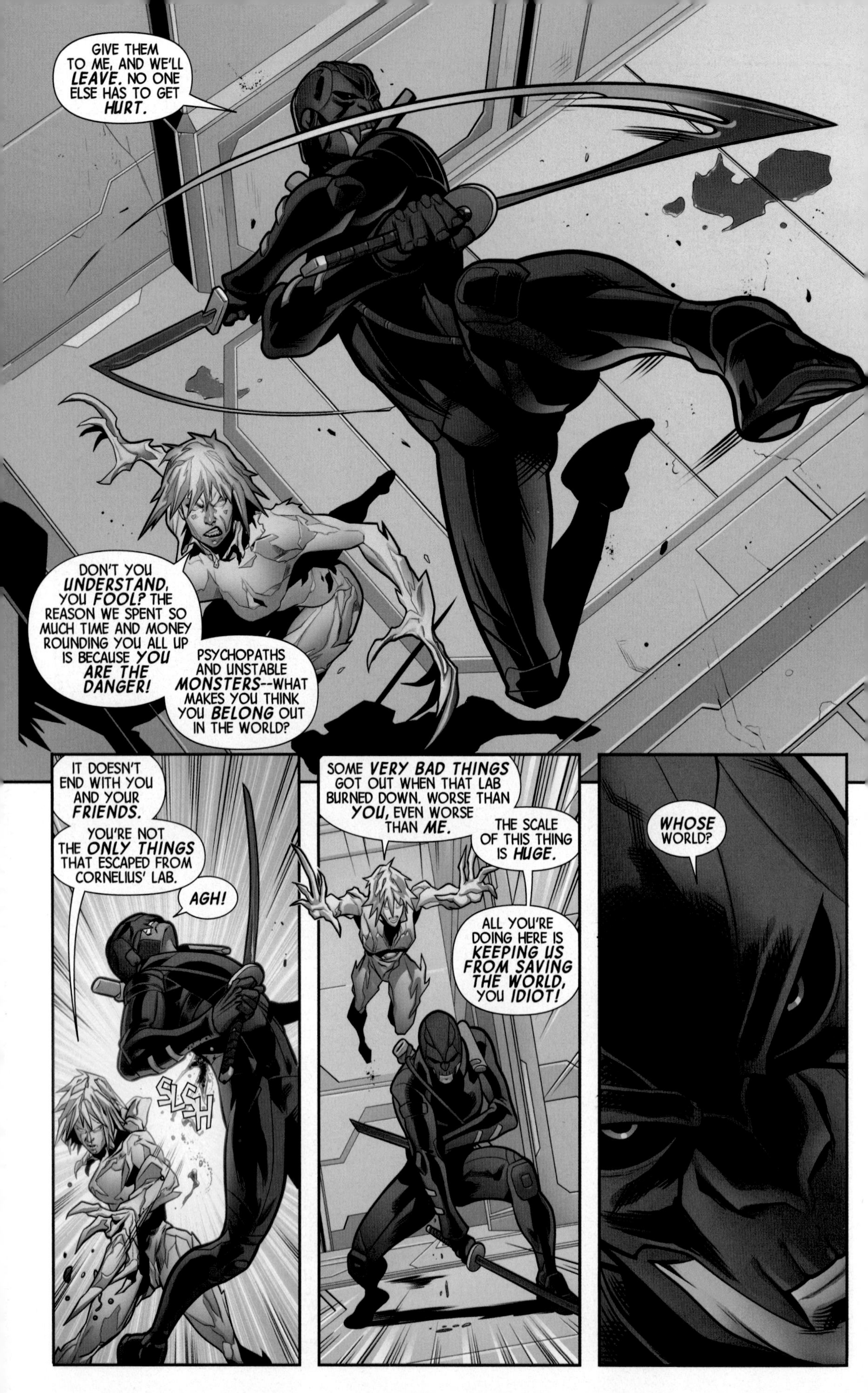
GIVE THEM TO ME, AND WE'LL LEAVE. NO ONE ELSE HAS TO GET HURT.
DON'T YOU UNDERSTAND, YOU FOOL? THE REASON WE SPENT SO MUCH TIME AND MONEY ROUNDING YOU ALL UP IS BECAUSE YOU ARE THE DANGER!
PSYCHOPATHS AND UNSTABLE MONSTERS--WHAT MAKES YOU THINK YOU BELONG OUT IN THE WORLD?
IT DOESN'T END WITH YOU AND YOUR FRIENDS.
YOU'RE NOT THE ONLY THINGS THAT ESCAPED FROM CORNELIUS' LAB.
AGH!
SLSH
SOME VERY BAD THINGS GOT OUT WHEN THAT LAB BURNED DOWN. WORSE THAN YOU, EVEN WORSE THAN ME.
THE SCALE OF THIS THING IS HUGE.
ALL YOU'RE DOING HERE IS KEEPING US FROM SAVING THE WORLD, YOU IDIOT!
WHOSE WORLD?

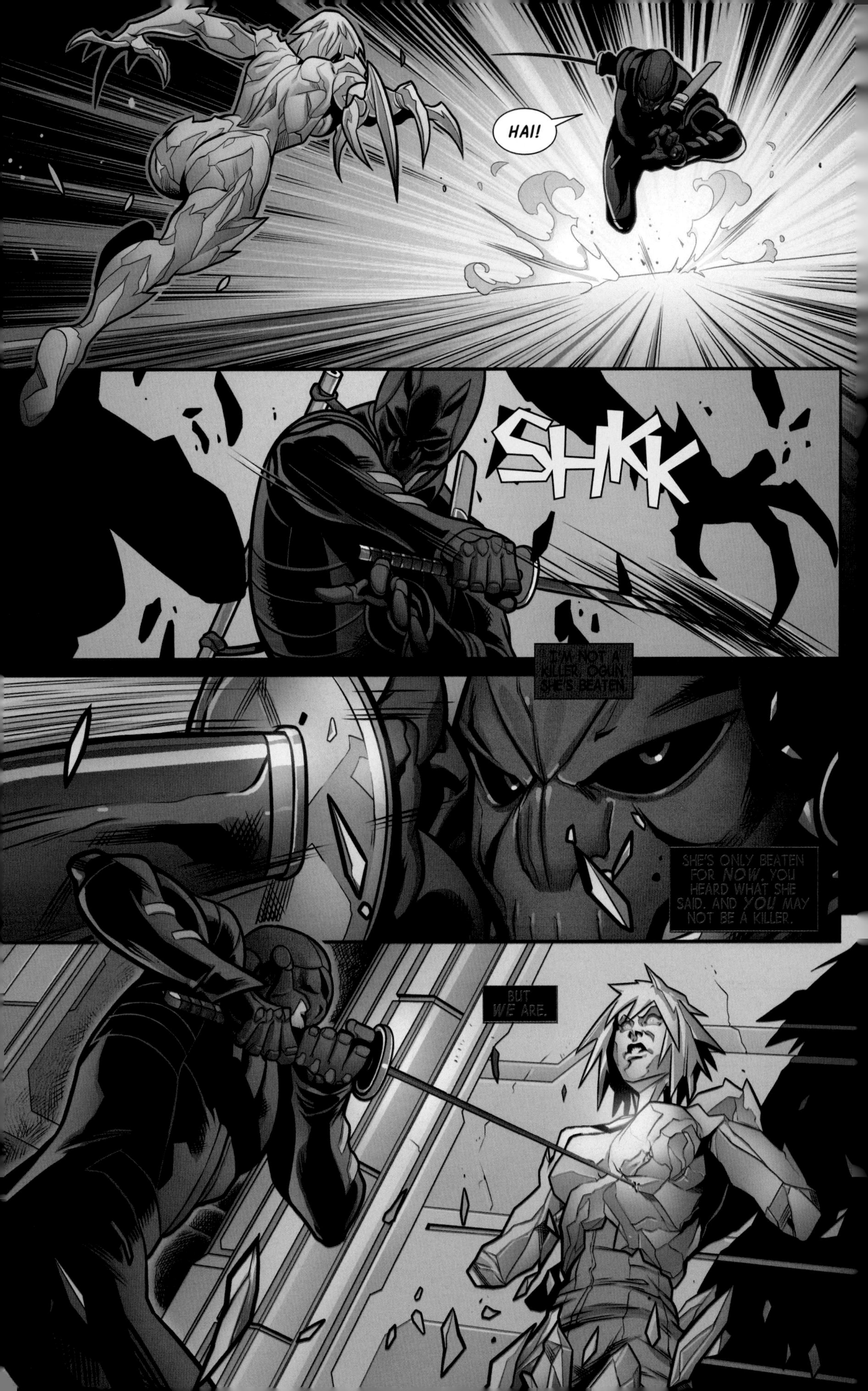
HAI!
SHKK
I'M NOT A KILLER, OGUN. SHE'S BEATEN.
SHE'S ONLY BEATEN FOR NOW. YOU HEARD WHAT SHE SAID. AND YOU MAY NOT BE A KILLER.
BUT WE ARE.

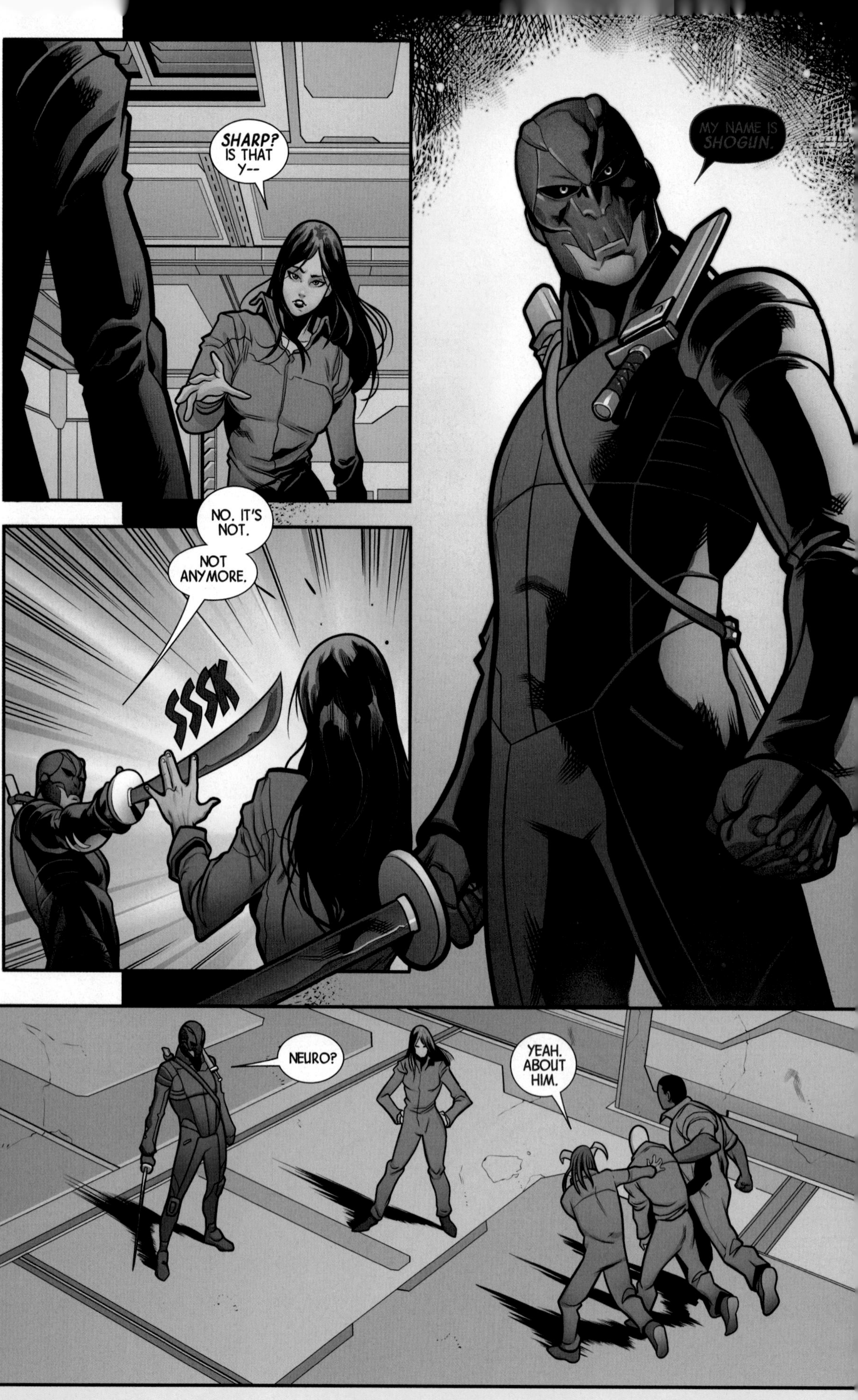
SHARP? IS THAT Y--
MY NAME IS SHOGUN.
NO. IT'S NOT.
NOT ANYMORE.
SSSK
NEURO?
YEAH. ABOUT HIM.

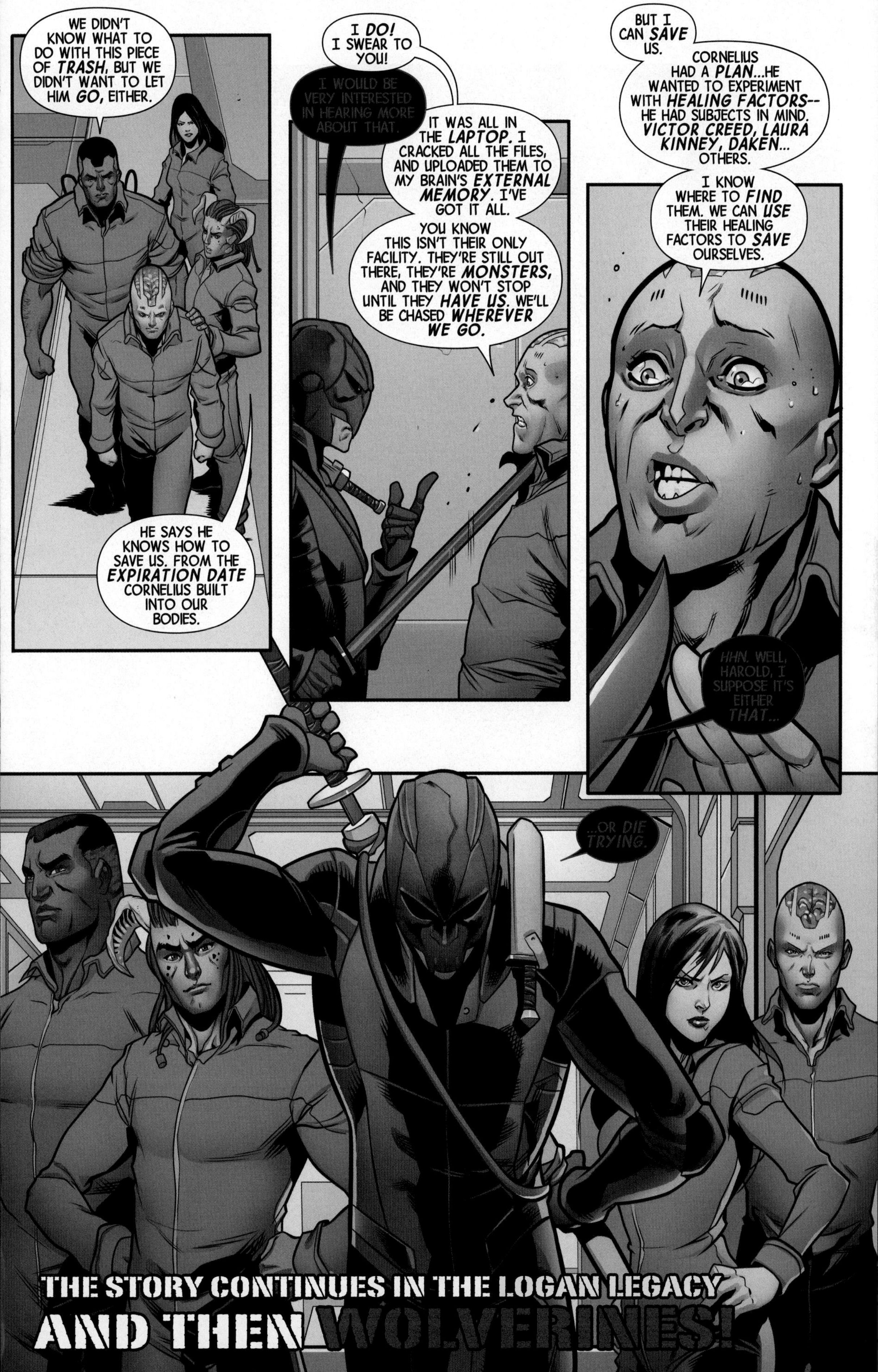

WE DIDN'T KNOW WHAT TO DO WITH THIS PIECE OF TRASH, BUT WE DIDN'T WANT TO LET HIM GO, EITHER.
HE SAYS HE KNOWS HOW TO SAVE US. FROM THE EXPIRATION DATE CORNELIUS BUILT INTO OUR BODIES.
I WOULD BE VERY INTERESTED IN HEARING MORE ABOUT THAT.
I DO! I SWEAR TO YOU!
IT WAS ALL IN THE LAPTOP. I CRACKED ALL THE FILES, AND UPLOADED THEM TO MY BRAIN'S EXTERNAL MEMORY. I'VE GOT IT ALL.
YOU KNOW THIS ISN'T THEIR ONLY FACILITY. THEY'RE STILL OUT THERE, THEY'RE MONSTERS, AND THEY WON'T STOP UNTIL THEY HAVE US. WE'LL BE CHASED WHEREVER WE GO.
BUT I CAN SAVE US.
CORNELIUS HAD A PLAN...HE WANTED TO EXPERIMENT WITH HEALING FACTORS--HE HAD SUBJECTS IN MIND. VICTOR CREED, LAURA KINNEY, DAKEN... OTHERS.
I KNOW WHERE TO FIND THEM. WE CAN USE THEIR HEALING FACTORS TO SAVE OURSELVES.
HHN. WELL, HAROLD, I SUPPOSE IT'S EITHER THAT...
...OR DIE TRYING.
THE STORY CONTINUES IN THE LOGAN LEGACY
AND THEN WOLVERINES!

1 LIFE AFTER LOGAN

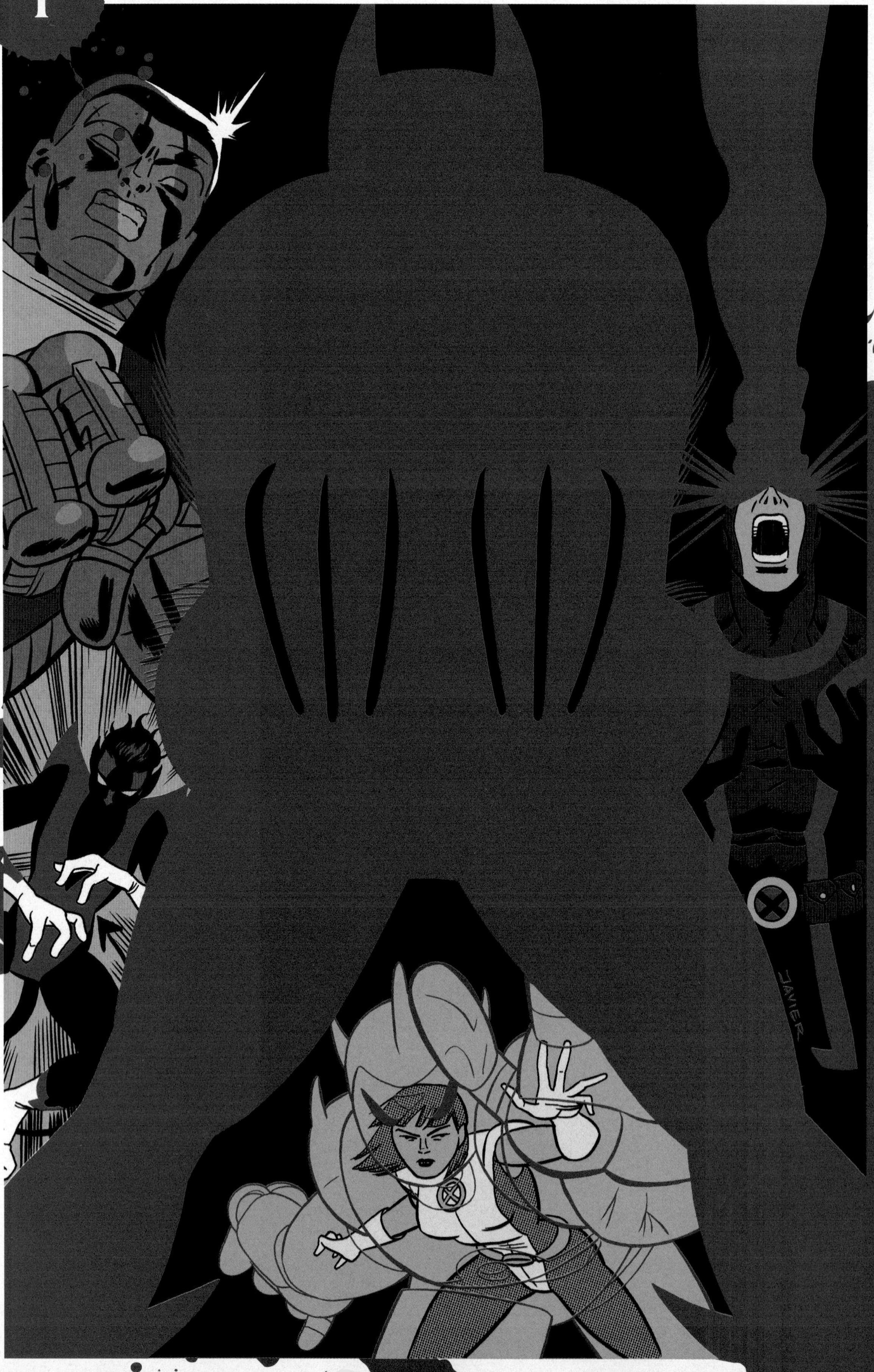

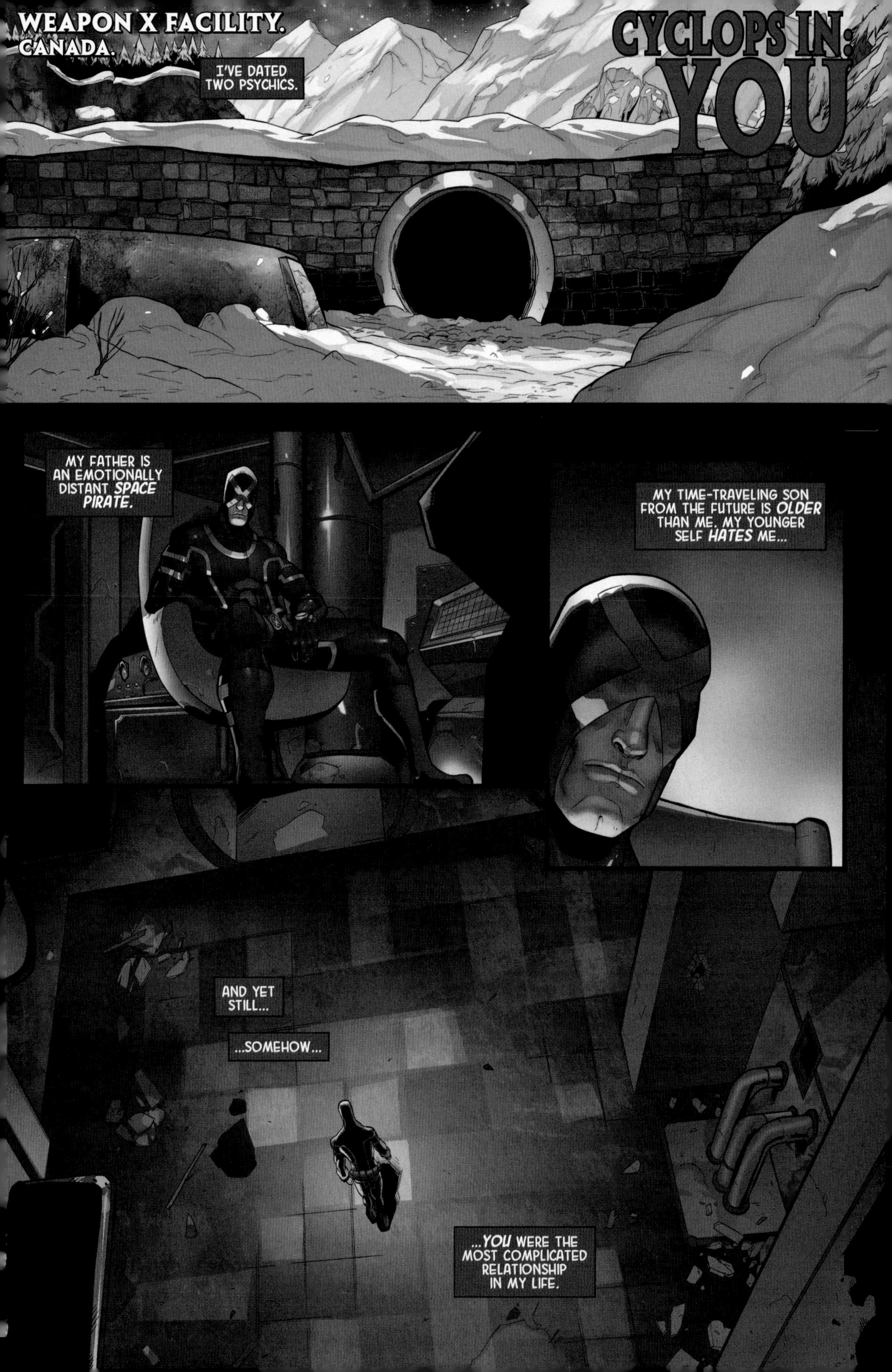
WEAPON X FACILITY.
CANADA.
CYCLOPS IN:
YOU
I'VE DATED TWO PSYCHICS.
MY FATHER IS AN EMOTIONALLY DISTANT SPACE PIRATE.
MY TIME-TRAVELING SON FROM THE FUTURE IS OLDER THAN ME. MY YOUNGER SELF HATES ME...
AND YET STILL...
...SOMEHOW...
...YOU WERE THE MOST COMPLICATED RELATIONSHIP IN MY LIFE.

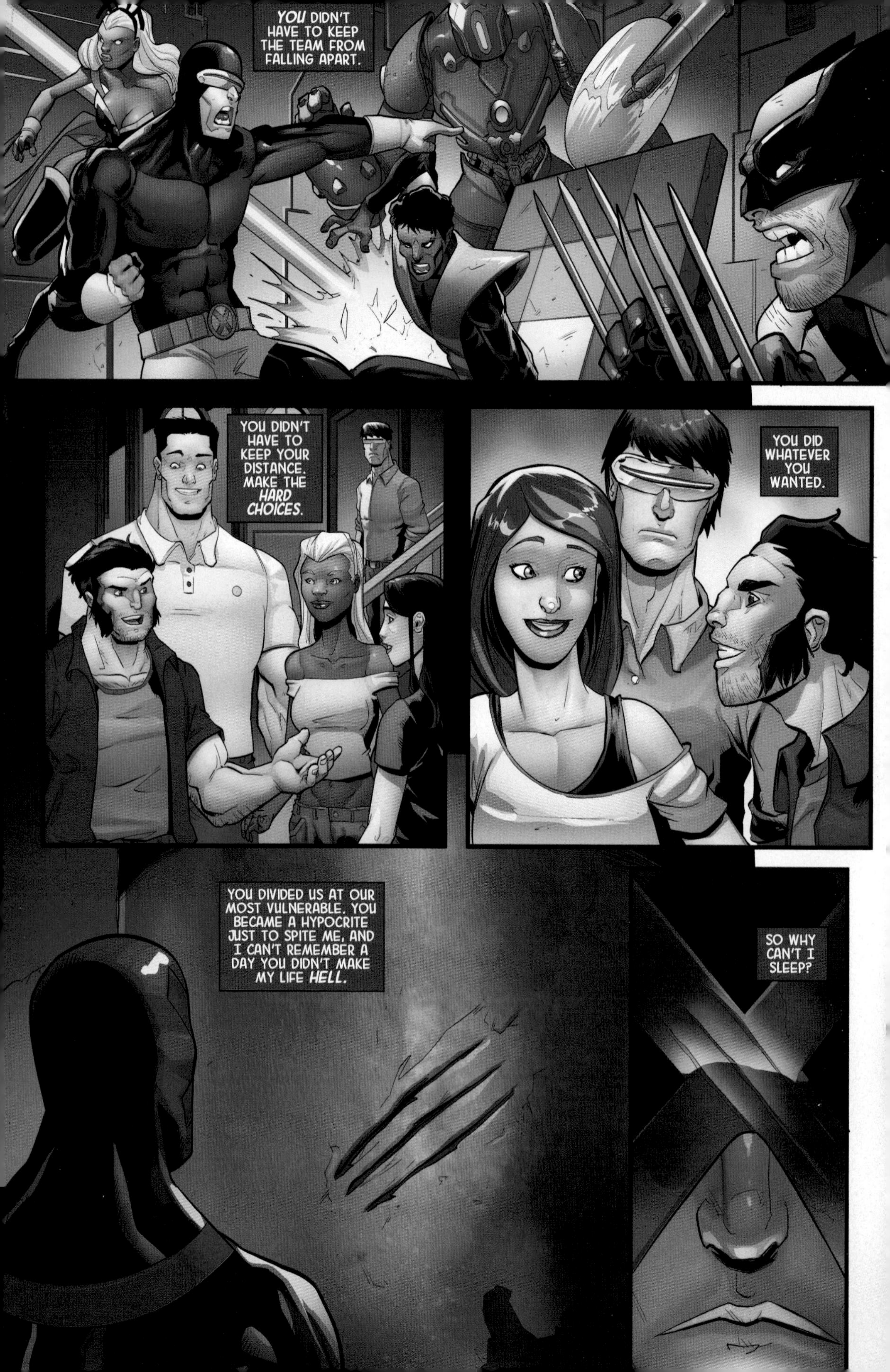
YOU DIDN'T HAVE TO KEEP THE TEAM FROM FALLING APART.
YOU DIDN'T HAVE TO KEEP YOUR DISTANCE. MAKE THE HARD CHOICES.
YOU DID WHATEVER YOU WANTED.
YOU DIVIDED US AT OUR MOST VULNERABLE. YOU BECAME A HYPOCRITE JUST TO SPITE ME, AND I CAN'T REMEMBER A DAY YOU DIDN'T MAKE MY LIFE HELL.
SO WHY CAN'T I SLEEP?

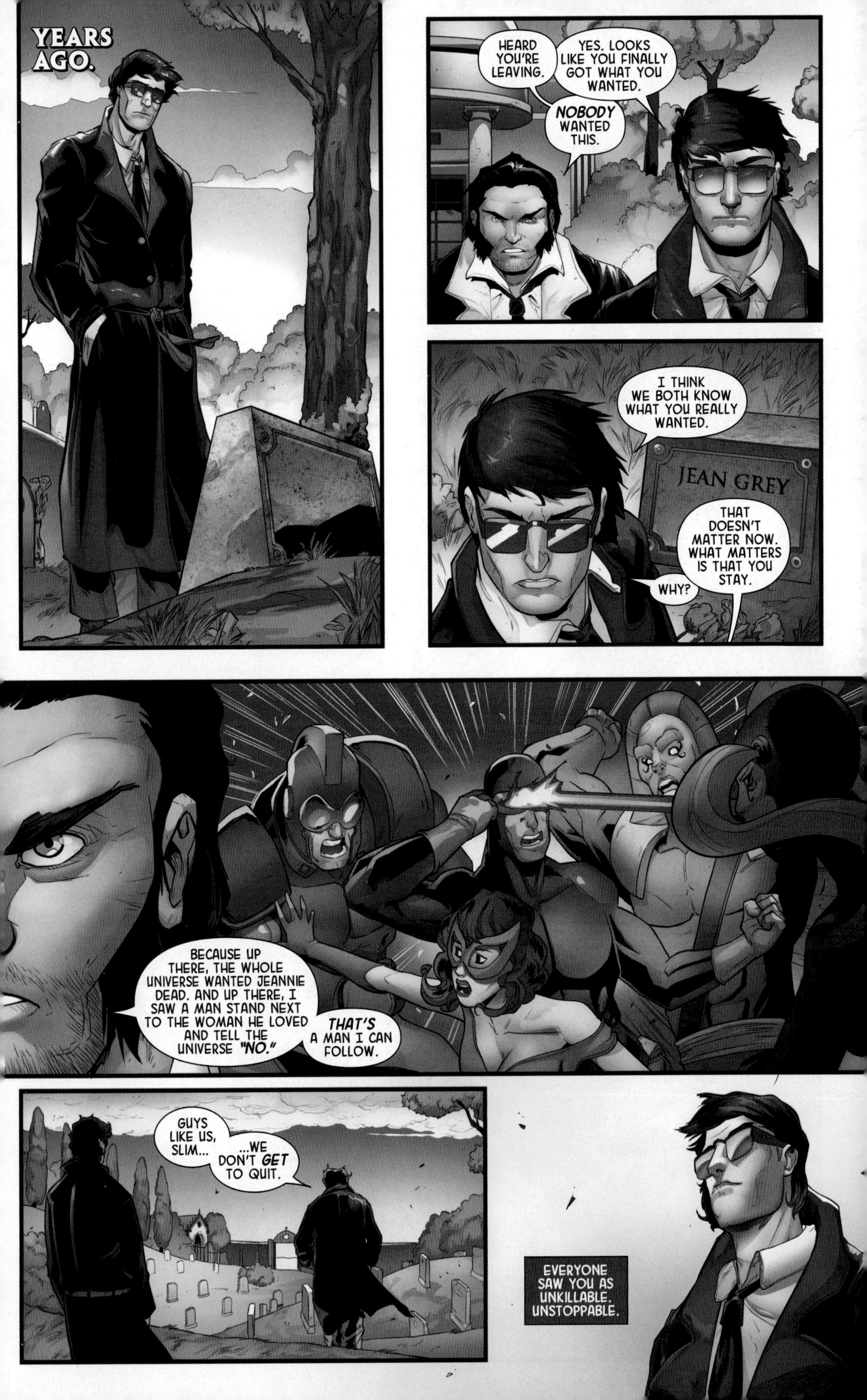
YEARS AGO.
HEARD YOU'RE LEAVING.
YES. LOOKS LIKE YOU FINALLY GOT WHAT YOU WANTED.
NOBODY WANTED THIS.
I THINK WE BOTH KNOW WHAT YOU REALLY WANTED.
JEAN GREY
THAT DOESN'T MATTER NOW. WHAT MATTERS IS THAT YOU STAY.
WHY?
BECAUSE UP THERE, THE WHOLE UNIVERSE WANTED JEANNIE DEAD. AND UP THERE, I SAW A MAN STAND NEXT TO THE WOMAN HE LOVED AND TELL THE UNIVERSE "NO."
THAT'S A MAN I CAN FOLLOW.
GUYS LIKE US, SLIM...
...WE DON'T GET TO QUIT.
EVERYONE SAW YOU AS UNKILLABLE. UNSTOPPABLE.

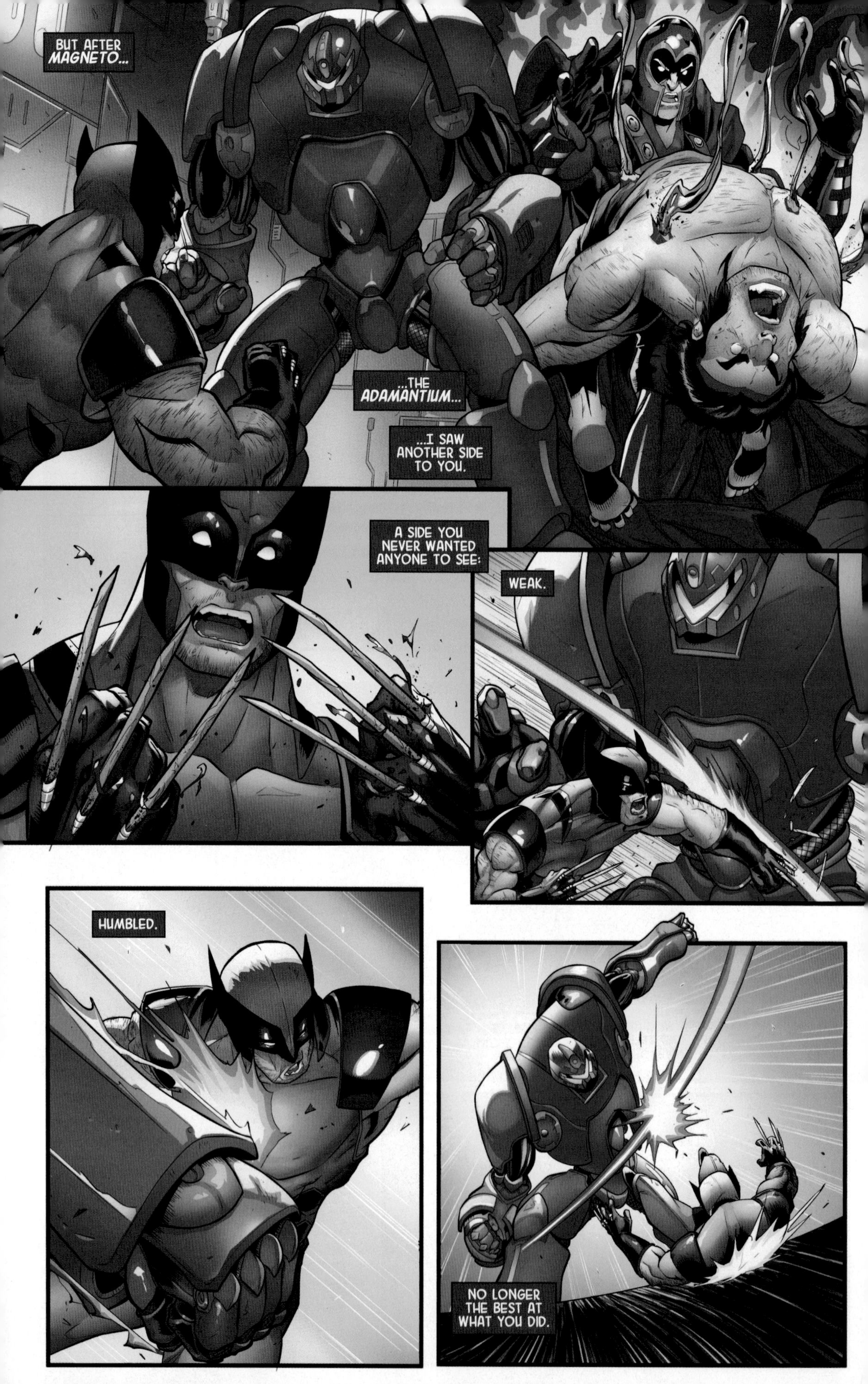

BUT AFTER MAGNETO...
...THE ADAMANTIUM...
...I SAW ANOTHER SIDE TO YOU.
A SIDE YOU NEVER WANTED ANYONE TO SEE:
WEAK.
HUMBLED.
NO LONGER THE BEST AT WHAT YOU DID.

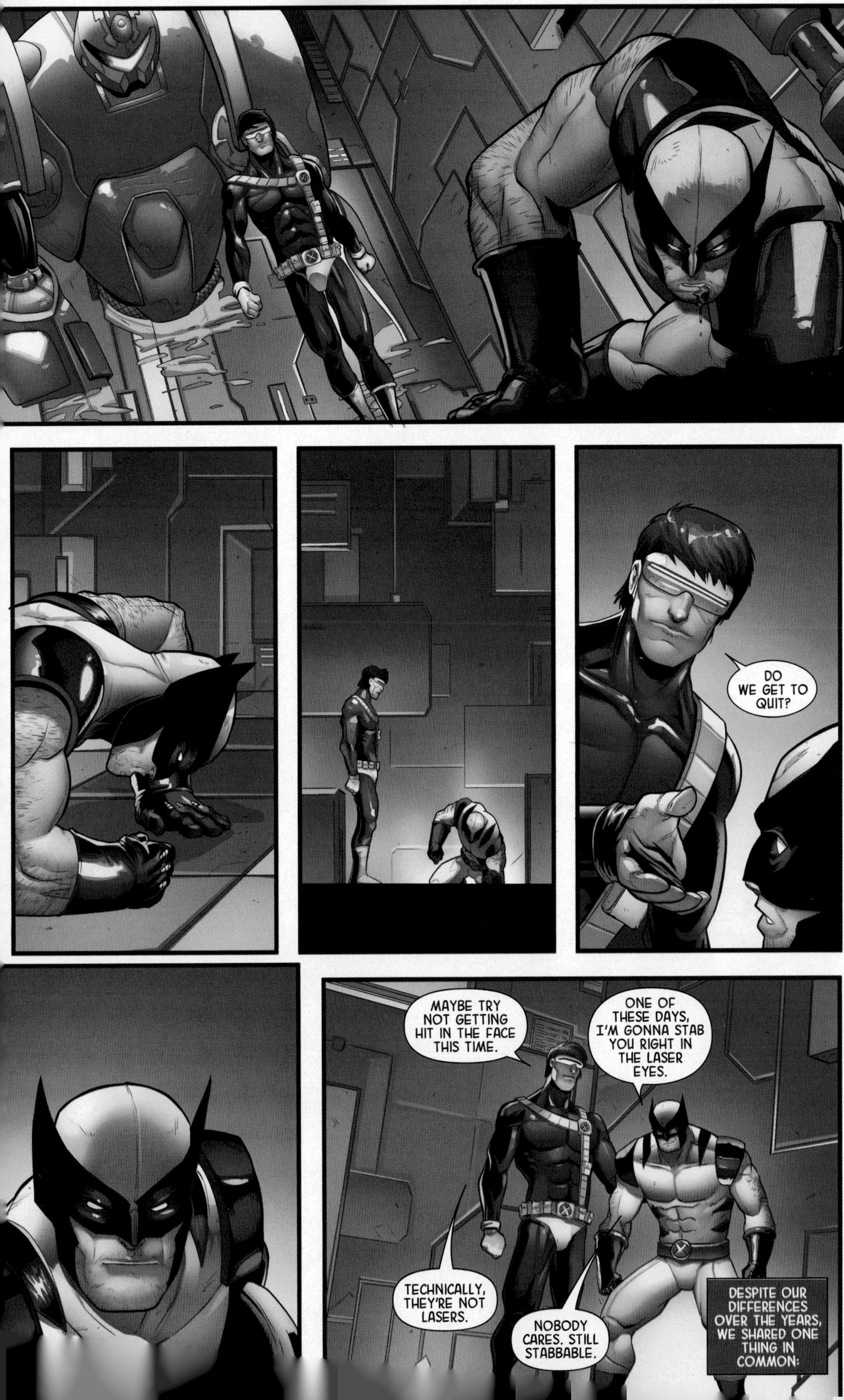
DO WE GET TO QUIT?
MAYBE TRY NOT GETTING HIT IN THE FACE THIS TIME.
ONE OF THESE DAYS, I'M GONNA STAB YOU RIGHT IN THE LASER EYES.
TECHNICALLY, THEY'RE NOT LASERS.
NOBODY CARES. STILL STABBABLE.
DESPITE OUR DIFFERENCES OVER THE YEARS, WE SHARED ONE THING IN COMMON:

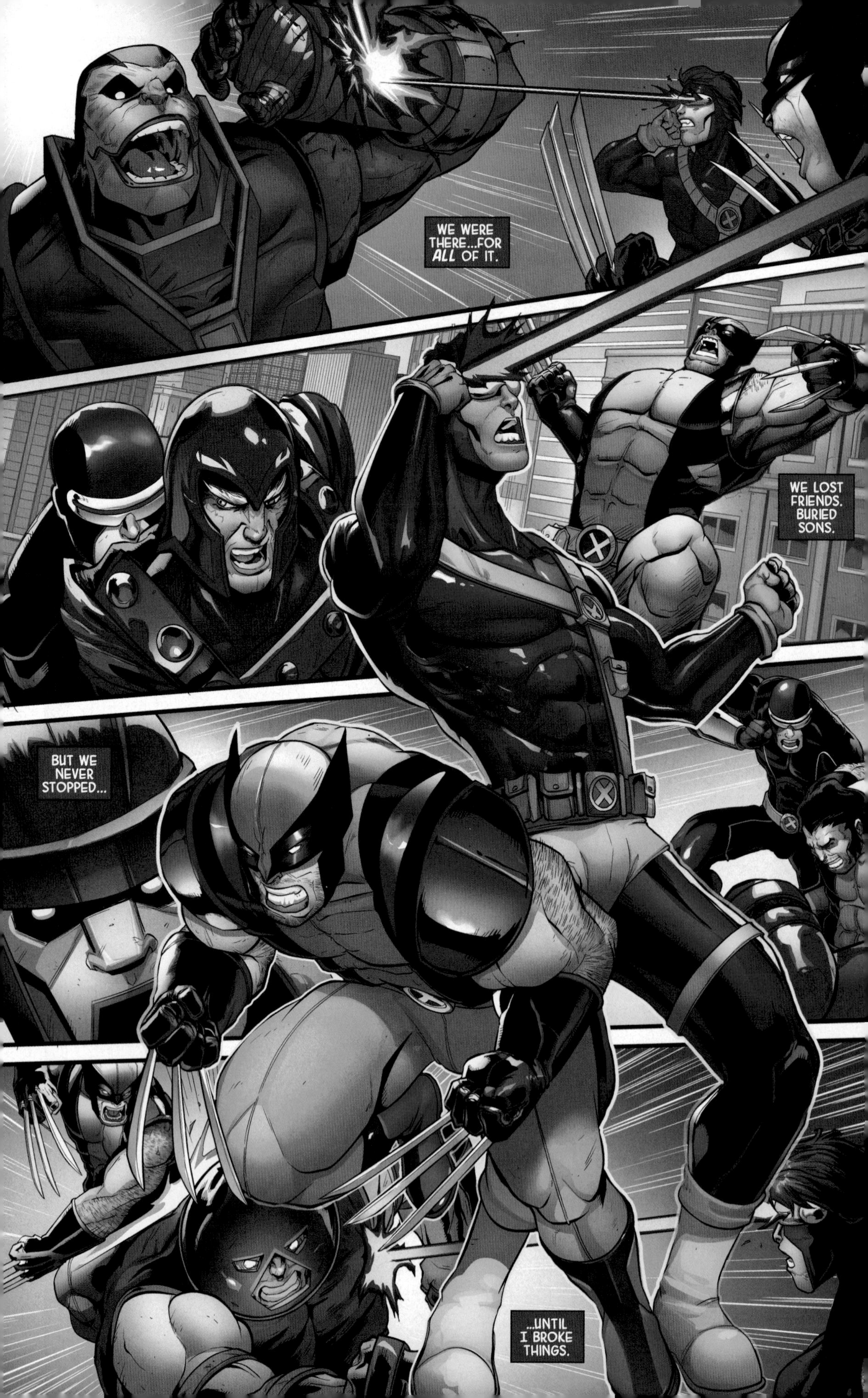
WE WERE THERE...FOR ALL OF IT.
WE LOST FRIENDS. BURIED SONS.
BUT WE NEVER STOPPED...
...UNTIL I BROKE THINGS.

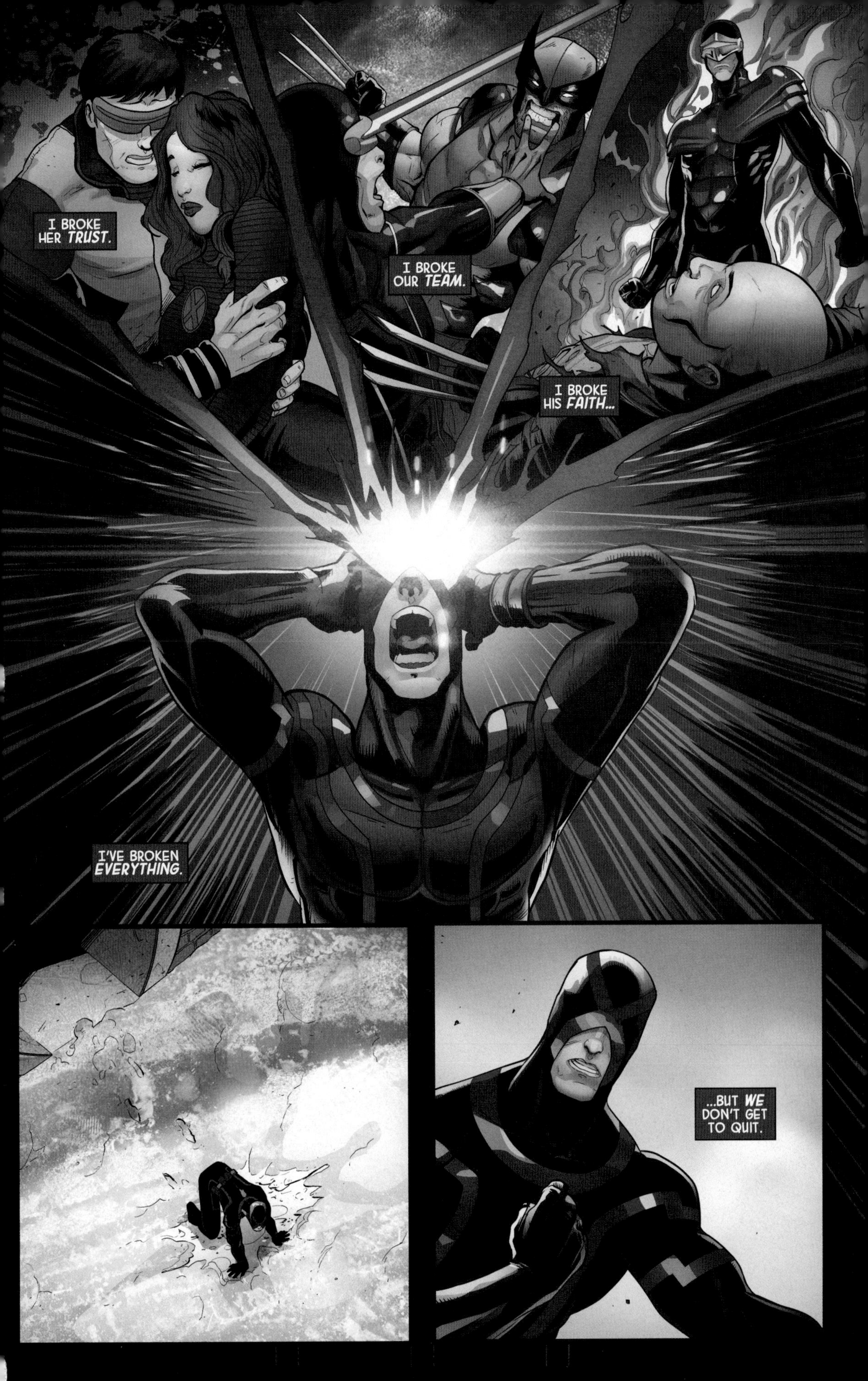
I BROKE HER TRUST.
I BROKE OUR TEAM.
I BROKE HIS FAITH...
I'VE BROKEN EVERYTHING.
...BUT WE DON'T GET TO QUIT.

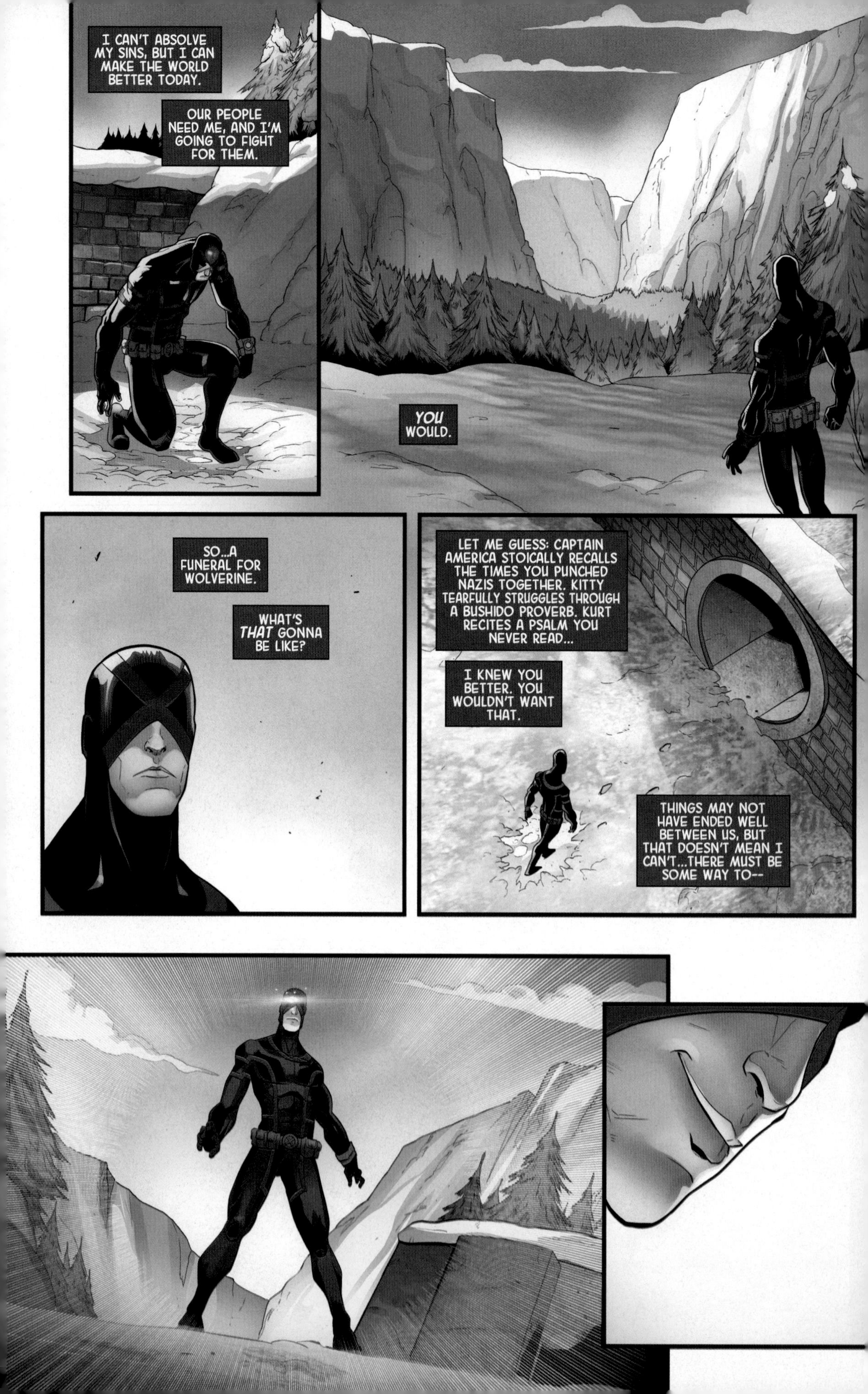
I CAN'T ABSOLVE MY SINS, BUT I CAN MAKE THE WORLD BETTER TODAY.
OUR PEOPLE NEED ME, AND I'M GOING TO FIGHT FOR THEM.
YOU WOULD.
SO...A FUNERAL FOR WOLVERINE.
WHAT'S THAT GONNA BE LIKE?
LET ME GUESS: CAPTAIN AMERICA STOICALLY RECALLS THE TIMES YOU PUNCHED NAZIS TOGETHER. KITTY TEARFULLY STRUGGLES THROUGH A BUSHIDO PROVERB. KURT RECITES A PSALM YOU NEVER READ...
I KNEW YOU BETTER. YOU WOULDN'T WANT THAT.
THINGS MAY NOT HAVE ENDED WELL BETWEEN US, BUT THAT DOESN'T MEAN I CAN'T...THERE MUST BE SOME WAY TO--

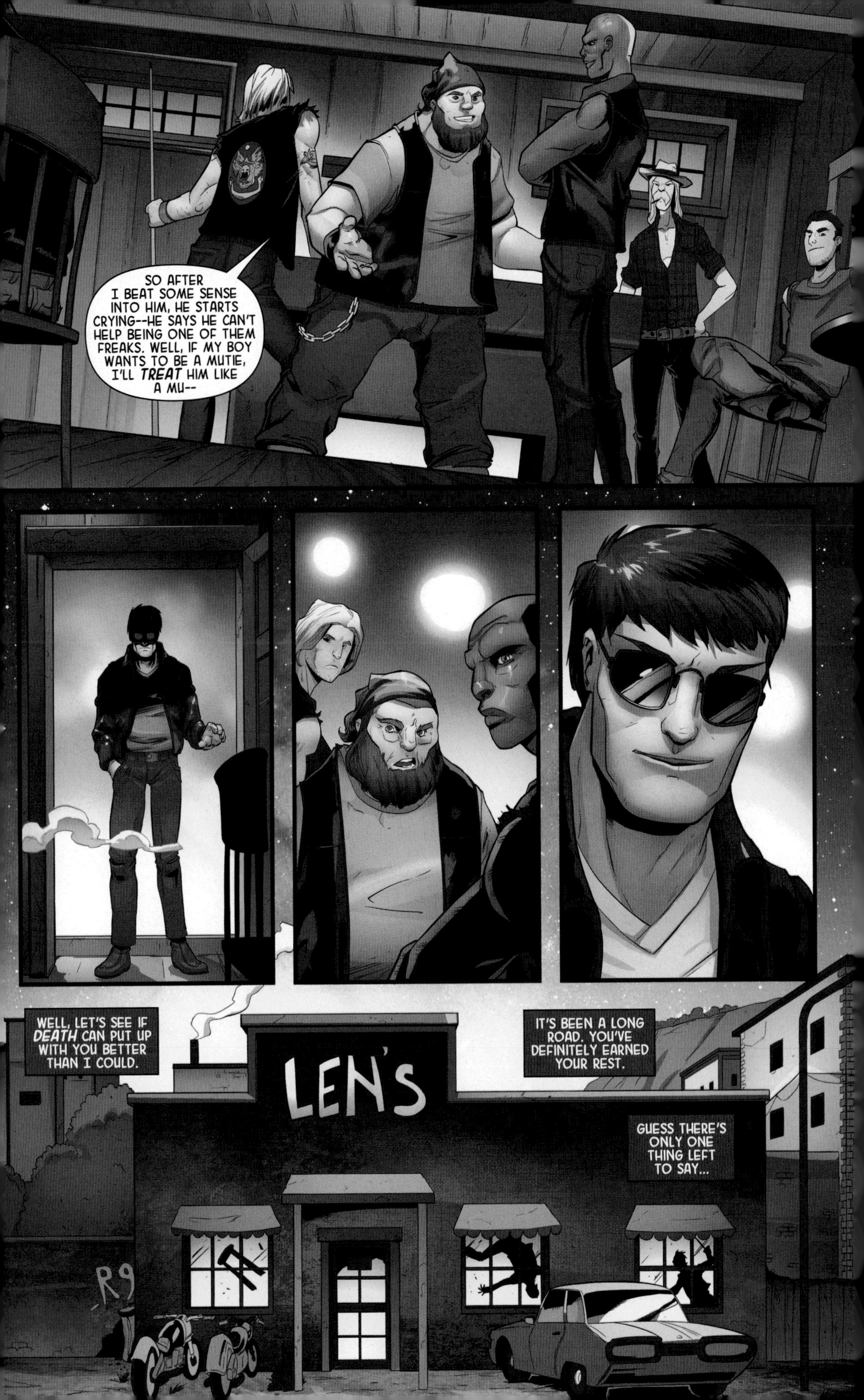
SO AFTER I BEAT SOME SENSE INTO HIM, HE STARTS CRYING--HE SAYS HE CAN'T HELP BEING ONE OF THEM FREAKS. WELL, IF MY BOY WANTS TO BE A MUTIE, I'LL *TREAT* HIM LIKE A MU--
WELL, LET'S SEE IF *DEATH* CAN PUT UP WITH YOU BETTER THAN I COULD.
LEN'S
IT'S BEEN A LONG ROAD. YOU'VE DEFINITELY EARNED YOUR REST.
GUESS THERE'S ONLY ONE THING LEFT TO SAY...

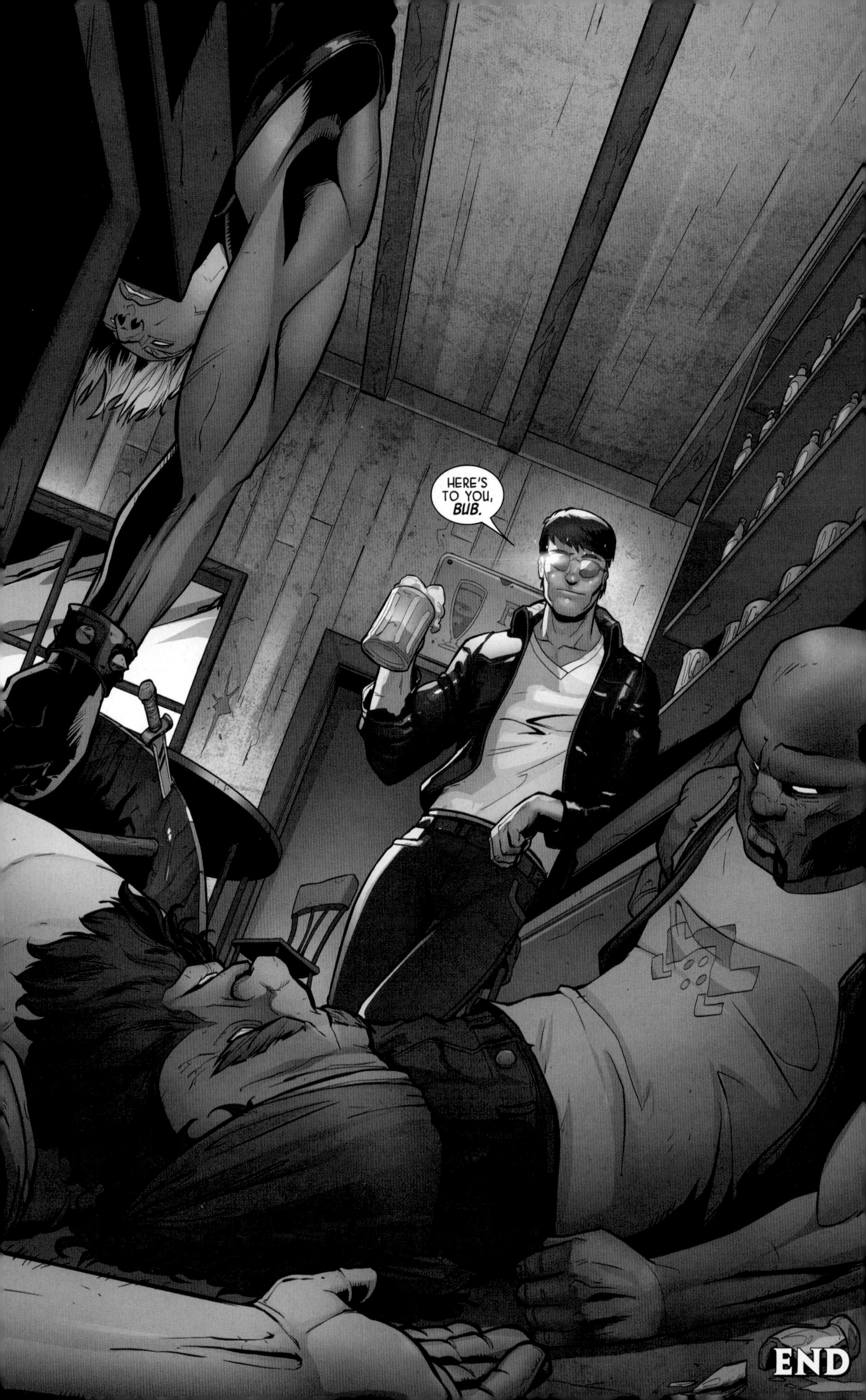
HERE'S TO YOU, BUB.
END

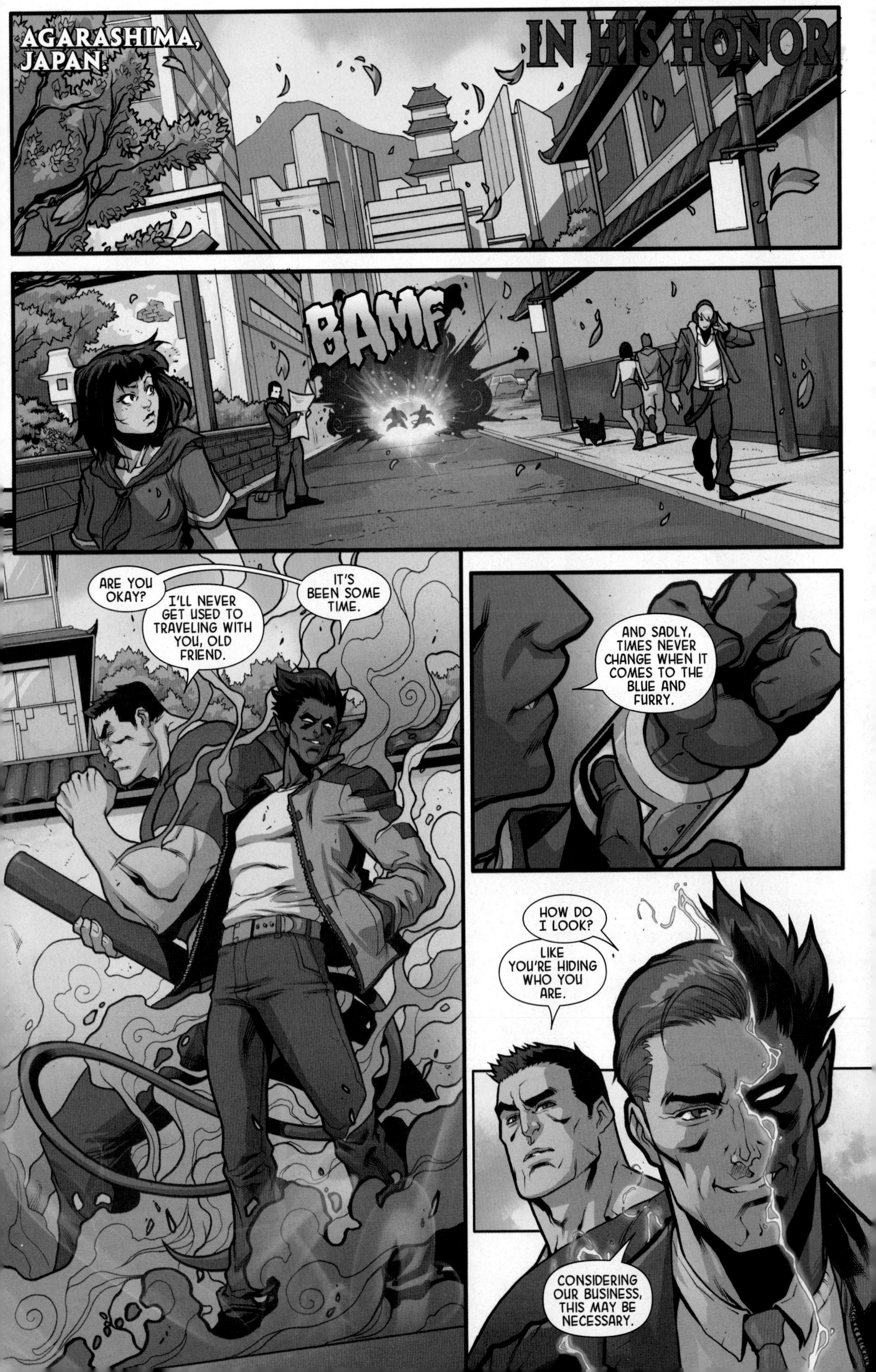
AGARASHIMA, JAPAN.
IN HIS HONOR
BAMF
ARE YOU OKAY?
I'LL NEVER GET USED TO TRAVELING WITH YOU, OLD FRIEND.
IT'S BEEN SOME TIME.
AND SADLY, TIMES NEVER CHANGE WHEN IT COMES TO THE BLUE AND FURRY.
HOW DO I LOOK?
LIKE YOU'RE HIDING WHO YOU ARE.
CONSIDERING OUR BUSINESS, THIS MAY BE NECESSARY.

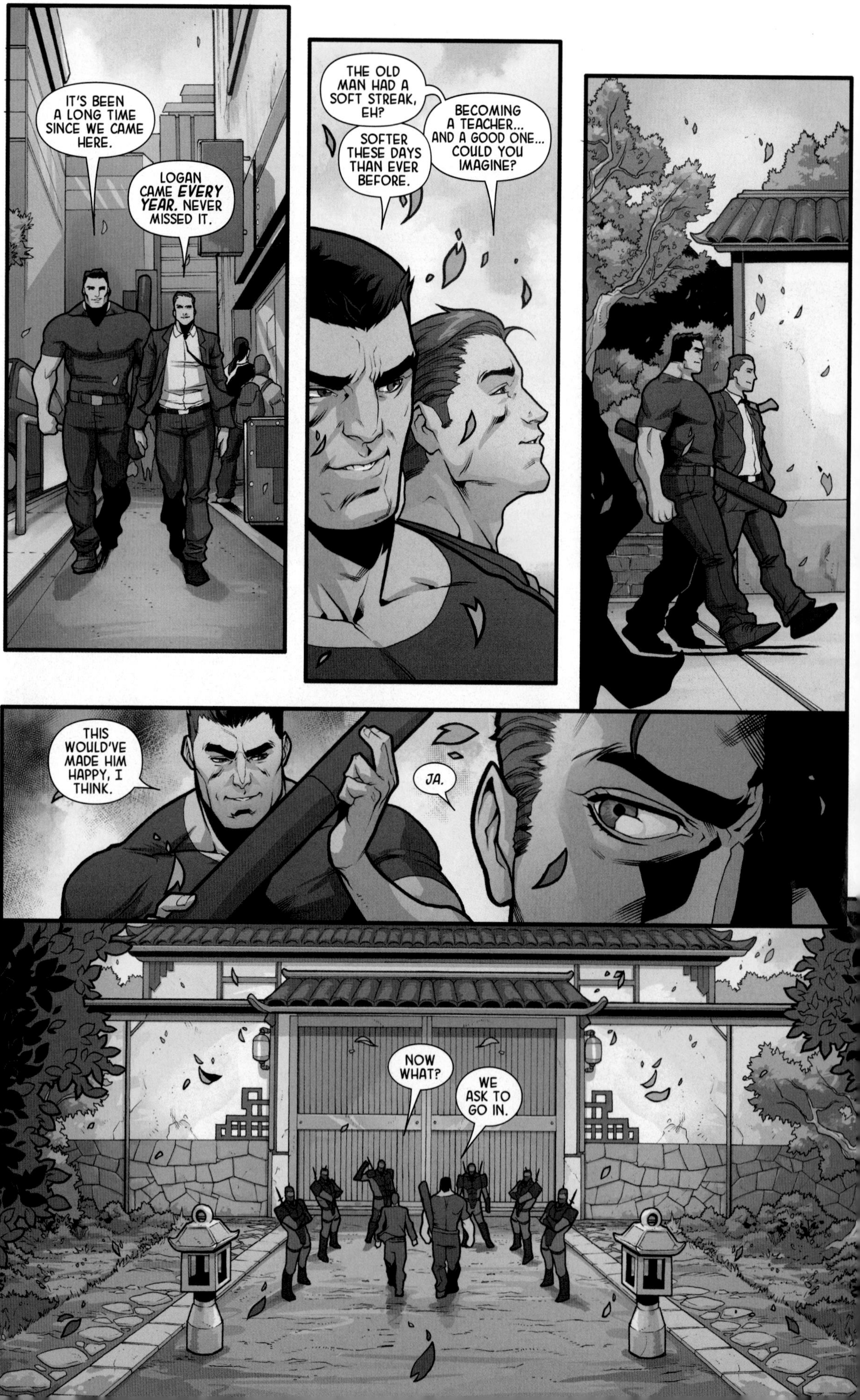
IT'S BEEN A LONG TIME SINCE WE CAME HERE.
LOGAN CAME EVERY YEAR. NEVER MISSED IT.
THE OLD MAN HAD A SOFT STREAK, EH?
SOFTER THESE DAYS THAN EVER BEFORE.
BECOMING A TEACHER... AND A GOOD ONE... COULD YOU IMAGINE?
THIS WOULD'VE MADE HIM HAPPY, I THINK.
JA.
NOW WHAT?
WE ASK TO GO IN.

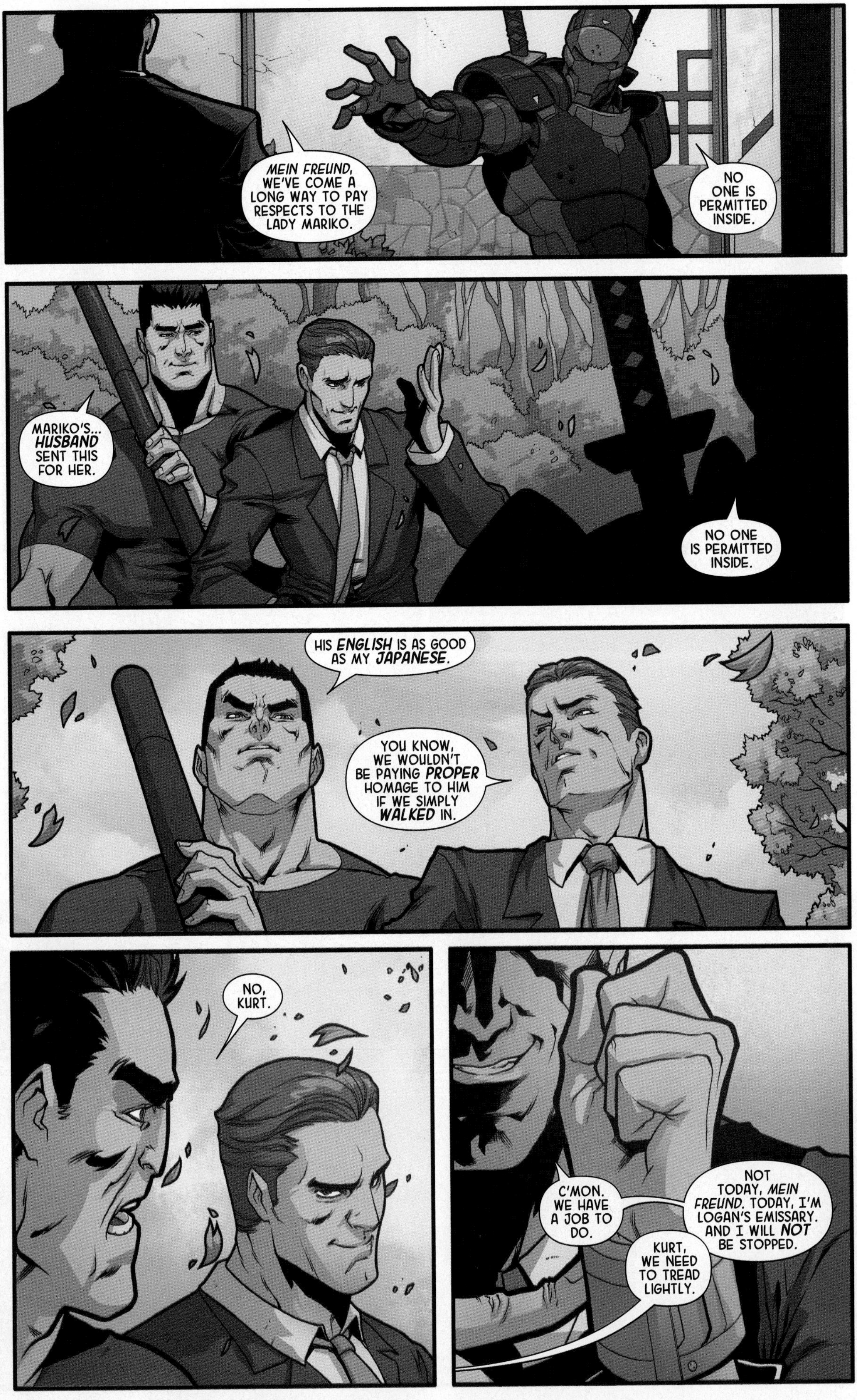

MEIN FREUND, WE'VE COME A LONG WAY TO PAY RESPECTS TO THE LADY MARIKO.
NO ONE IS PERMITTED INSIDE.
MARIKO'S... HUSBAND SENT THIS FOR HER.
NO ONE IS PERMITTED INSIDE.
HIS ENGLISH IS AS GOOD AS MY JAPANESE.
YOU KNOW, WE WOULDN'T BE PAYING PROPER HOMAGE TO HIM IF WE SIMPLY WALKED IN.
NO, KURT.
C'MON. WE HAVE A JOB TO DO.
NOT TODAY, MEIN FREUND. TODAY, I'M LOGAN'S EMISSARY. AND I WILL NOT BE STOPPED.
KURT, WE NEED TO TREAD LIGHTLY.

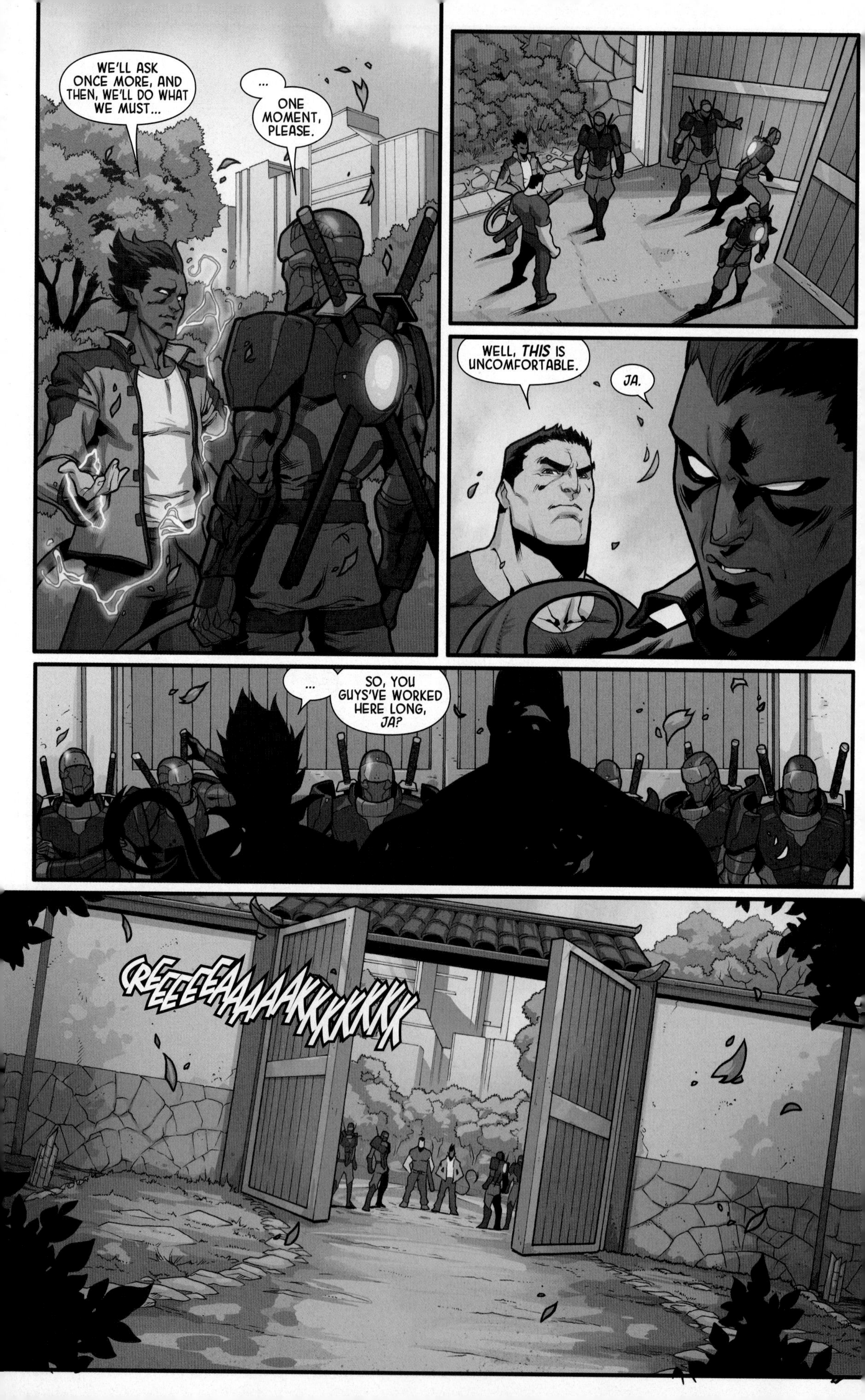
WE'LL ASK ONCE MORE, AND THEN, WE'LL DO WHAT WE MUST...
...
ONE MOMENT, PLEASE.
WELL, THIS IS UNCOMFORTABLE.
JA.
...
SO, YOU GUYS'VE WORKED HERE LONG, JA?
CREEEEEAAAAAKKKKKKK

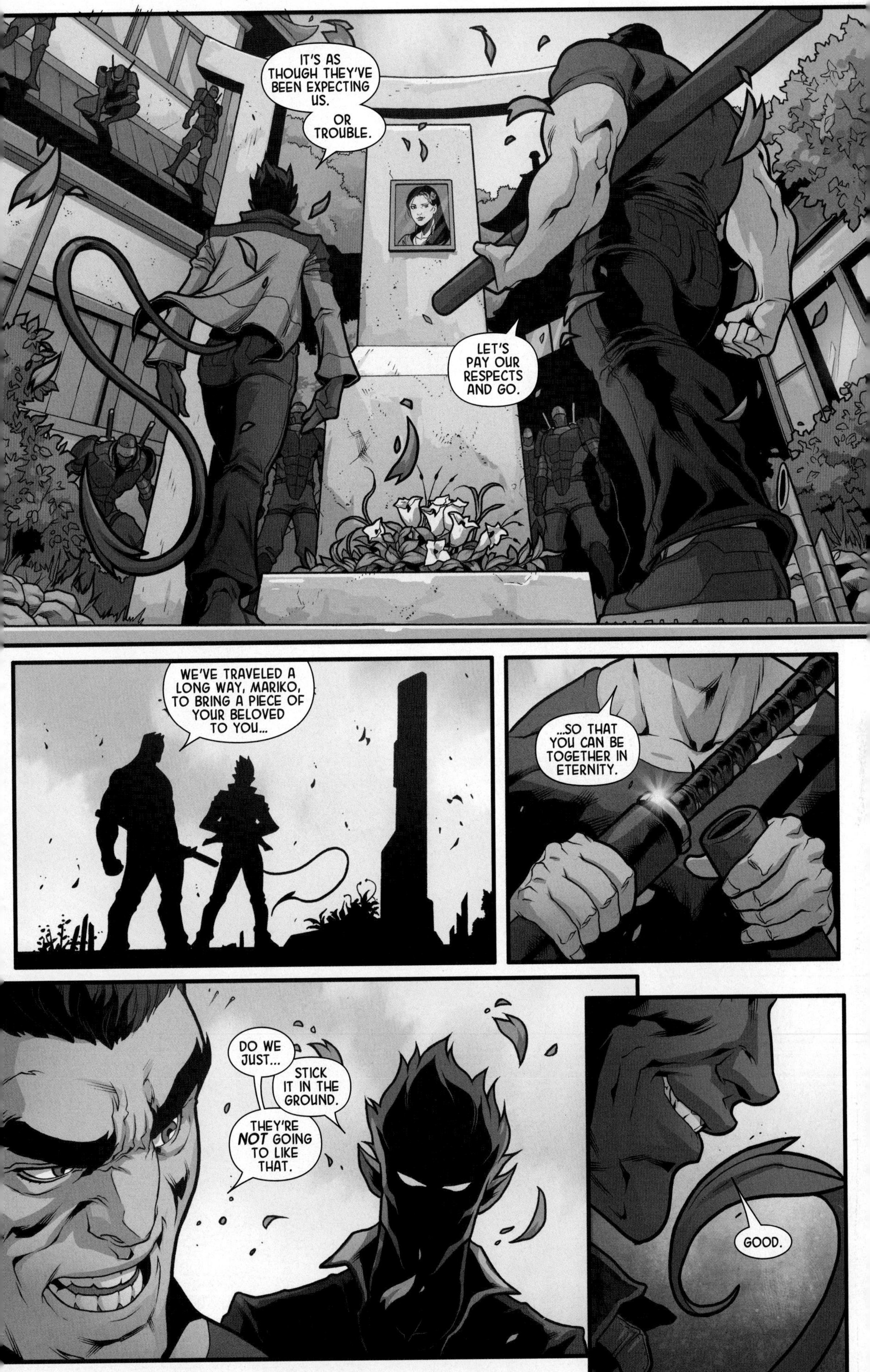
IT'S AS THOUGH THEY'VE BEEN EXPECTING US.
OR TROUBLE.
LET'S PAY OUR RESPECTS AND GO.
WE'VE TRAVELED A LONG WAY, MARIKO, TO BRING A PIECE OF YOUR BELOVED TO YOU...
...SO THAT YOU CAN BE TOGETHER IN ETERNITY.
DO WE JUST...
STICK IT IN THE GROUND.
THEY'RE NOT GOING TO LIKE THAT.
GOOD.

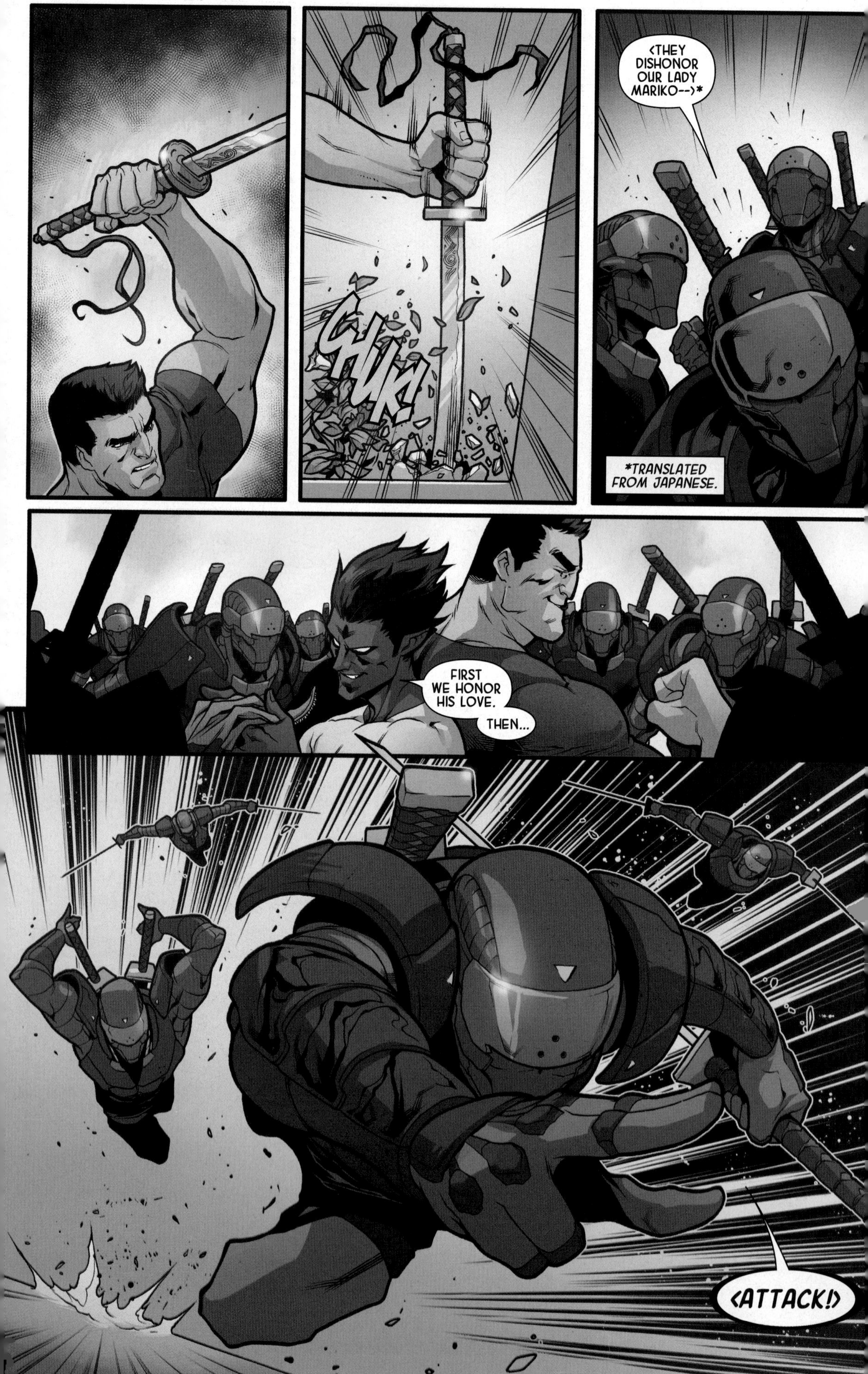

CHUK!
<THEY DISHONOR OUR LADY MARIKO-->*
*TRANSLATED FROM JAPANESE.
FIRST WE HONOR HIS LOVE.
THEN...
<ATTACK!>

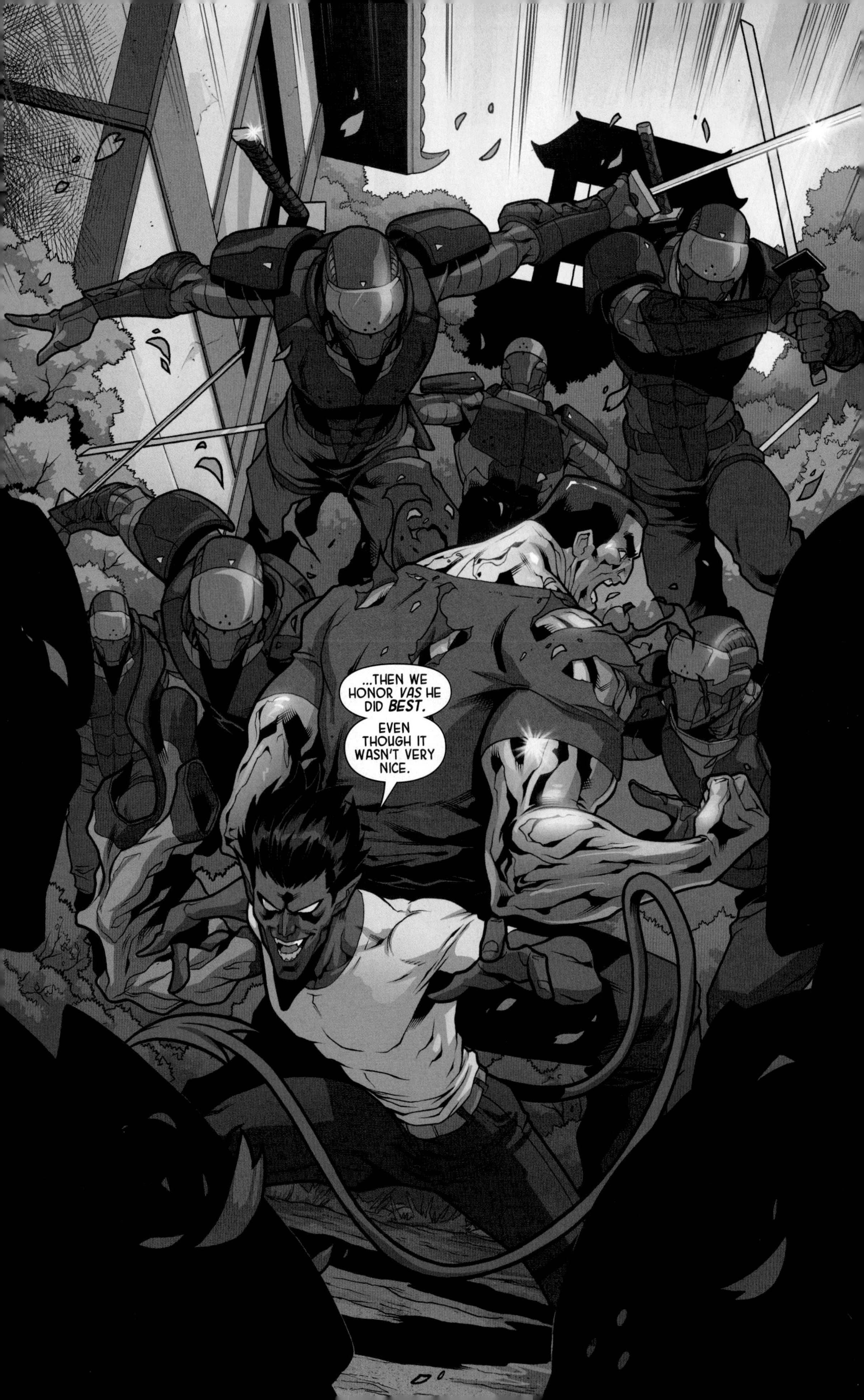
...THEN WE HONOR VAS HE DID BEST.
EVEN THOUGH IT WASN'T VERY NICE.

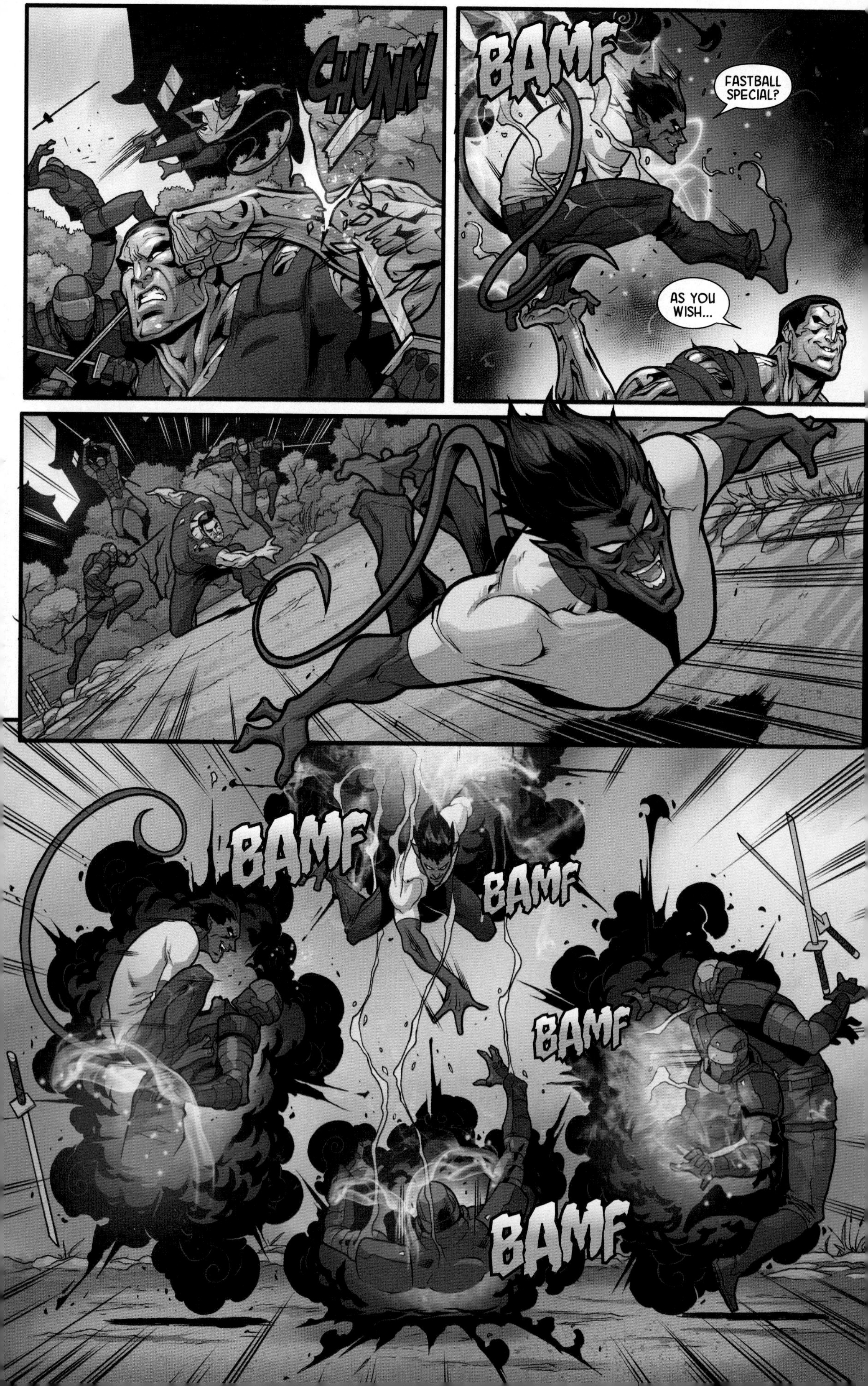
CHUNK!
BAMF
FASTBALL SPECIAL?
AS YOU WISH...
BAMF
BAMF
BAMF
BAMF

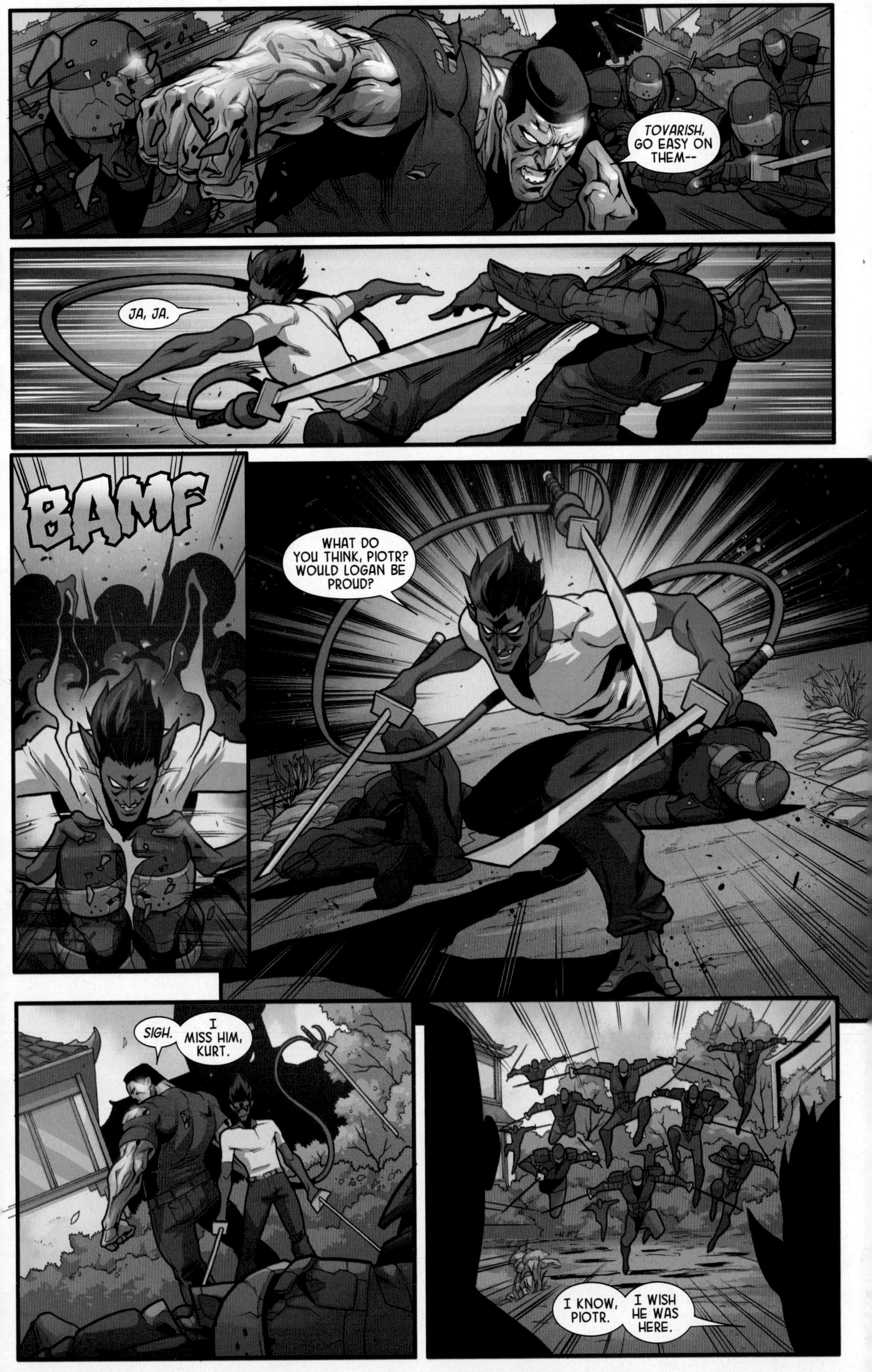
TOVARISH, GO EASY ON THEM--
JA, JA.
BAMF
WHAT DO YOU THINK, PIOTR? WOULD LOGAN BE PROUD?
SIGH.
I MISS HIM, KURT.
I KNOW, PIOTR.
I WISH HE WAS HERE.

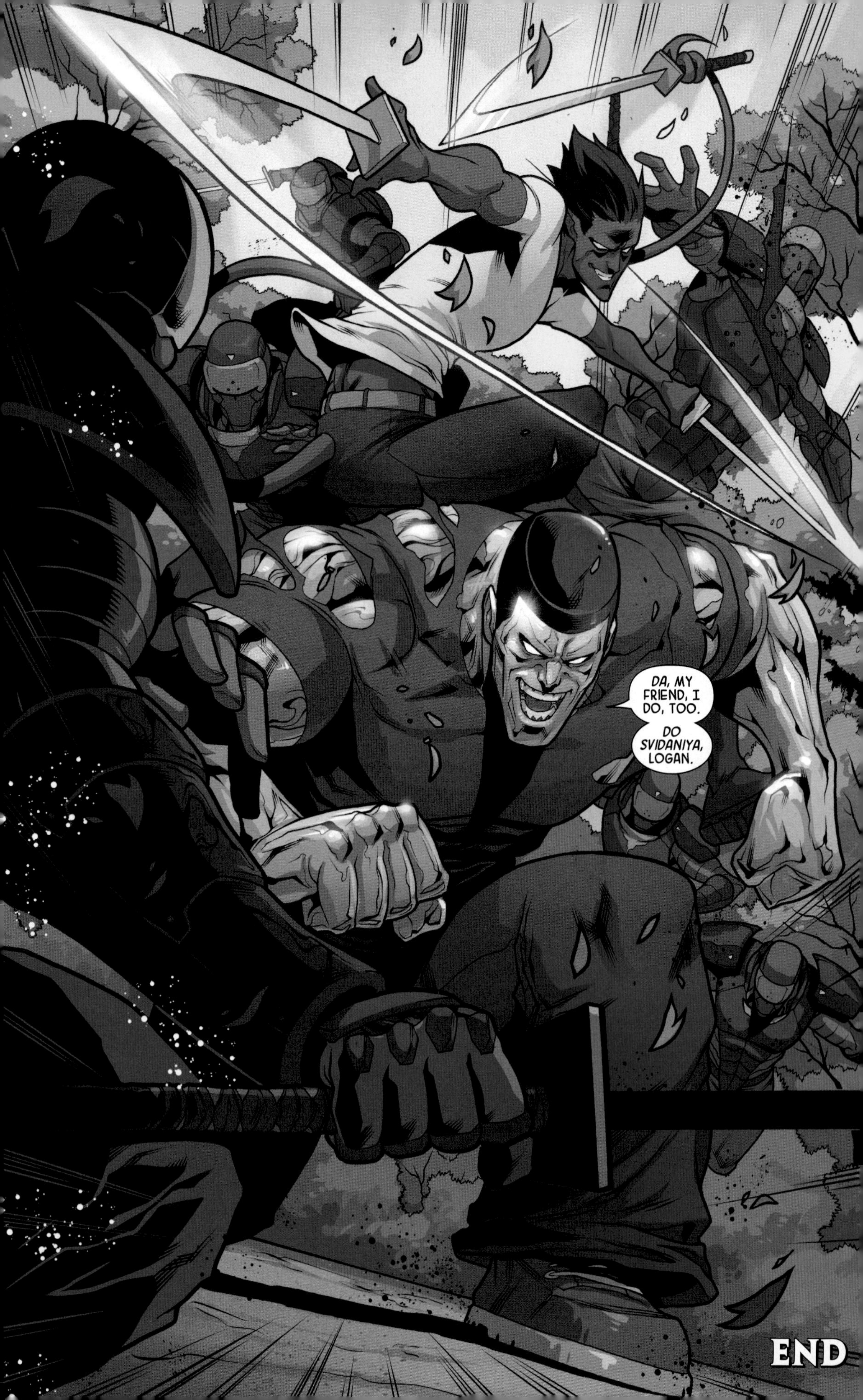
DA, MY FRIEND, I DO, TOO.
DO SVIDANIYA, LOGAN.
END

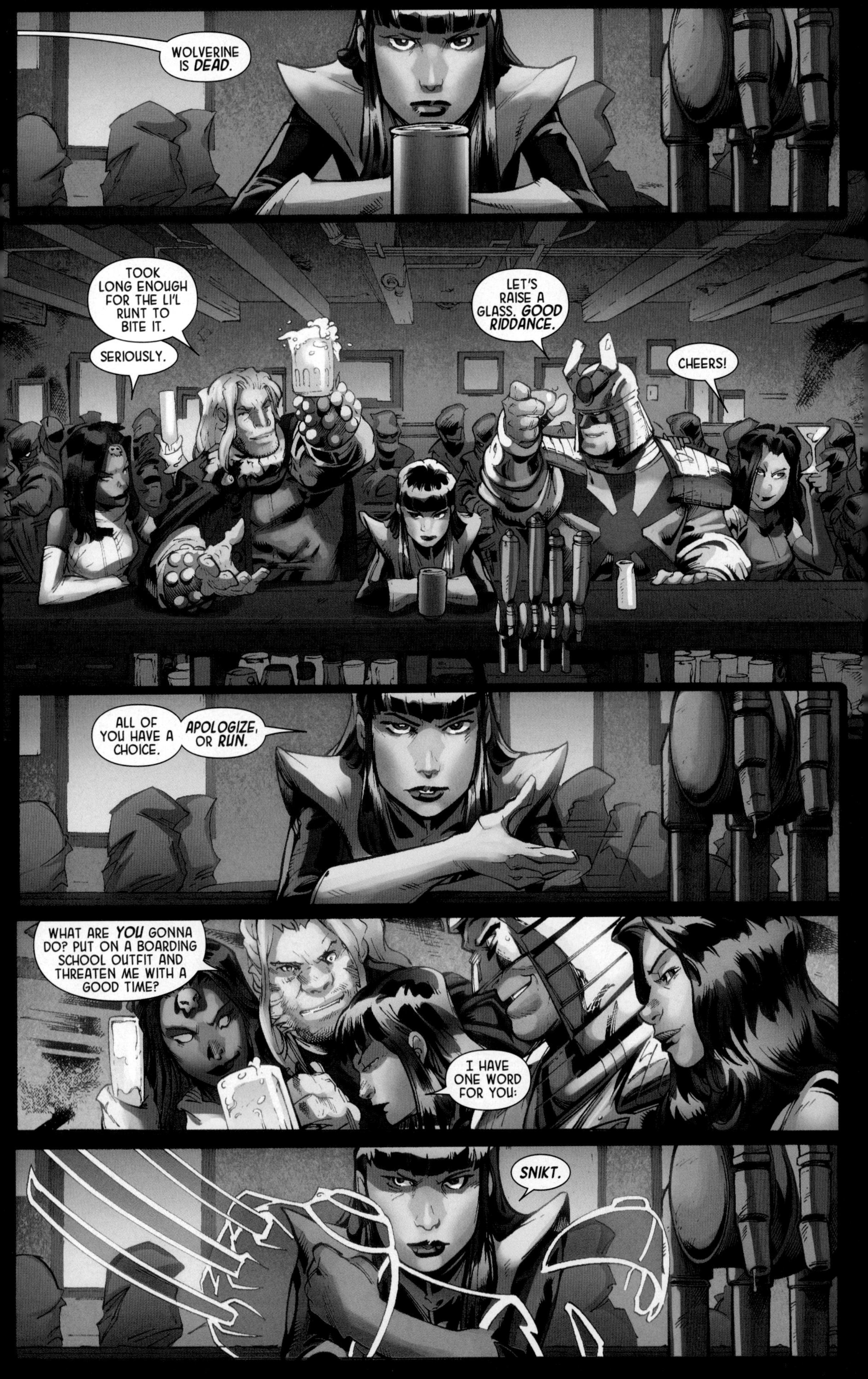
WOLVERINE IS DEAD.
TOOK LONG ENOUGH FOR THE LI'L RUNT TO BITE IT.
SERIOUSLY.
LET'S RAISE A GLASS. GOOD RIDDANCE.
CHEERS!
ALL OF YOU HAVE A CHOICE.
APOLOGIZE, OR RUN.
WHAT ARE YOU GONNA DO? PUT ON A BOARDING SCHOOL OUTFIT AND THREATEN ME WITH A GOOD TIME?
I HAVE ONE WORD FOR YOU:
SNIKT.

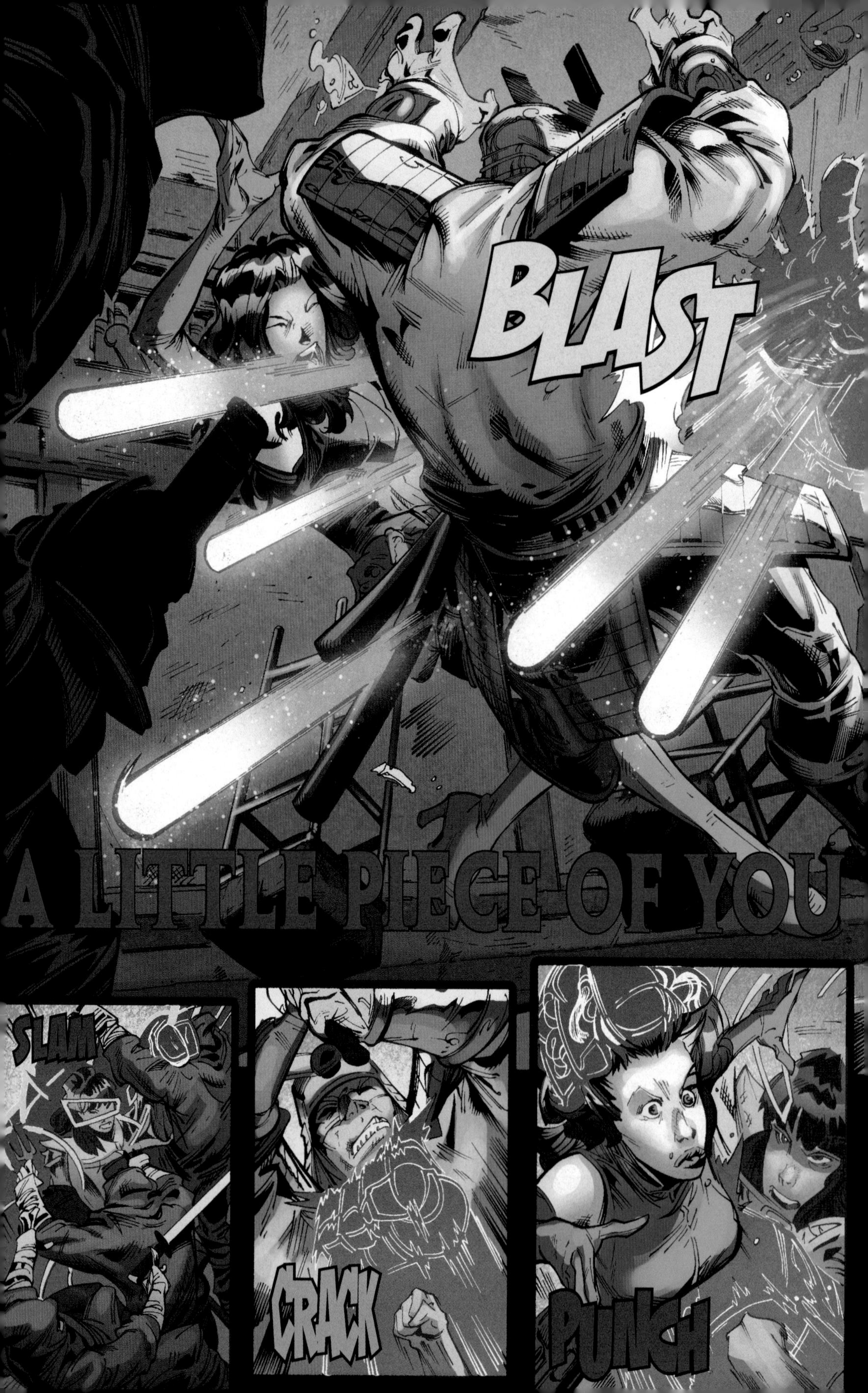
BLAST
A LITTLE PIECE OF YOU
SLAM
CRACK
PUNCH

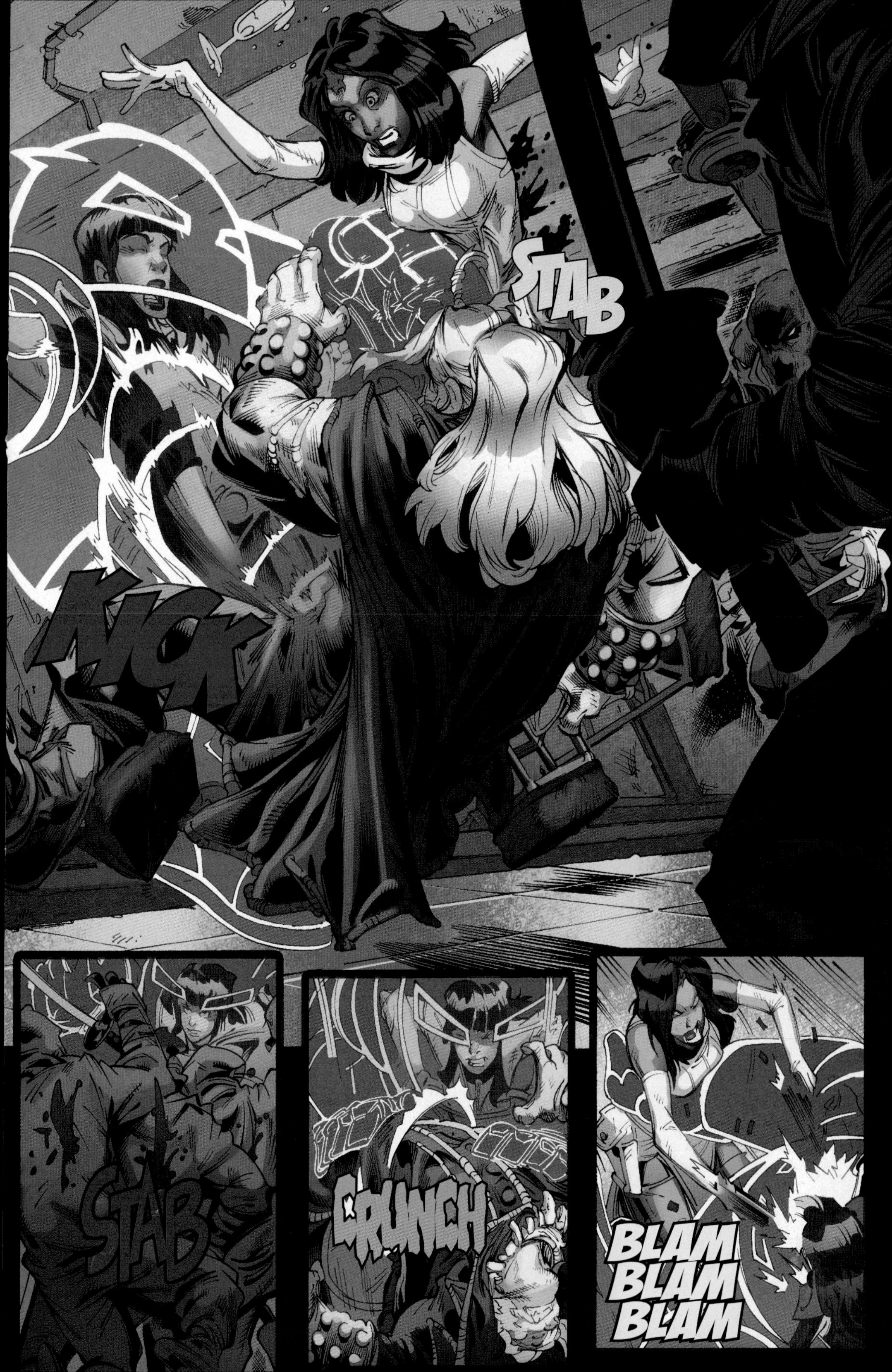
STAB
STAB
CRUNCH
BLAM
BLAM
BLAM

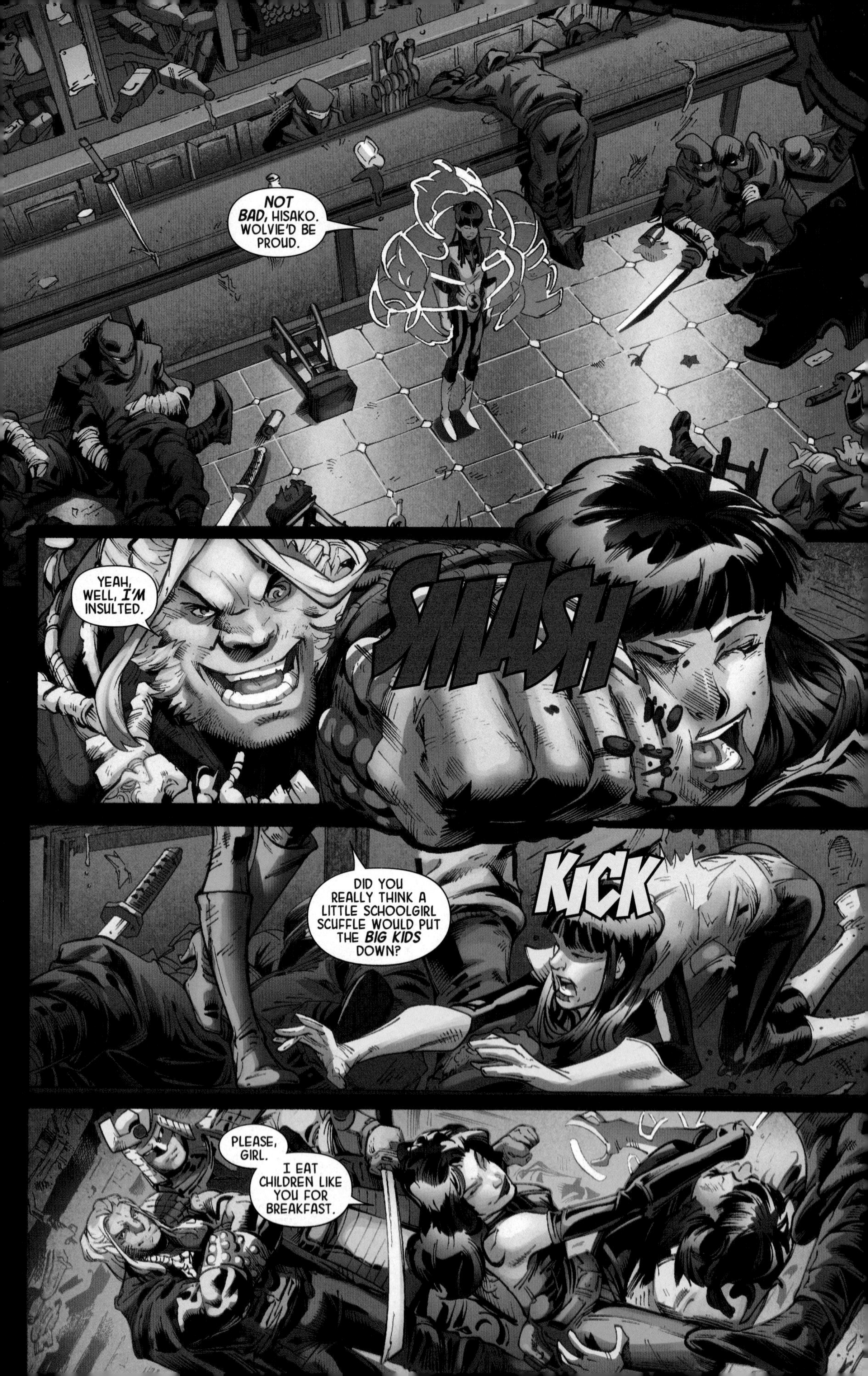
NOT BAD, HISAKO. WOLVIE'D BE PROUD.
YEAH, WELL, I'M INSULTED.
SMASH
DID YOU REALLY THINK A LITTLE SCHOOLGIRL SCUFFLE WOULD PUT THE BIG KIDS DOWN?
KICK
PLEASE, GIRL.
I EAT CHILDREN LIKE YOU FOR BREAKFAST.

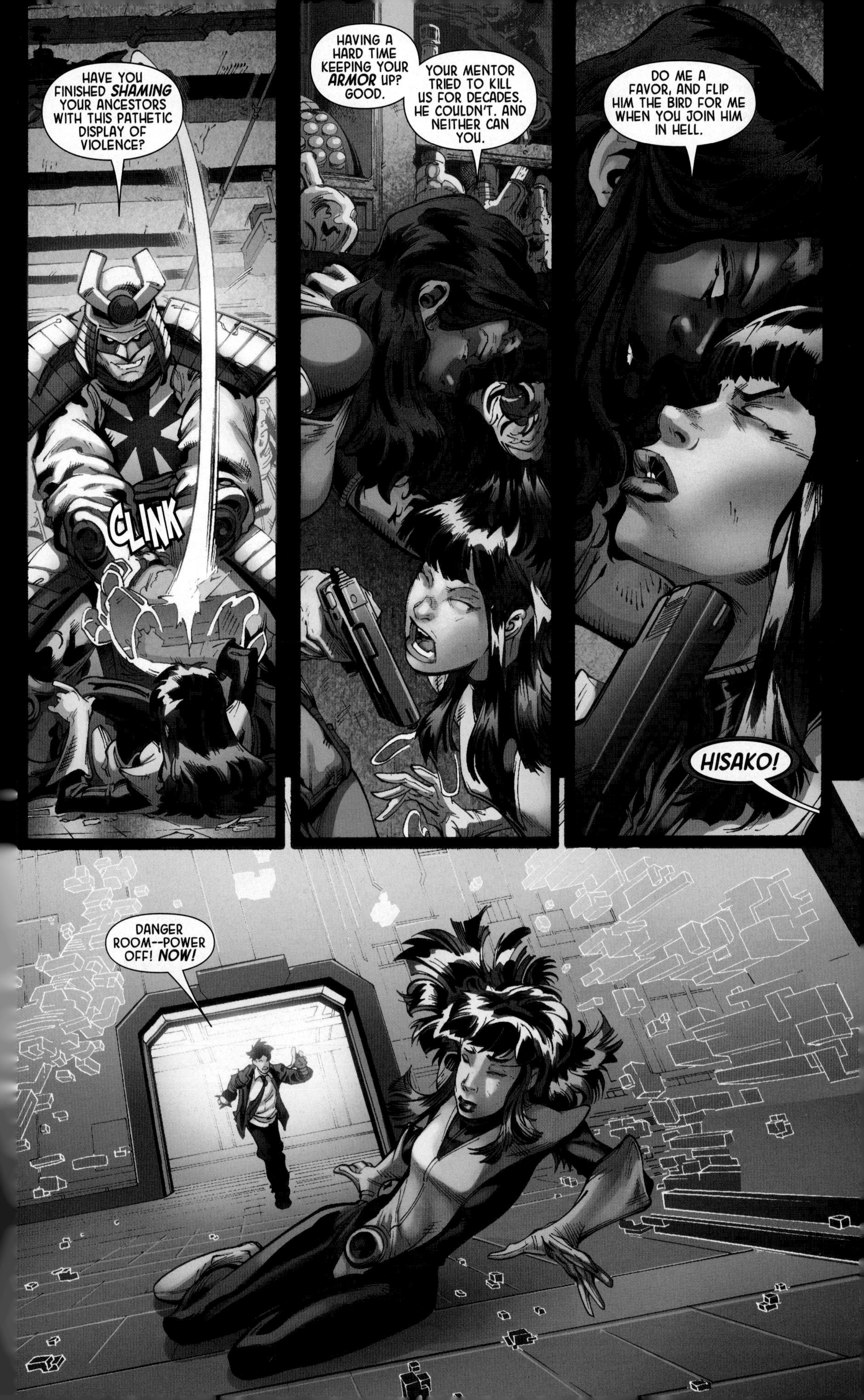
HAVE YOU FINISHED SHAMING YOUR ANCESTORS WITH THIS PATHETIC DISPLAY OF VIOLENCE?
CLINK
HAVING A HARD TIME KEEPING YOUR ARMOR UP? GOOD.
YOUR MENTOR TRIED TO KILL US FOR DECADES. HE COULDN'T. AND NEITHER CAN YOU.
DO ME A FAVOR, AND FLIP HIM THE BIRD FOR ME WHEN YOU JOIN HIM IN HELL.
HISAKO!
DANGER ROOM--POWER OFF! NOW!

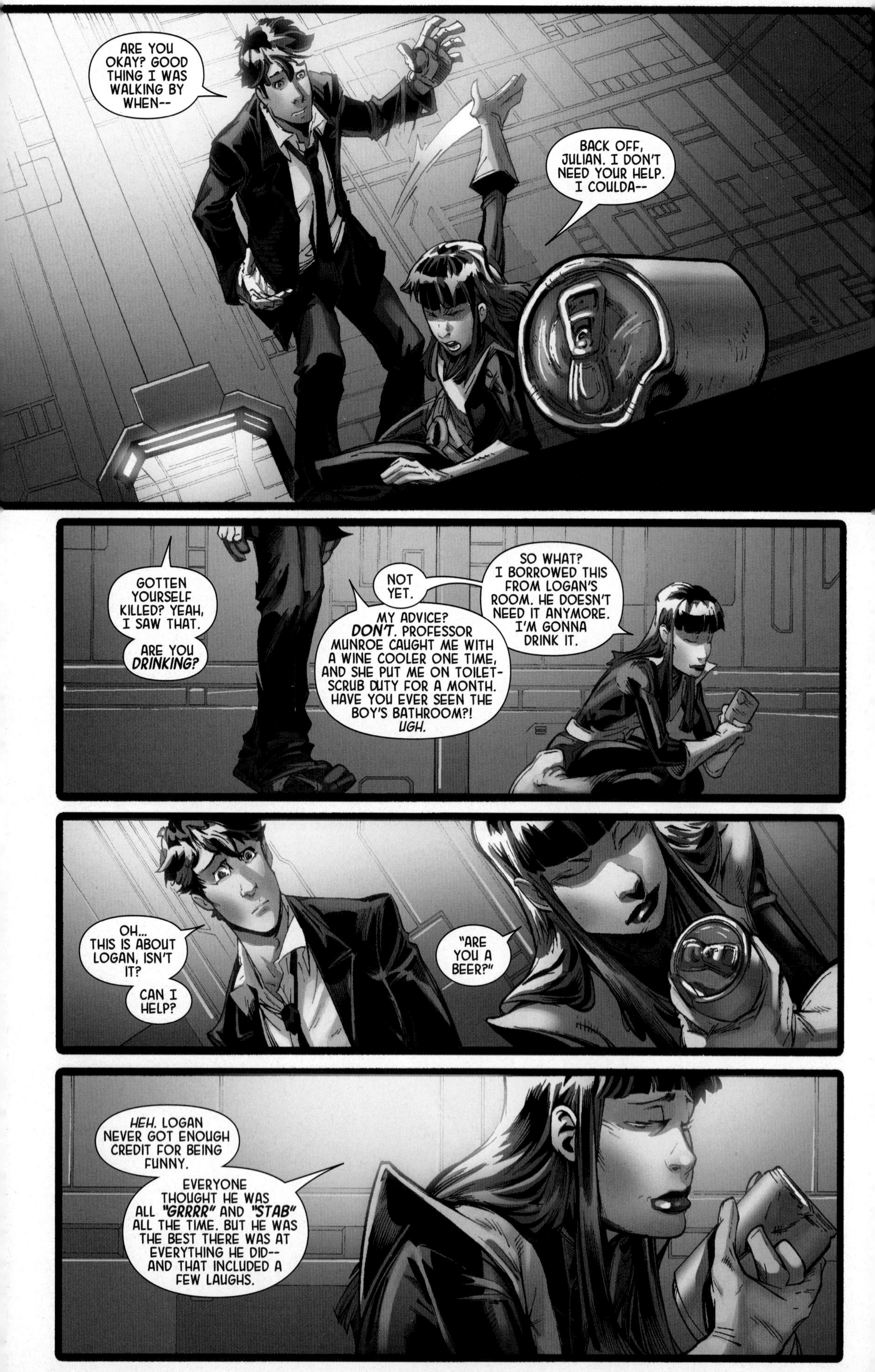
ARE YOU OKAY? GOOD THING I WAS WALKING BY WHEN--
BACK OFF, JULIAN. I DON'T NEED YOUR HELP. I COULDA--
GOTTEN YOURSELF KILLED? YEAH, I SAW THAT.
ARE YOU *DRINKING?*
SO WHAT? I BORROWED THIS FROM LOGAN'S ROOM. HE DOESN'T NEED IT ANYMORE. I'M GONNA DRINK IT.
NOT YET.
MY ADVICE? ***DON'T***. PROFESSOR MUNROE CAUGHT ME WITH A WINE COOLER ONE TIME, AND SHE PUT ME ON TOILET-SCRUB DUTY FOR A MONTH. HAVE YOU EVER SEEN THE BOY'S BATHROOM?! *UGH.*
OH... THIS IS ABOUT LOGAN, ISN'T IT?
CAN I HELP?
"ARE YOU A BEER?"
HEH. LOGAN NEVER GOT ENOUGH CREDIT FOR BEING FUNNY.
EVERYONE THOUGHT HE WAS ALL ***"GRRRR"*** AND ***"STAB"*** ALL THE TIME. BUT HE WAS THE BEST THERE WAS AT EVERYTHING HE DID-- AND THAT INCLUDED A FEW LAUGHS.

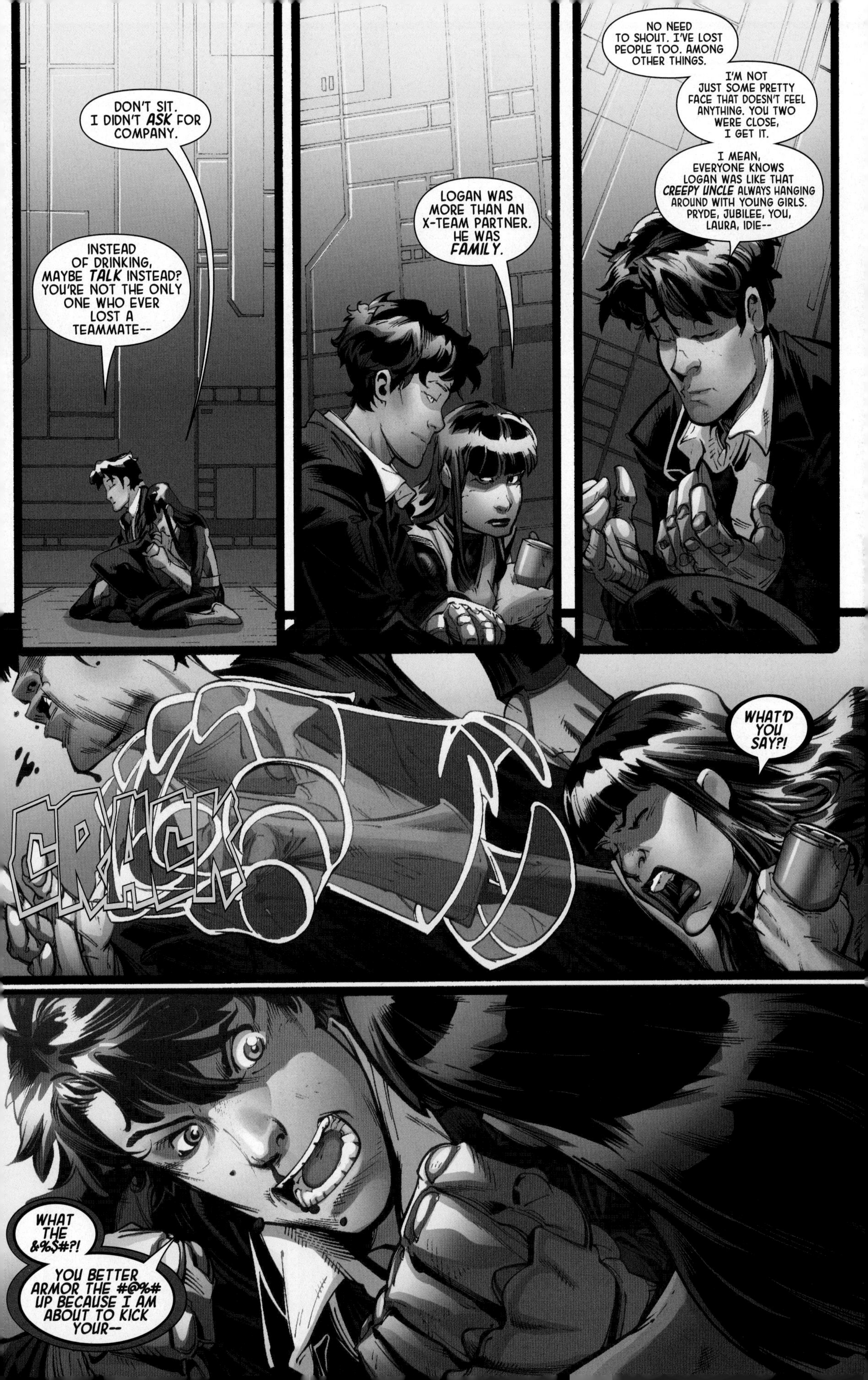
DON'T SIT. I DIDN'T ASK FOR COMPANY.
INSTEAD OF DRINKING, MAYBE TALK INSTEAD? YOU'RE NOT THE ONLY ONE WHO EVER LOST A TEAMMATE--
LOGAN WAS MORE THAN AN X-TEAM PARTNER. HE WAS FAMILY.
NO NEED TO SHOUT. I'VE LOST PEOPLE TOO. AMONG OTHER THINGS.
I'M NOT JUST SOME PRETTY FACE THAT DOESN'T FEEL ANYTHING. YOU TWO WERE CLOSE, I GET IT.
I MEAN, EVERYONE KNOWS LOGAN WAS LIKE THAT CREEPY UNCLE ALWAYS HANGING AROUND WITH YOUNG GIRLS. PRYDE, JUBILEE, YOU, LAURA, IDIE--
WHAT'D YOU SAY?!
CRACK
WHAT THE &%$#?!
YOU BETTER ARMOR THE #@%# UP BECAUSE I AM ABOUT TO KICK YOUR--

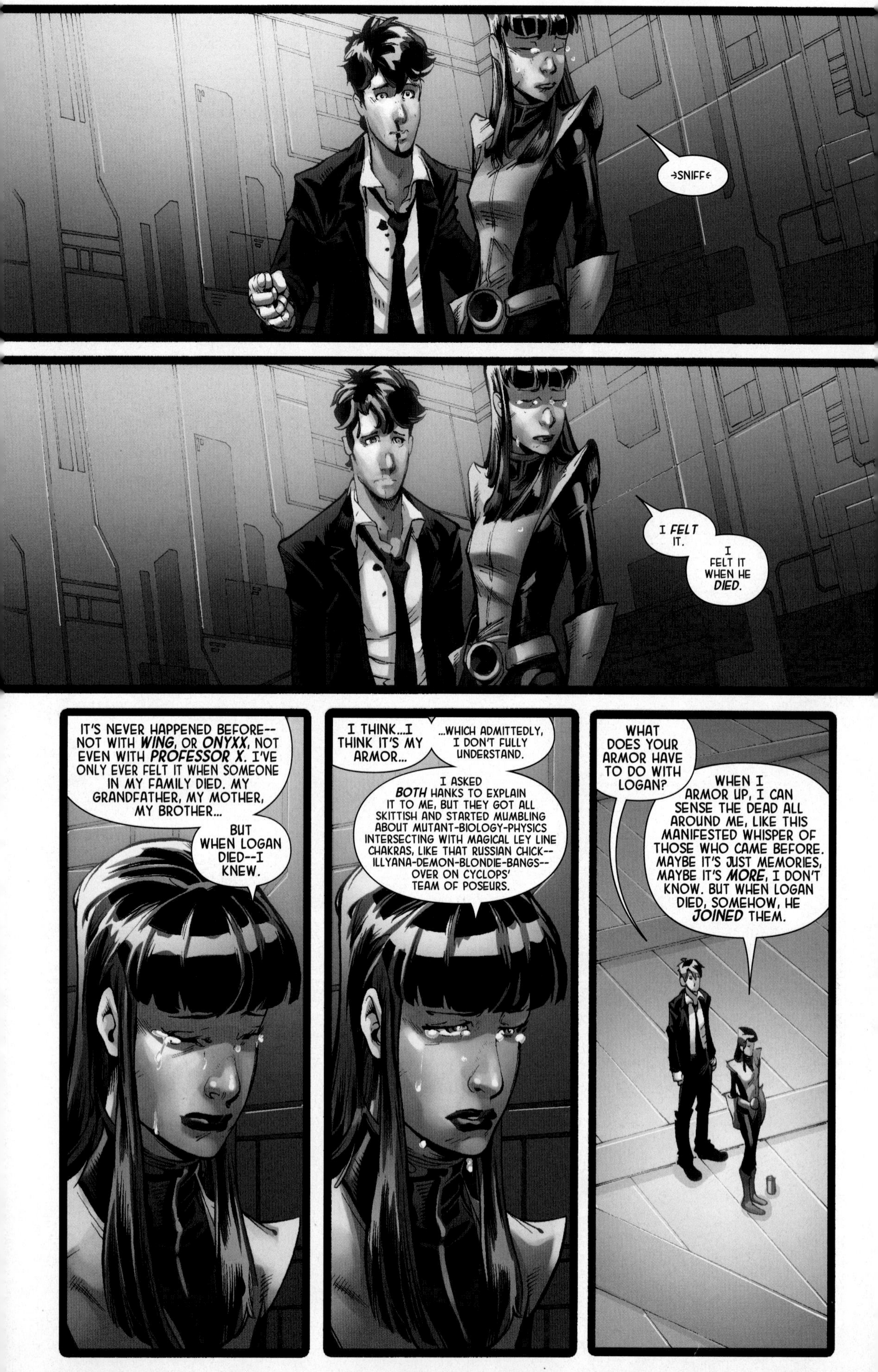

→SNIFF←
I FELT IT.
I FELT IT WHEN HE DIED.
IT'S NEVER HAPPENED BEFORE-- NOT WITH WING, OR ONYXX, NOT EVEN WITH PROFESSOR X. I'VE ONLY EVER FELT IT WHEN SOMEONE IN MY FAMILY DIED. MY GRANDFATHER, MY MOTHER, MY BROTHER...
BUT WHEN LOGAN DIED--I KNEW.
I THINK...I THINK IT'S MY ARMOR...
...WHICH ADMITTEDLY, I DON'T FULLY UNDERSTAND.
I ASKED BOTH HANKS TO EXPLAIN IT TO ME, BUT THEY GOT ALL SKITTISH AND STARTED MUMBLING ABOUT MUTANT-BIOLOGY-PHYSICS INTERSECTING WITH MAGICAL LEY LINE CHAKRAS, LIKE THAT RUSSIAN CHICK-- ILLYANA-DEMON-BLONDIE-BANGS-- OVER ON CYCLOPS' TEAM OF POSEURS.
WHAT DOES YOUR ARMOR HAVE TO DO WITH LOGAN?
WHEN I ARMOR UP, I CAN SENSE THE DEAD ALL AROUND ME, LIKE THIS MANIFESTED WHISPER OF THOSE WHO CAME BEFORE. MAYBE IT'S JUST MEMORIES, MAYBE IT'S MORE, I DON'T KNOW. BUT WHEN LOGAN DIED, SOMEHOW, HE JOINED THEM.

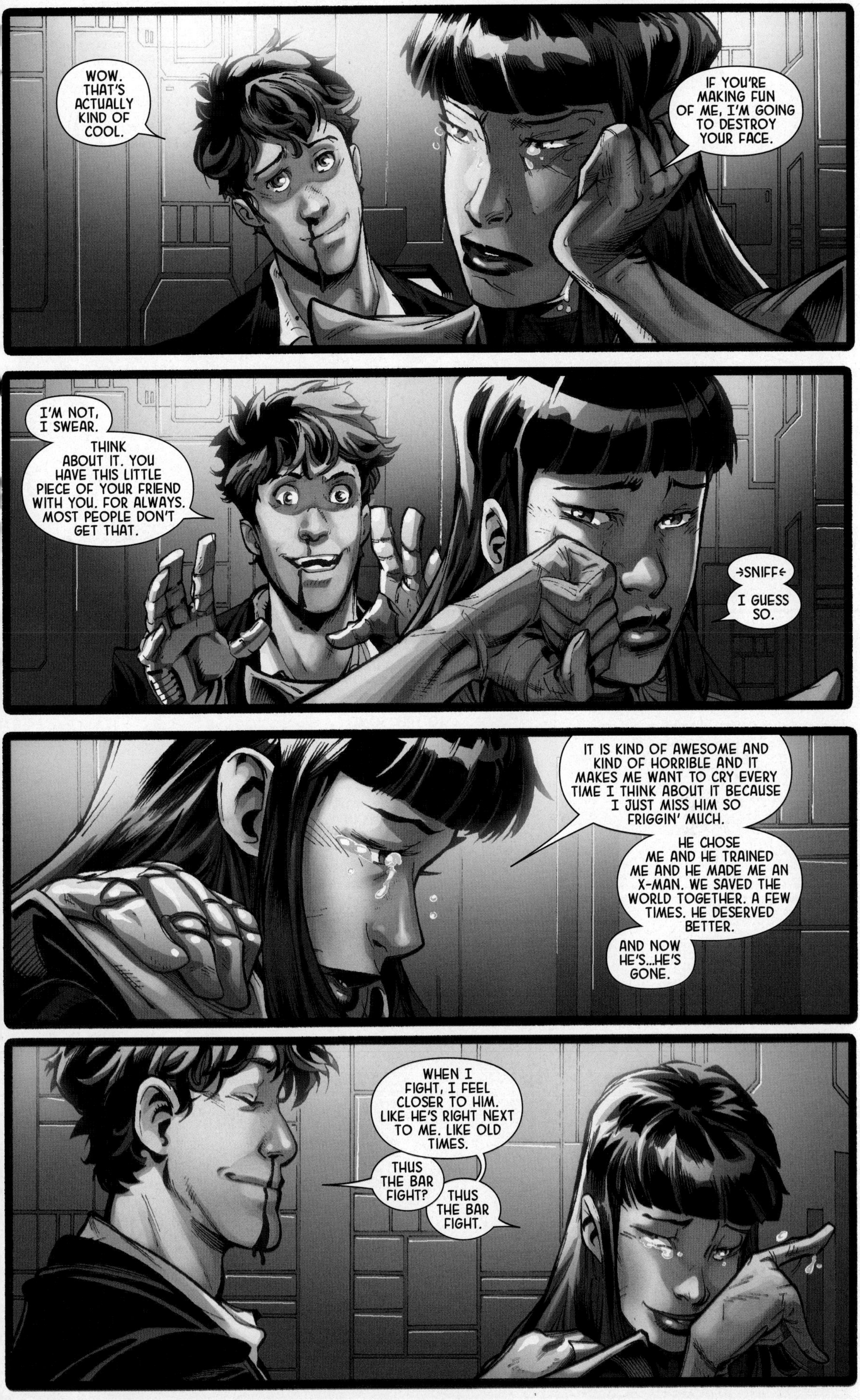
WOW. THAT'S ACTUALLY KIND OF COOL.
IF YOU'RE MAKING FUN OF ME, I'M GOING TO DESTROY YOUR FACE.
I'M NOT, I SWEAR.
THINK ABOUT IT. YOU HAVE THIS LITTLE PIECE OF YOUR FRIEND WITH YOU. FOR ALWAYS. MOST PEOPLE DON'T GET THAT.
SNIFF
I GUESS SO.
IT IS KIND OF AWESOME AND KIND OF HORRIBLE AND IT MAKES ME WANT TO CRY EVERY TIME I THINK ABOUT IT BECAUSE I JUST MISS HIM SO FRIGGIN' MUCH.
HE CHOSE ME AND HE TRAINED ME AND HE MADE ME AN X-MAN. WE SAVED THE WORLD TOGETHER. A FEW TIMES. HE DESERVED BETTER.
AND NOW HE'S...HE'S GONE.
WHEN I FIGHT, I FEEL CLOSER TO HIM. LIKE HE'S RIGHT NEXT TO ME. LIKE OLD TIMES.
THUS THE BAR FIGHT?
THUS THE BAR FIGHT.

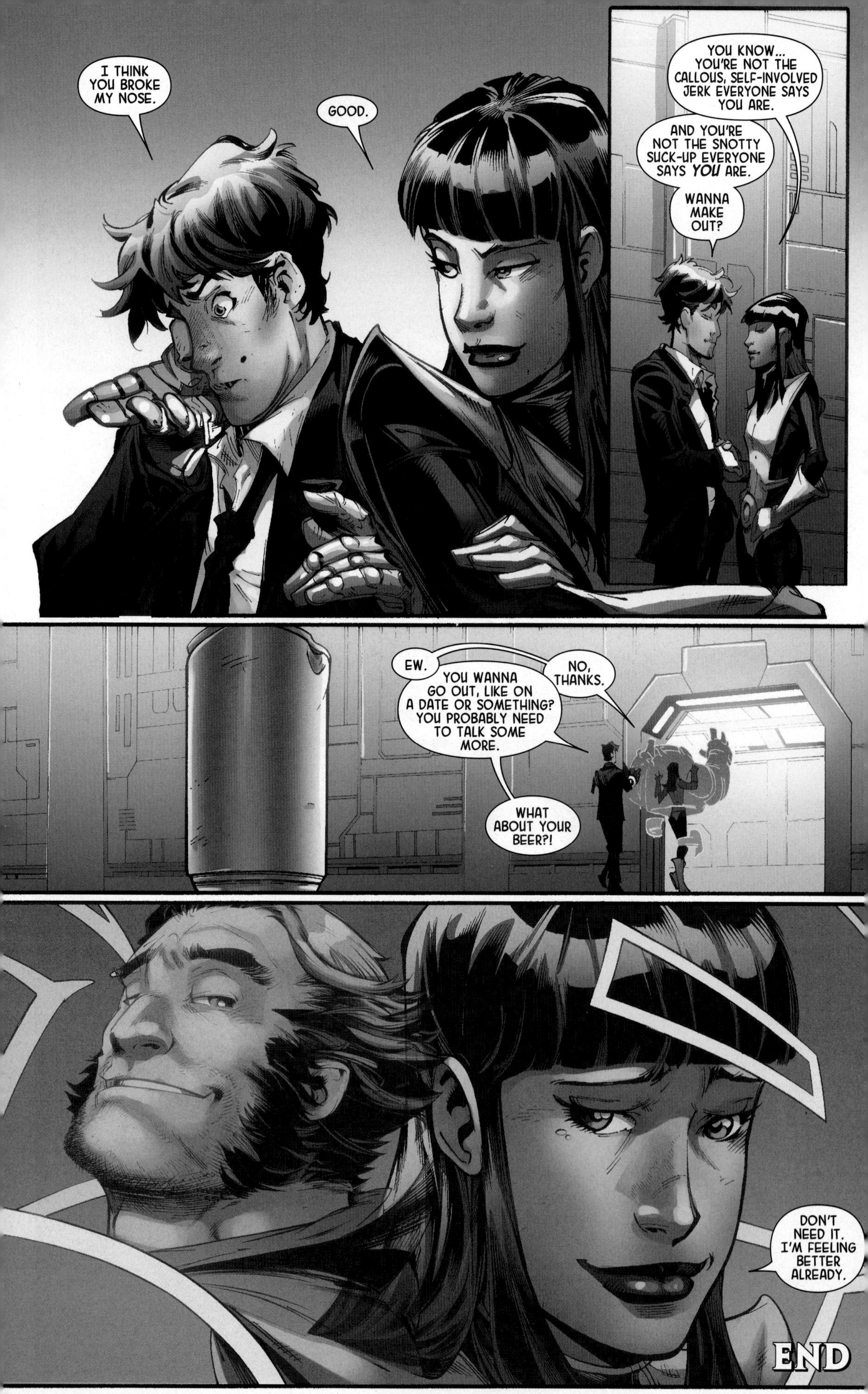
I THINK YOU BROKE MY NOSE.
GOOD.
YOU KNOW... YOU'RE NOT THE CALLOUS, SELF-INVOLVED JERK EVERYONE SAYS YOU ARE.
AND YOU'RE NOT THE SNOTTY SUCK-UP EVERYONE SAYS *YOU* ARE.
WANNA MAKE OUT?
EW.
NO, THANKS.
YOU WANNA GO OUT, LIKE ON A DATE OR SOMETHING? YOU PROBABLY NEED TO TALK SOME MORE.
WHAT ABOUT YOUR BEER?!
DON'T NEED IT. I'M FEELING BETTER ALREADY.
END

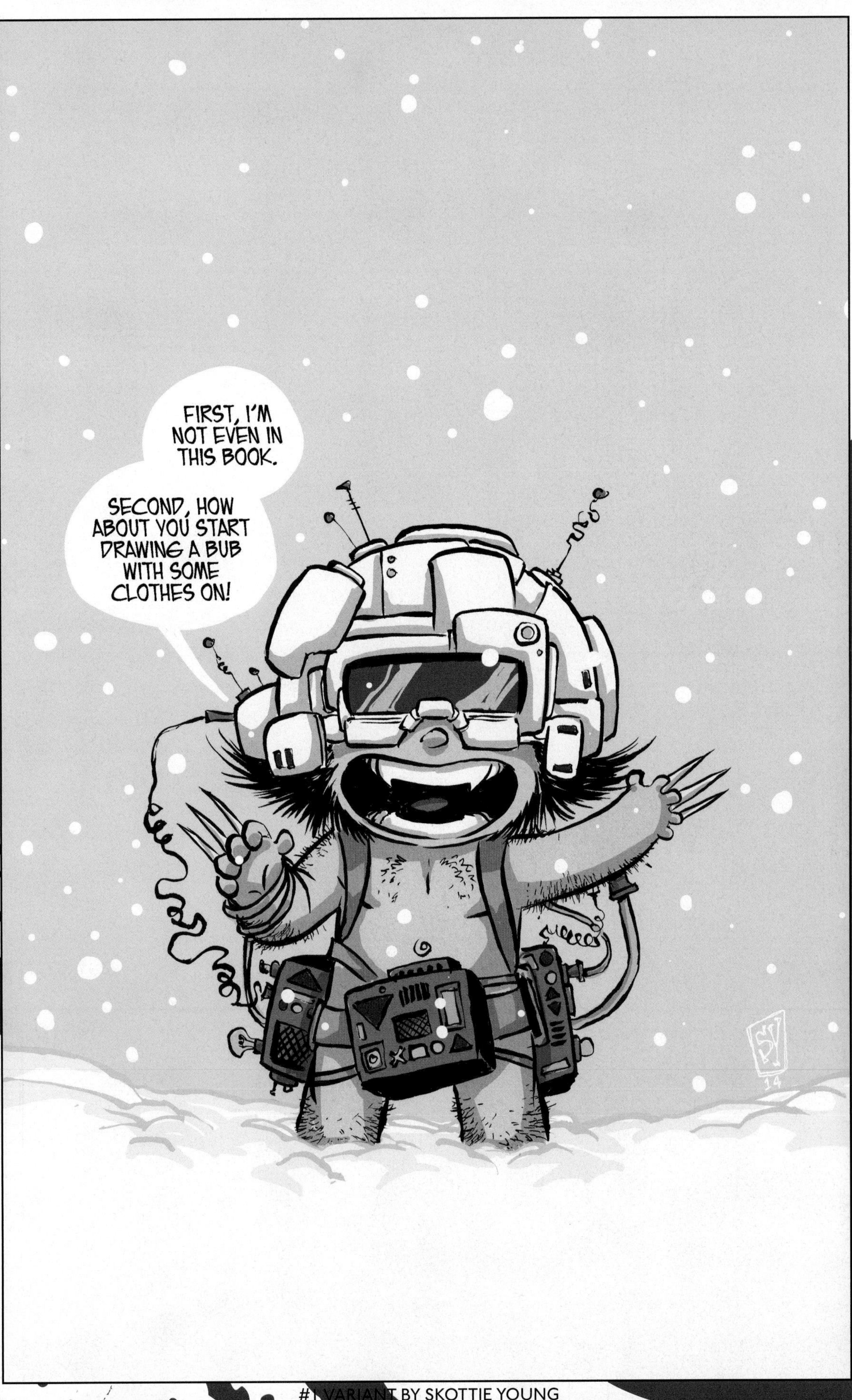
FIRST, I'M NOT EVEN IN THIS BOOK.
SECOND, HOW ABOUT YOU START DRAWING A BUB WITH SOME CLOTHES ON!

#1 VARIANT BY SKOTTIE YOUNG

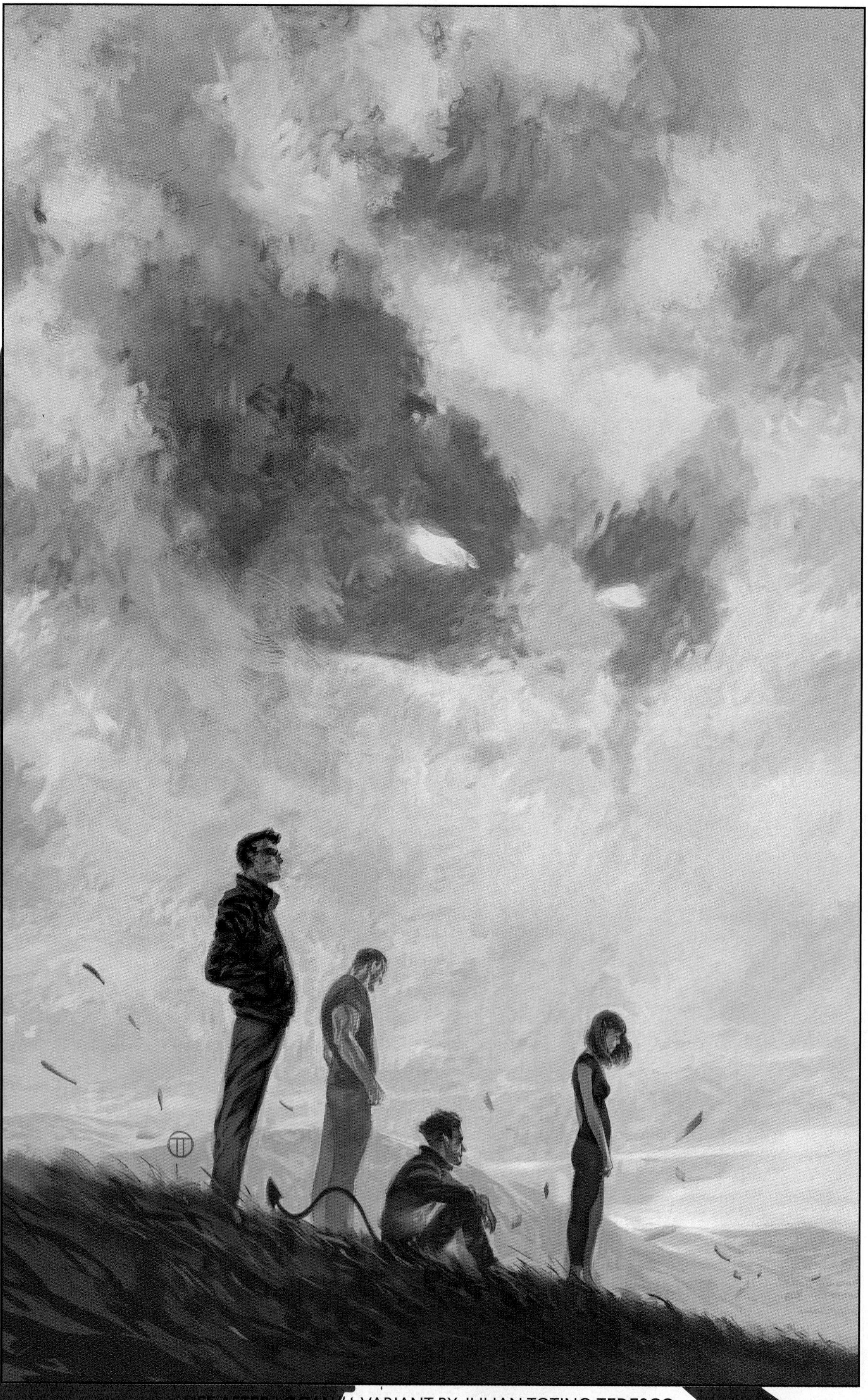

LIFE AFTER LOGAN #1 VARIANT BY JULIAN TOTINO TEDESCO

CHARACTER DESIGNS
BY SALVADOR LARROCA

ENDO

WIRES

ENDO

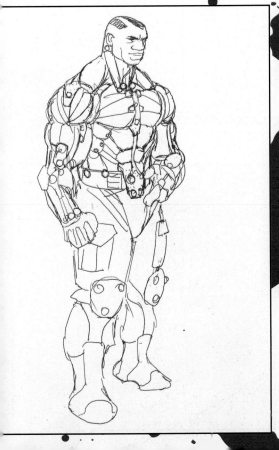

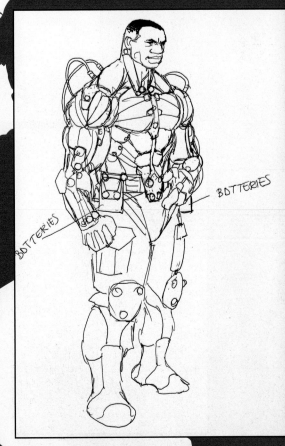

BOTTERIES

BOTTERIES

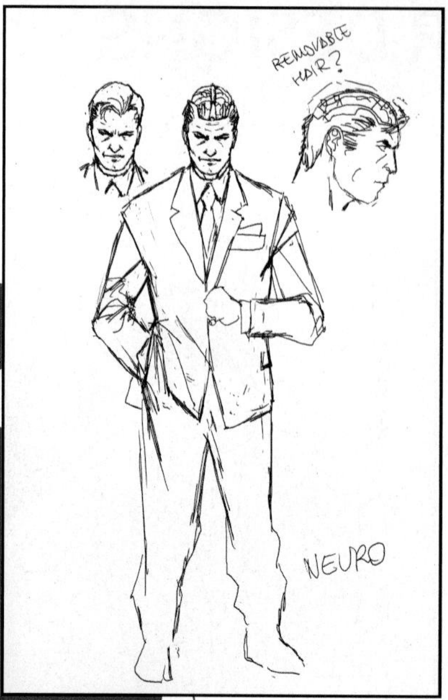
REMOVABLE HAIR?
NEURO

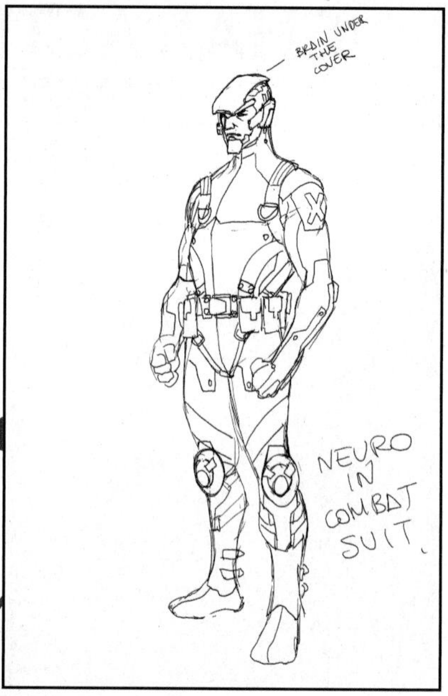
BRAIN UNDER THE COVER
NEURO IN COMBAT SUIT.

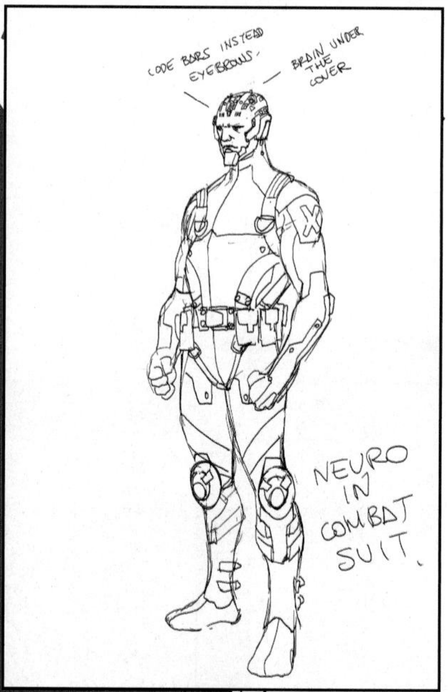
CODE BARS INSTEAD EYEBROWS.
BRAIN UNDER THE COVER
NEURO IN COMBAT SUIT.

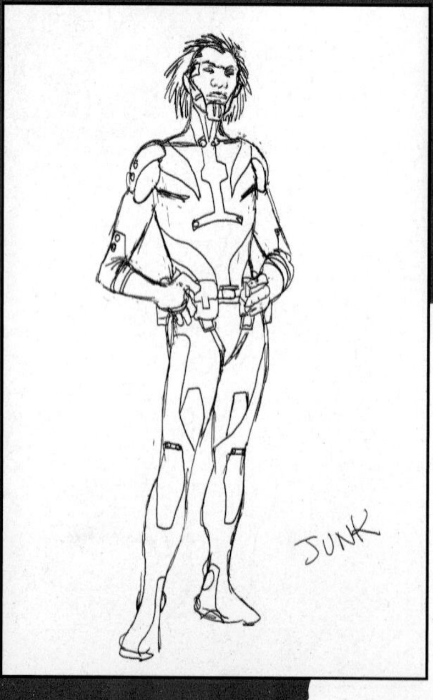
JUNK

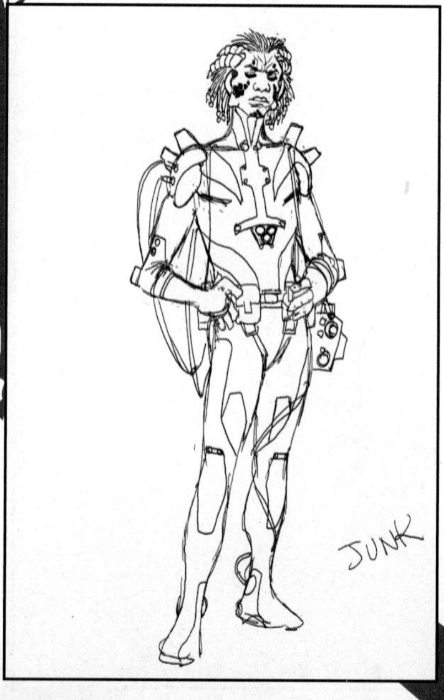
JUNK

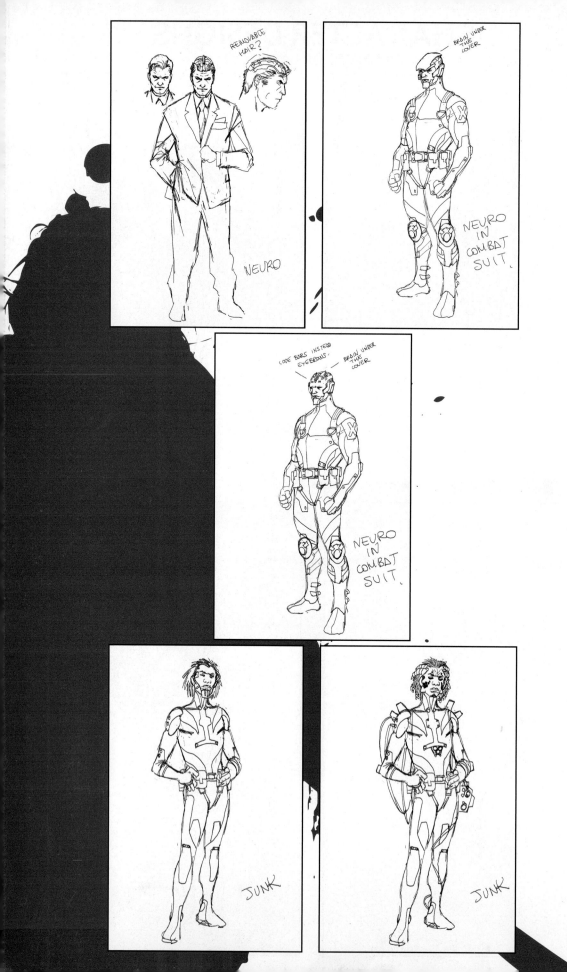